RUM WAR AT SEA

Rum War at Sea

By MALCOLM F. WILLOUGHBY

Commander USCGR(T)

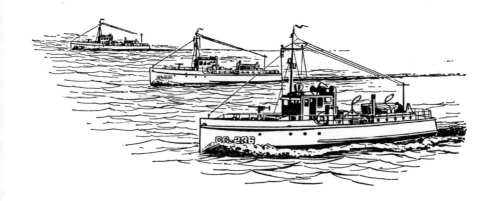

TREASURY DEPARTMENT

UNITED STATES COAST GUARD

UNITED STATES

GOVERNMENT PRINTING OFFICE

WASHINGTON : 1964

For sale by the Superintendent of Documents, U.S. Government Printing Office
Washington, D.C. 20402 - Price $2.75

DEDICATED

TO THE OFFICERS AND MEN

OF THE

UNITED STATES COAST GUARD

WHO SERVED THEIR COUNTRY

FROM 1920 TO 1935

Foreword

PROBABLY NO OTHER ERA in American history has been more controversial than the prohibition period, extending from the middle 1920's through the early 1930's. As one of the law enforcement agencies charged with the suppression of the illegal liquor traffic, the United States Coast Guard was deeply involved in what has come to be known as "The Rum War." It was a hard, unremitting war with few of the rewards normally accompanying performance of such duty. Yet under the law, the Coast Guard had no alternative but to conduct it with zeal and dedication, utilizing all the resources at its command. The story of the "Noble Experiment" is in large part a Coast Guard story. In this carefully researched, well documented history, students of this turbulent chapter of American history will find rewarding reading.

E. J. Roland

ADMIRAL, U.S. COAST GUARD
Commandant

Preface

THE PERIOD OF NATIONAL PROHIBITION which this Nation suffered between 1920 and 1934 challenged each individual American. It was also a challenge to Congress, State governments, the courts, local and State police, the clergy, customs and prohibition authorities, and the U.S. Coast Guard. The experience proved to be one replete with lessons for posterity. Never before had the power of the underworld touched, directly or indirectly, such a tremendous proportion of the U.S. citizenry. It was a period which, decades later, claims the interest and imagination of the American public.

Many interesting books have been written about this historic experiment. None, however, has presented an adequate history of perhaps the most colorful enforcement agency of those days—the U.S. Coast Guard. The desirability of such a work has become apparent with the passing years.

The purpose of this book is to set forth the history of the U.S. Coast Guard in its battle with the rum runners.

During prohibition the Coast Guard seized literally thousands of vessels which were engaged in transporting liquor into the United States from the sea. Obviously, it would be impracticable and almost repetitive to attempt to cover all seizures, particularly the predominating ones of routine nature. Seizures of special interest or significance are, for the most part, recounted in these pages.

Many of the incidents were highly dramatic. There is always a temptation to let one's imagination rise above the basic facts to produce an exciting and gripping story! That is not the way of history, and it has been assiduously avoided! Every effort has been made toward a factual presentation.

In mentioning the name of a Coast Guard vessel, the commanding officer at the time of the incident is usually indicated, if known. Ranks, grades, or ratings given are those prevailing at the time regardless of further attainments by the individual officer or enlisted man. Photographic illustrations are all from official Coast Guard photographs unless otherwise indicated.

By far the chief source of information has been the official Coast Guard records on file at the National Archives in Washington, D.C.

Herbert Asbury's *The Great Illusion* has been valuable as a reference for background material for the prohibition era in general. Many pertinent items were gleaned from the *New York Times* and checked with official records. A number of retired Coast Guard officers who were in the Service during this era have provided helpful memoranda on their experiences. Among these, special acknowledgment is due to Capt. Frank M. Meals, Capt. Roderick S. Patch, Capt. Frank K. Johnson, and Commodore John S. Baylis.

Captain Meals furnished much of the basic material for chapter VIII on Aids to Information. Mr. William D. Wilkinson of New York, who has a great fund of knowledge on Coast Guard small craft, prepared a very helpful memorandum on that subject.

The author has also had the benefit of cheerful and wholehearted cooperation from Capt. W. K. Thompson, USCG, Chief, Capt. R. L. Mellen, USCG, formerly Chief, Comdr. J. D. Doyle, USCG, Assistant Chief, and Mr. Hyman Kaplen, of the Public Information Division at Coast Guard Headquarters, Washington, D.C., and from Mr. Lyle J. Holverstott, Archivist in Charge, Fiscal Branch, General Records Division and Mr. William Sherman of the National Archives.

To all who have so kindly and willingly assisted in this endeavor, the author extends his sincere thanks.

MALCOLM F. WILLOUGHBY

Boston, Mass.

Contents

RUM WAR AT SEA

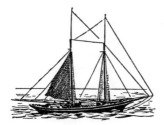

CHAPTER I

The Trail to

Prohibition

BIG "RED" SHANNON cast a satisfied glance over his powerful white 30-foot motorboat *Goose* and the piled cases of liquor it contained as he left Gun Cay, near Bimini, and steered for Miami one clear February afternoon. If all went as planned, he would make port under cover of semidarkness, mingle with the yachts in the harbor, and ease into the Flamingo Hotel dock with his illicit cargo. The success of similar previous missions gave him confidence.

This time, however, word of his departure reached the U.S. Coast Guard Base at Fort Lauderdale. Ens. Philip E. Shaw, the executive officer at the Base, was summoned and directed to intercept personally this boat and bring the notorious smuggler in. Shaw immediately got his expert boat crew of four experienced North Carolinians, and set out for Biscayne Bay in 35-foot *K–1445*—a captured rum runner converted to Coast Guard use.

Moving quietly in the deep twilight shadows of Star Island off Miami, these five coast guardsmen watched intently through their night glasses for sign of the white rum runner. Suddenly a red running light appeared, approaching at about 12 knots from under the Causeway Bridge, and a white hull could be seen below it. "Come left slowly, Otis," said Shaw to his helmsman. "Put slugs in the chambers of your pistols, you two in the bow, and keep your safeties on. Don't fire those guns unless I tell you to. Rev up your motors a bit, Otis, and keep astern of him— let him get well up into the bay before we try to catch him."

The rum runner was deeply laden, and appeared to be heading for the Flamingo Hotel dock. *K–1445* followed 300 yards astern, then opened up wide to get alongside. Aware of a chase, a crew member in the leading boat began throwing case after case of liquor overboard. Shaw could make out the name *Goose* on her stern. This was the boat!

She turned hard left at 18 knots and fled southward. *K–1445* turned also to keep the runner on an inside course. *Goose* disappeared behind

1

the hull of the anchored *Shadow K,* and Shaw ordered Otis to head the boat across that vessel's bow. As he did so, *Goose* roared down *Shadow K's* starboard side close aboard headed straight for the Coast Guard boat in the hope of ramming. The latter swung hard right to parallel the rummy's course in the opposite direction, and avoid a high speed collision. *Goose* missed the stern by 6 inches.

Shaw yelled: "This is the Coast Guard—heave to immediately. I'm coming aboard." *Goose* continued on. Shaw fired two quick shots across her bow. This had no effect, and the rum runner roared off into the darkness, jettisoning more liquor and picking up speed. *K–1445* crossed *Shadow K's* stern, but the quarry became lost momentarily among the anchored yachts. She then appeared again flying along the shore of Star Island and *K–1445* went after her. *Goose* swung around and again headed straight for her pursuer with obvious intent to ram. The Coast Guard boat turned sharply right to avoid collision but the rum runner struck her a heavy glancing blow, bashing in her guard rail and heeling her over violently to port, nearly knocking the men overboard.

"Fire into that vessel" cried Shaw. Three 45s spoke almost at once. Shaw aimed at the engine room hoping to cripple the boat's motors. The man at the wheel of the rum runner grabbed his back, then slumped across nearby bags of liquor.

"Cease firing" called the ensign. Both boats slowed and drifted close together. A man in *Goose's* cockpit, who had come from the engine room, had his hands over his head, and a coast guardsman kept a rifle on him. The man said his mate had been wounded by shot. The two boats were lashed together and were soon at the hotel dock, the rum runner secured inside *K–1445.*

The ensign turned his attention to the wounded man who was unconscious. The latter groaned and turned sidewise. Shaw was shocked as he recognized him as Duncan W. "Red" Shannon with whom, years earlier, he had sailed out of Boston in his father's fishing schooner! Shannon was sent to the Allison Memorial Hospital, where he died.

This shooting caused much furor among the local populace and in the press. There was a continuous series of editorials and articles which inflamed the public mind against the coast guardsmen involved in particular, and the Coast Guard in general. Charges of murder were leveled at Ensign Shaw and a long and involved court case followed. Shaw eventually was absolved of all culpability.

The incident was one of thousands of captures by the Coast Guard in its war against the highly organized rum runners of the prohibition era. This era was not a sudden occurrence; it was brought about by over a hundred years of gradually accelerating agitation. The trail to prohibition should be summarized as a preliminary to the story of the Coast Guard in the hectic years of the 18th amendment.

It would be incorrect to say that human consumption of alcoholic beverages is as old as man, but it may be correct to say that it is about as old as "civilization." It flourished grandly when the Roman Empire was in its glory, as vividly described in Henryk Sienkiewicz's *Quo Vadis;* it was an old, old story then, and it has thrived to the present day. As long as liquor in any form has existed, there have been those who considered it a friend in the exuberance of celebration or in the depths of despond, and those who have regarded it as a curse on humanity. The two viewpoints probably will continue as long as liquor exists, perhaps *ad infinitum.*

In America, alcoholic beverages were a part of colonial life from the earliest days. In some sections they seemed to become too great a part of life, and this brought about opposition in various forms.

The colony of Georgia experimented with prohibition from 1735 until 1742, following an act passed by the British Parliament in 1734 prohibiting the importation of rum and brandies into Georgia. Legally deprived of ardent spirits, Georgia's citizens immediately went about the business of getting their liquor. When stills were set up in the back country, rum runners provided most of the supply; they ran boats down from South Carolina and put cargoes ashore on the unguarded beaches. Bootleggers sold the liquor inland. Speakeasies flourished. Violators of the law, if caught, demanded jury trials, and were usually acquitted. After 7 years, prohibition in Georgia was abandoned; rum runners, bootleggers, and speakeasies vanished, and the colony again prospered.

Probably America's most intemperate period began in the last half of the 18th century and continued for 80 or 90 years. Almost everybody drank, and liquor was considered a virtual necessity of life. Drunkenness was quite common. While all kinds of liquor were easily available, rum was the most abundant. Taverns thrived.

In the earlier days of the 17th century licenses had been granted only to citizens of good reputation and character and the tavern keepers enjoyed prestige and good social standing. Eventually, however, licenses were often given on political and other grounds, and gradually the drinking places came under control of a less desirable element. The quality of the taverns declined, and in the 18th century most were dirty and disorderly places. The characteristics of the saloon gradually appeared, presenting lawmakers with a problem which would last indefinitely.

The distillation of whiskey in this country began about 1760 in western Pennsylvania. Thirty-four years later, the Federal Government imposed an excise tax of 9 cents a gallon on all distilled spirits which, of course, invited evasion. The Whiskey Insurrection of 1794 broke out among the backwoods farmers in the Monongahela Valley as a result of this tax.

As always, there were those who opposed the use of intoxicating liquor. By 1800 they were becoming a factor of some importance. In

1823 the *Boston Recorder,* which was a temperance journal, published some amazing figures on the great consumption of spirits in various cities and towns of New England. Small temperance movements appeared but made no progress for a long time.

Drinking created many nuisances, and it was only natural that the authorities, despite a general approval of liquor as such, should promulgate many strict statutes. There were curfews; time limits were established at some places on how long a man might sit and drink, and limitations on the amount that could be served him. There were more arrests for drunkenness. But all this was ineffective.

The early laws were directed not against the use of intoxicants but against their misuse. However, as the 18th century progressed, there was a growing awareness of the dangers of intemperance. Opposition became more manifest among individuals and small groups, and appeals were made to convert people from the use of hard liquor to that of wine and beer. The idea of total abstinence did not appear until about 1819, and it was not until 1830 that it became the main objective of the temperance advocates.

The first formal temperance society in the world was organized at Moreau, N.Y., county of Northumberland, in April 1808. It was called the Union Temperance Society of Moreau and Northumberland. It lasted a few years, and though it was relatively unsuccessful, it encouraged other reform elements. Several similar societies sprang up in various States during the next decade, mostly to promote moderation rather than total abstinence. They had a short life, and did little to improve conditions.

Efforts of three New England preachers, including the Reverend Lyman Beecher, father of Harriet Beecher Stowe, succeeded in revitalizing the temperance movement in 1826. Beecher's sermons on the subject gained wide circulation and their influence was great. That same year another of the 3, Rev. Justin Edwards, together with 16 prominent Boston citizens, organized a prospective national society, first known as American Society for the Promotion of Temperance, and then as the American Temperance Society. The first journal devoted to the cause began publication, and by 1836 the number had increased to 11. Old societies were revived, new ones organized. In 1831 there were around 3,000. This growth mushroomed through the early 1830s. In 1836 the American Temperance Society was succeeded by the American Temperance Union; there were 8,000 societies most of which had some affiliation with the national organization. Several members of Congress joined the movement giving it far greater prestige. Temperance finally became a religious issue. And so, like an incipient fire gaining headway, the movement grew and the reformers frankly advocated total abstinence from all alcoholic beverages.

Gen. James Appleton of Massachusetts was in 1832 the first to recommend outright prohibition. He soon moved his family to Maine and was elected to the Maine Legislature. His influence brought about a committee recommendation to prohibit the sale of ardent spirits in that State. Though it was tabled, it was the first such recommendation in American history to be made by a legislative committee. In 1838 Maine legislators defeated by a single vote a proposal to forbid the sale of liquor in less than 28-gallon quantities.

Several States passed laws restricting sales to minimum quantities all the way from 1 quart to 15 gallons. The first local option laws were passed in 1839 by Rhode Island and New Hampshire. Many were soon repealed or modified, and none was particularly effective. But the reformers had become deeply engaged in politics, and by 1840 the movement was fully committed to lawful prohibition of ardent spirits.

Interest centered in Maine, even then considered the bellwether of American politics, and if Maine could vote a prohibitory law other States might follow. A prosperous Portland merchant named Neal Dow wielded great influence as a "dry," and after some years of frustration succeeded in having Portland become the first important city to prohibit liquor by popular vote. However, liquor continued to be sold, judges were uncooperative, and it was concluded that only a statewide law would be effective.

By the middle 1840s there were temperance lobbies in about every State legislature. In New York, this finally resulted in a local option law, passed in 1845, and of the 856 cities and towns, 728 voted against licensing grogshops. The local option law, however, was voted down by the legislature in 1847. That year the U.S. Supreme Court ruled that the States had full power to regulate or prohibit the sale of intoxicating liquors, and this gave great impetus to movements for statewide prohibition. The lobbyists in the State capitols went to work with a vengeance.

Dow immediately expanded his efforts on a statewide basis. Temperance forces endorsed candidates for the legislature. A bill abolishing the license system and prohibiting sale of liquor passed the Maine House and Senate and became law on 7 August 1846. Loopholes were plentiful and it proved unsatisfactory. Dow tried again, but without success, in 1850. Nothing daunted, he became mayor of Portland in April 1851, and promptly submitted a new and liquor-tight bill which became law on 2 June 1851.

The "Maine Law" excited temperance groups and gave them new life. The National Temperance Convention at Saratoga Springs 2 months later adopted a resolution urging other States to enact similar laws. During the next 4 years, 12 States and 1 territory did so. But for the following 25 years not another State adopted such a law; the temperance movement steadily declined, and except for Maine, the States which had enacted the laws repealed or greatly modified them.

As a means of obtaining additional revenue during the Civil War, the Internal Revenue Act established a tax on each liquor dealer and manufacturer; this became an important source of revenue, and thereafter the temperance leaders had to meet and combat the argument that prohibition would cause the Government a great loss of income. In fact, during the 1860s dry leaders found little but discouragement.

Until the middle of the 19th century, the temperance movement had been conducted entirely by men. In 1852 women became interested and some, like Susan B. Anthony, were very active. It was some time, however, before women were influential. In the early 1870s Dr. Dioclesian Lewis inspired "The Women's Crusade" and women began marching on the saloons. They caused great commotions. As a result of the women's crusade, which was most effective in Ohio, many thousands of saloons were closed, over 700 breweries went out of business throughout the country, and production of malt beverages declined by 5,500,000 gallons between 1873 and 1875. The collection of liquor taxes by the Federal Government dropped substantially. But the crusade did not affect the laws which permitted the saloons to operate, or the alliance between the liquor interests and politicians. While things soon returned to normal, the campaign served to revive nationwide interest and affected events of the coming years.

The most important outcome was organization of the National Women's Christian Temperance Union in November 1874, the goal of which was legal prohibition of all intoxicating liquor. Under the later guidance of Frances W. Willard, it became the most powerful temperance organization in the world.

A prohibition party came into being which, in 1876, proposed an entirely new approach. It denounced importation, exportation, manufacture and sale of all alcoholic drinks as "high crimes against society"; demanded a constitutional amendment to prohibit these; and nominated Gen. Green Clay Smith, for the presidency. Most temperance organizations and many dry periodicals supported him. But the great competition given by Rutherford B. Hayes, himself a dry, completely overwhelmed Smith.

The first constitutional amendment for prohibition to be submitted to Congress was introduced in the House in December 1876 and was buried in committee. A stronger one, introduced in 1880, fell by the wayside. A third in 1887 was comprehensive, favorably reported to the Senate, and roundly defeated in 1889. Not until 1914 was another such amendment to go before Congress.

Many States, however, experimented with prohibition amendments to their own constitutions. In 1880 Kansas became the first State to have constitutional prohibition; it remained in force for 67 years. Several other States followed; Maine became constitutionally dry in 1884 and Rhode Island followed 2 years later. Some other States adopted such amendments, revised them, watered them down, repealed them. Only Maine, Kansas, and North Dakota survived as dry States. Even there, enforcement machinery was poor and bootleggers and speakeasies did a thriving business.

The antiliquor forces met plenty of resistance from the distilling and brewing interests. The latter raised a great deal of money, spent it where it would do the most good, propagandized, and published. But they, like their adversaries, were in a state of flux; for decades it was a tug of war between the two opposing factions.

In 1893, the Anti-Saloon League of Ohio was permanently organized. Two years later the Anti-Saloon League of America was formed, with the Ohio and District of Columbia organizations as a nucleus. These and 45 other national, State, and local organizations were merged into this League. It took 10 years, however, to become satisfactorily organized on a nationwide basis, with paid full-time employees and agents. Dominating the entire antiliquor crusade throughout the country, this League became powerful and eventually achieved national prohibition.

It was during these early days of the Anti-Saloon League that Carry Nation made her spectacular hatchet-swinging assaults on the liquor dispensaries of Kansas, and became known as the most violent foe of liquor. Her chief objects of attack were speakeasies, but saloons came in for their share of destruction. She used stones, bricks, and iron bars to destroy bottles, kegs, counters, and fixtures before resorting to a hatchet. She swept through other States, carrying speakeasies and saloons before her, and was a ferocious symbol of the antiliquor forces for 10 years. She was many times arrested and imprisoned for disorderly conduct and for wanton destruction of property, but was soon back on her rampages. The Anti-Saloon League ignored her and her methods, but the W.C.T.U. supported her with enthusiasm. Whatever else may be said, she did contribute to the cause of prohibition.

In commenting somewhat respectfully on the Anti-Saloon League in 1907, *Bonfort's Wine and Spirit Circular* hãd this to say:

"The Anti-Saloon League is not a mob of long-haired fanatics, as some of the writers and speakers connected with our business have declared, but it is a strongly centralized organization, officered by men with unusual ability, financiered by capitalists with very long purses, subscribed to by hundreds of thousands of men, women, and children who are solicited by their various churches, advised by well-paid attorneys of great ability, and it is working with definite ideas to guide it in every State, in every county, in every city, in every precinct . . . ."

By the mid-1900s, dry leaders had discovered the efficacy of supporting dry candidates for office; they controlled the legislatures of six Southern States. The League then shifted its attention from local to statewide prohibition. Georgia, Oklahoma, Mississippi, and North Carolina were legislated dry in 1907, followed by Tennessee in 1909.

The League set up its own publishing house in 1909 at Westerville, Ohio, not far from Columbus, and its publications became highly efficient propaganda. The League wooed the churches, the clergy, and politicians. There was no lack of funds. It became a real nonpartisan political power in line with its original intention. Several years later West Virginia, Virginia, Oregon, Washington, Colorado, and Arizona joined the dry States.

The League again raised its sights. Under the Wilson Law of 1890 shipment of liquor into dry States for personal use was not prohibited, and mail order concerns did a thriving business of this sort. This came under attack by the League and, as a result, the Webb-Kenyon Law was passed over President Taft's veto in 1913; the law removed interstate commerce in liquor from jurisdiction of the Federal Government and placed it in the hands of States which could then enforce their own laws regarding such shipments. It was hailed by the League as a great national victory.

Thereupon, the official organ of the League—American Issue—advocated a prohibition amendment to the Federal Constitution. On 13 November 1913, former Governor Hanly of Indiana, in a speech before the Jubilee Convention at Columbus, Ohio, declared for such an amendment. This declaration was received with wild enthusiasm. One month later, resolutions for a constitutional amendment prohibiting traffic in intoxicating liquors were submitted to Congress.

The armed services became affected by the dry movement; in 1914, Navy ships were forbidden to have liquor on board, 13 years after the sale of liquor on Army posts had been banned.

World War I began in Europe in August 1914, and in the United States resentment against Germany grew like a prairie fire. In the next year or two, the German-American Alliance, which for a long time had been the principal clearing house for antiprohibition work among foreign-born in this country, became generally known. Brewers tied in with the Alliance had made vast contributions to political campaigns, violating Federal statutes and State laws, and had sought to influence public opinion through "subsidizing" various segments of the public press. A later investigation of this Alliance resulted in Federal grand jury indictments of conspiracy against two brewers' associations and a large number of corporations concerned directly or indirectly with the brewing industry. Most pleaded guilty. The Anti-Saloon League made the most of the opportunity offered by the exposure of the German-American Alliance, which had also disseminated pro-German and anti-American propaganda.

Now the League needed still greater congressional support. The resolutions had been defeated by failure to receive a two-thirds vote. The

League concentrated on building its strength in Congress for the next 2 years. By the time of the elections of 1916 the fight for prohibition had been all but won.

The Webb-Kenyon Law had provided no penalities, and consequently the law really had no teeth. Early in 1917, the "Reed-Randall Bone Dry Act," prohibiting all shipment of liquor into dry States and providing for heavy penalties, passed both Houses of Congress.

On 6 April 1917, Congress declared a state of war with Germany. War legislation held priority and dry leaders held off temporarily on the constitutional amendment. On 8 September 1917, however, a law was passed which, among other things, forbade the manufacture of distilled liquors. The drys succeeded in obtaining a ban on the sale of liquor to servicemen. Finally the advocates of the 18th amendment succeeded in bringing the matter to a vote; on 1 August 1917, the Senate approved the amendment 65 to 20. The measure then went before the House which added this to the amendment: "The Congress and the several States shall have concurrent power to enforce this article." In its final form the House voted in favor, 282 to 128, on 18 December 1917.

The 18th amendment, having been adopted by Congress, went to the States for ratification. It should be pointed out that 33 States were already dry. Mississippi was the first to ratify—on 8 January 1918. The 36th State, Nebraska, did so on 14 January 1919. The war was doubtless a factor in the speed with which ratification was accomplished. Prohibition became the law of the land, effective 1 year later, on 16 January 1920.

In October 1919, the National Prohibition Act—usually called the Volstead Act—was passed by Congress, vetoed by President Wilson, and passed over his veto. This act was designed to provide the enforcement apparatus for the 18th amendment, and placed the administration of the law under the Bureau of Internal Revenue, a subdivision of the Treasury Department. This Department viewed the new responsibility with no relish whatsoever. John F. Kramer of Mansfield, Ohio, who was an ardent prohibitionist, was appointed as the first Commissioner of Prohibition.

The *New York Times* of 11 January 1920 quoted Kramer in describing his organization:

"The machinery will consist of two branches. One branch will operate in the States as units, the other in districts of which there will be 10 in the United States . . . . In each there will be a Federal Prohibition Director. Under each Director there will be inspectors . . . . The State organization will have charge of the permissive features of the law. It will issue all permits for the sale and use of beverage alcohol . . . At the head of each of the 10 districts will be a prohibition agent. Under each prohibition agent will be a staff of men . . . . All these men will be experienced in police and secret service duties. They will have particular charge of the discovery of the illicit sale and illicit manufacture of intoxicating liquors. They will make raids and arrests . . . ."

It was estimated that the cost of enforcement would be $5 million a year; this is interesting in the light of later experience.

The advent of prohibition was hailed by the majority as the solution to most of the problems of mankind. Little did the American people foresee the insuperable problems which prohibition was to engender, or the Frankenstein which was born of the 18th amendment!

CHAPTER II

The "Noble Experiment"

As Prohibition went into effect on 17 January 1920, enforcement personnel were ready. The U.S. Treasury Department had been given the enforcement task, and several subdivisions stood ready—the Customs Service, the Coast Guard, the prohibition agents, and other divisions of the Bureau of Internal Revenue. On the local level were sheriffs and the police. Authorities expected few violations, however, for penalties under the Volstead Act were severe. Even the wets expected that prohibition would prohibit. Naturally, a large segment of the populace had prepared for the event by hoarding. Rather frantic private buying had been going on for months. As the day approached, there was a country-wide rush to buy up the existing supply. Little was wasted.

On the morning of the first day of prohibition, agents seized trucks loaded with liquor in Peoria, Ill., and in New York City; they issued 12 warrants for the arrest of violators in New York, and raided stills in several other large cities. From this point forward until 5 December 1933, when the amendment was finally repealed, the prohibition law was broken on a wide-spread scale during every minute of that 14-year period, despite everything the Federal Government and its agencies could do in an effort to prevent it.

Once liquor was legally banned, it seemed to gain in desirability. The old drinkers were not to be denied if they could help it; new drinkers discovered something akin to a thrill in possessing and partaking of the forbidden spirits. A person who was able to get some liquor was looked upon by himself and his friends as "smart." Liquor could not be sold openly, of course, but there were thousands all over the country who risked arrest by selling it under cover, and so speakeasies sprang up like mushrooms. The business became very lucrative. Citizens who were otherwise law-abiding patronized the speakeasies along with the less meticulous, and thus became lawbreakers.

The scarcity of liquor inspired many to manufacture their own. It was almost invariably wretched stuff. In no time, stores sprang up which sold hops, malt, yeast, corn meal, and other supplies, as well as apparatus with which one could produce at home what was generally called "home brew." Even portable 1-to-5-gallon stills made their appearance in the stores. Hip pocket flasks broke out like a rash on the shelves of stores ranging from the lowliest to the swankiest right across the United States. Before the first year was out, thousands and thousands of homes had become little breweries and distilleries for "home consumption."

The younger generation of boys and girls caught the spirit, and drinking became the "thing to do." Women became much more interested in what had been largely a men's province. Boys and girls in colleges became good customers, and bootleggers and speakeasies in college vicinities did a brisk business. Social conditions in the schools and colleges deteriorated considerably. The same was true of the older group, and country clubs and many other organizations had a new lease on life. Not only did all this involve law-breaking, but it seemed to engender a wider contempt for law generally at all levels of society.

Liquor came from three principal sources. There was that manufactured in many thousands of homes; that which was produced in thousands of stills, chiefly in the back country but also in cities and towns; and that which entered the country from outside its borders. The best quality of liquor, of course, came from the third source.

The various law enforcement agencies kept a watch for liquor being illegally transported by truck, train or ship, raided hotels, clubs, speakeasies, and other establishments, and made arrests. These activities were not always peaceful. In the first 12 months, prohibition officials claimed that one Federal agent and one civilian had been killed. The Bureau of Internal Revenue announced in April 1926 that up to then 89 civilians and 47 enforcement personnel (including two coast guardsmen) had been killed. By October 1930, 200 civilians and 86 prohibition agents had been killed according to one report. The Wickersham Commission differed somewhat, reporting that, by the beginning of 1931, the figures were 144 and 60 respectively. These numbers did not include State enforcement personnel, or officers of counties, cities, and towns, or killings by such personnel. Probably three times as many killings occurred at the local level. Many shootings were in self defense, but, regardless of the "merits" of the cases, these killings aroused much public indignation.

The Department of Justice made no particular preparations to handle violators of the Volstead Act; only a relatively few cases of this sort were expected. But in only a few months the Federal courts throughout the country were literally overwhelmed by the number of cases awaiting trial; penitentiaries could hardly hold the rum runners, bootleggers, and others who had been arrested. In 3 years the population of Federal prisons had about doubled.   During the first 6 years prohibition agents alone arrested 313,940 suspected violators according to Department of Justice figures—a number just about matched by the local authorities. The peak of arrests by Federal agents was 75,307 in 1928.   Federal court convictions ranged between 37,181 in 1921 and 58,813 in 1928.

Around 25,000 cases pended at each year-end; most were finally dismissed.   While a majority of cases were handled honestly, bribery and corruption were prevalent.   U.S. attorneys across the country spent at least 44 percent of their time on dry law cases, and in many States much more.   The U.S. courts staggered under the load.   Enforcement by many States was dilatory.   Throughout the entire period of prohibition, enforcement suffered for lack of funds, personnel, and detention space. Violators were well aware of all this.

The padlock method during the earlier years was fairly effective.   A large number of speakeasies, restaurants, saloons, and hotels were closed as a result of being caught at liquor sales.

Corruption among some of the prohibition agents themselves is a matter of public record, as well as corruption in other agencies.   Certainly, the numerous and generous offers from brewing and distilling interests, rum runners, bootleggers, and speakeasies were highly tempting to law enforcement personnel.   That many succumbed to the temptations is not surprising.   And it is said that the so-called Government bootleggers were free from molestation.

One of the most important agencies concerned with law enforcement was the U.S. Coast Guard.   As a result of its additional duties to prevent smuggling of liquor into the United States from the sea, a rapid expansion of its facilities and personnel was required, as will be related presently. The Coast Guard turned in a fine performance throughout the period of prohibition.   Its personnel were almost entirely immune from the temptations of the day, though there were some exceptions.   In the first 2 years a few temporary warrant officers and enlisted men were convicted of scheming with rum runners and bootleggers.   In 1925 the crews of two patrol boats were court-martialed for assisting or protecting smugglers.   There were a few other isolated cases.   Far more numerous were the instances of attempted bribery which were unsuccessful.

There were instances, too, in the Customs Service and among other Government employees, and State, county, and municipal officials. These were the cases that made the news; routine and honest enforcement rarely did so, and such publicity gave false impressions.   The great majority of Government agents were honest, conscientious people who endeavored to do their assigned duties according to the book regardless of their personal feelings or reactions about an obviously unpopular law.

Prohibition brought about a great change in New York and particularly along Broadway.   Many famous hotels and cabarets found it necessary to go out of business, for in the past the difference between profit and loss had depended largely upon their liquor sales. Some of the old places were converted, but new drinking places of a different type cropped up which were in tune with the times. Gradually, the most famous drinking and dancing resorts came under the domination of the big-shot criminal element.

This element grew rapidly and soon became wealthy. It acquired control over the flow of liquor into the city. It dictated distribution and sale, financed night clubs, operated syndicates, and directed the New York liquor wars. It had liquor and other alliances which became literally country-wide; the influence of this element extended to Chicago and Detroit, to Miami and New Orleans, and to Los Angeles and San Francisco. In large measure these men were responsible for the deaths of hundreds of bootleggers and gangsters through various means but especially through the employment of gunmen to whom such work was merely a means of livelihood.

This upsurge of the underworld as a result of prohibition was undoubtedly its most vicious development. Not only did it advance the old-time thugs and racketeers in their chosen professions, but it brought in and developed thousands of new ones. This was the element which, in large part, eventually controlled the great inflow of liquor from the sea, which was to become one of the greatest problems of the period and the particular concern of the U.S. Coast Guard.

But the interests of these barons of crime did not end with the liquor traffic itself; there were many corollary activities which included narcotics traffic, gambling, racketeering, extortion, robbery, prostitution, and murder. Even within the high-up criminal element itself things were not always peaceful. Hijacking and doublecrossing were almost common. These men were terrorists in their field, and many of the enforcement agents avoided getting mixed up with them. To bring such people to book was pretty much a major operation.

When they were taken to court, the perpetrators of widespread crime were ably defended by skilled, well-paid, and unscrupulous lawyers who, in innumerable instances, succeeded in impressing courts which seemed very willing to be impressed.

The story of the rise of these gangsters and racketeers, of whom Al Capone and "Legs" Diamond were perhaps the most famous, the fortunes which they amassed, and the intrigues, murders, and doublecrossing in which they engaged, constituted a shameful byproduct of prohibition. The details need not be recounted in this particular work; they would fill volumes of the most sordid type of reading.

At any rate, during the "Noble Experiment," as President Hoover called it, liquor was profitably dispensed all over New York City, and speakeasies and other places in the city where it was sold numbered high in the thousands. In the other major cities the same was generally true in proportion to the size of the population. There were raids, arrests, and court convictions by the thousands, but the flow of liquor in these cities was never stemmed or even perceptibly retarded.

At the beginning of prohibition there was probably a supply of 40 to 70 million gallons of distilled liquor in the warehouses; of this about 38 million were held by the Government as of 1 July 1922. Under special dispensation, certain distilleries and breweries were permitted to continue production for uses other than beverage. Medicinal liquor was removed from the warehouses in large quantities—much of this went to bootleg gangs. By 1926, probably one-half of the warehouse supplies had been withdrawn, and 2 years later only about a third remained.

Alcohol was manufactured by licensed distilleries, placed in bonded warehouses, and sold by the Government in three classifications—pure, specially denatured, and completely denatured. Industry used these in large and increasing quantities, and production was unrestricted. Much of the pure alcohol which was manufactured found its way into the illicit liquor field. Many new chemical companies came into existence which never manufactured anything, but drew alcohol to the limit of their legal permits, stored it temporarily, and then sold it indirectly to bootleg rings. Since the Prohibition Bureau had no power to investigate beyond the original purchase, it was a pretty safe way of doing business. After some years, this type of transaction fell off materially.

Then of course, there were the moonshiners. In the first few years of the dry era, illicit distillers produced whiskey of a sort, but after 1925 most shifted over to making alcohol. This was easier and more profitable and storing was unnecessary. Production assumed large proportions, and eventually this source exceeded all others combined. There were many hundreds of thousands of stills operating day and night across this broad land. One thinks of stills as typically in the mountains and backwoods. They were there, in quantity, but also in the cities and towns. The stills produced not only whiskey and alcohol, but a lot of money for their operators. They ranged from crude homemade devices to distilleries capable of making 2,000 gallons a day; the large ones often enjoyed excellent police and political protection.

In the larger cities the producers were often controlled by the gang leaders in a well organized operation. The leaders sometimes provided the stills and materials, paid the operators a wage or a share of the profit, collected the alcohol regularly by truck, and sold to wholesale bootleggers. Alcohol thus produced became "gin" after a little treatment by the consumer. Moonshiners in many country areas were also controlled by hoodlums and criminal gangs with connections in the big cities.

As would be expected, prohibition agents seized a tremendous number of stills. In the first 5 years alone, the seizures totaled 696,933. It was estimated in 1926 that at least 500,000 persons were engaged in this type of distilling. With all this widespread activity one might well ask how the authorities allowed it, but it should be remembered that at no time did the Prohibition Bureau have more than 2,300 field agents; protection was widespread; and thus it was an almost impossible situation.

It can be readily appreciated that most of the liquor produced by these various means could not be classed as good. Yet, a great deal of good liquor was available. Most of this, along with much liquor of poor quality, found its way into the country from outside of the borders. All of this had to be smuggled in either from across the Canadian or Mexican borders, or from the sea. Tremendous quantities flowed in from Canada, particularly through Detroit. These were chiefly the concern of the customs men and prohibition agents, though smuggling across the St. Lawrence River and the Great Lakes was also the concern of the Coast Guard.

Those smuggling spirits in from Canada and Mexico had certain advantages. Liquor was not contraband until it had actually crossed the border into the United States. Smugglers by land had 6,000 miles of border country in which to choose their point of entry. From Canada there were more than 400 reasonably good roads, plus 150 which were passable, and a good number of trails. From Mexico, the figures can be divided by about four. Boats in the St. Lawrence, the Great Lakes, and the Rio Grande were often of great assistance. The Coast Guard, the Customs Service, and the prohibition agents were unable to maintain stations at more than a relatively few strategic points due mainly to personnel limitations. In the earlier years there were only about 35 agents for the Mexican border and scarcely 100 for the Canadian boundary. Even with enforcement efforts at their best, it was like trying to stem a flood with a rake. And the flood started within 2 weeks of the advent of prohibition.

Automobiles and trucks took the supplies in over the border roads, while boats transported liquor across rivers and lakes. On the American side, they were usually met and escorted by gunmen. This meant some shooting, of course. Eight guards had been killed and 23 civilians, mostly smugglers, had been slain by the guards by late 1929. Liquor was even smuggled in by air, and railroad freight cars were convenient when railroad employees were cooperative for a liberal remuneration.

These smuggling operations, as well as those on salt water, were not haphazard activities. The entire operations, from importation to final dispensers, were largely controlled by the organized gangsters and racketeers. Large sums of money were expended for the most modern and efficient equipment to defeat the plans of the Coast Guard and other enforcement agencies.

For a few years the combinations worked quite harmoniously together, but rivalries developed, hijacking became frequent, gang wars broke out. Syndicates became bigger, fewer, and more powerful. Those in New York controlled in large measure the flood of liquor from Rum Row with which we shall be presently concerned. Most syndicates operated their own cutting plants, speedboats, and trucks. Some ran as much as 20,000 to 40,000 cases a month. The largest syndicates maintained substantial offices, kept their files and records, paid income taxes chiefly to avoid investigation, employed a large number of persons, and retained smart legal talent. They kept in close touch with politicians and local law enforcement authorities.

Of the liquor smuggled into the United States in 1924, for example, Department of Commerce figures indicate that about two-thirds came in from Canada over the border, and about one-third from Rum Row. That from Mexico never assumed important proportions. Ships of the rum fleet loaded their cargoes chiefly in the West Indies, at some Canadian ports, and at St. Pierre et Miquelon, the French island possession 15 miles off the Burin Peninsula on the south coast of Newfoundland. But the sources of cargoes were not confined to these places.

Smuggling of liquor on the Pacific coast was a minor operation compared with that on the Atlantic. While rum runners were active all along the Atlantic seaboard and the Gulf coast, there were five principal points where entry by sea was chiefly concentrated. The largest and most important was, of course, the New York area, including Long Island and the New Jersey shores. It was in these waters that Rum Row was established. A subsidiary Rum Row existed at times off Boston. A great deal of liquor was run into the country in Florida waters, partly because of the proximity of Cuba and the British-owned Bahama Islands. And much found its way between the Virginia Capes, and also into the New Orleans market.

The usual procedure was to load fairly large vessels with the cargoes of liquor at the various foreign ports of supply and depart for points off the coast where the vessels were anchored. These were the supply, or mother ships. The larger ones were mostly New England or Canadian fishing schooners, able to carry one to three thousand cases on a trip. They were good sea boats and could ride out almost anything the weatherman ordered. But there were also steam trawlers, converted yachts, tramp steamers, and old windjammers. Rum Row consisted of a motley collection of craft of many types.

Contact with shore was made through smaller boats. These came out to the rum ships from shore, lay alongside, took on their cargoes, paid for the load, and returned to shore where they were unloaded. In the earlier days Rum Row was only just beyond the 3-mile limit, and boats of every description went out for their supplies. Liquor was sold to all comers. Even rowboats and small boats with outboard motors were used. Gradually, speedboats came into preference, and before long they predominated. As time went on, and Rum Row was pushed outside the 12-mile zone by international agreement, larger and faster craft became the rule.

The business of bringing the liquor ashore became concentrated in the hands of the big-shot syndicates. They sent their buyers to the West Indies, St. Pierre et Miquelon, England, and elsewhere, chartered vessels, built their own speedboats, and used larger ships as ocean carriers. Some of the speedboats were 75-footers with three Liberty engines, capable of speeds exceeding 40 knots, and of carrying up to a thousand cases. Some were protected by armor plate.

Capt. Bill McCoy claims in his autobiography that he founded Rum Row. He bought and sold his own liquor, but was not tied in with the big syndicates; he did occasionally operate in partnership with Nassau wholesalers and others in the United States. McCoy was no gangster and, strange as it may seem, was not a drinking man. He was noted in Rum Row for handling good liquor and being fair in his dealings. His liquor became known as "the real McCoy"; this term had quality connotations, and has become an American slang phrase meaning genuine and on the level. McCoy says he was the first to run liquor out of St. Pierre et Miquelon; this eventually came to be a most important point of departure for Rum Row. He is also credited with inventing the "burlock"—a package holding six bottles jacketed in straw, three on the bottom, then two, then one, the whole sewed tightly in burlap. It was economical of space and easy to handle and stow. These were generally known in the Coast Guard as "sacks."

McCoy had been captain of the schooner *Henry L. Marshall* which had run a cargo of liquor in to Savannah in 1921. He then bought the fast New England fishing schooner *Arethusa* which he renamed *Tomoka,* and changed her to British registry—a procedure followed by many American rum ships as protection against seizure. He bought a third schooner and began operating out of St. Pierre. After making a few trips and considerable money, he was arrested. A Federal Grand Jury indicted him, but he was freed on bail until 1925 when he served 9 months at the Atlanta penitentiary. On release he found that the big syndicate competition was too much for him; he sold his ships, and retired to Florida where he died in 1948.

The smuggling of liquor from the sea began in a small way but grew to immense proportions. At first, the enforcement of the prohibition law fell chiefly upon the customs and prohibition agents. Through 1920 and 1921, customs officers seized contraband liquor in increasing quantities both along the borders and along the shores. Prohibition agents could intercept liquor being landed on the wharves of New York and other large coastal cities to some extent, and in some ports they had boats of their own to catch the small craft operating in local waters. The task, however, proved far beyond their capabilities. After about 2 years of the dry law, Commissioner Kramer said that prohibition enforcement was a failure due to the antagonism of the people.

It soon fell squarely upon the U.S. Coast Guard to suppress the smuggling from the sea. The Treasury Department had been given the responsibility for enforcement of the prohibition laws, and the Coast Guard, operating under the Treasury Department, is responsible for the protection of the revenues and the prevention of smuggling of all types. Every commissioned officer of the Coast Guard is also a customs officer. With its fleet of cutters for offshore work and a large number of small craft for coastal and inshore activity, this was the logical service for the duty of enforcement on salt water.

From the beginning to the end, the Coast Guard undertook to wage the Rum War at sea, distasteful as it was, and it did a most creditable job considering the personnel and facilities which were placed at its disposal in comparison with the magnitude of the assignment and the problems involved.

CHAPTER III

The
Rising Tide

ONCE UPON A TIME, according to a British folktale, King Canute, in whose power his subjects had supreme confidence, ordered the tide to stop rising.   But the tide kept right on coming in.   With almost equal confidence the U.S. Government, through the 18th amendment and its prohibition law enforcement agencies, ordered the rising tide of liquor to stop, with about as effective results.   Like Old Man River, the flood of liquor just kept rolling along; this surprised the authorities, who had expected few violations and an annual enforcement cost of $5 million.

At the inception of prohibition, the Coast Guard was under the top command of Rear Adm. William E. Reynolds, Captain Commandant, whose title was changed to Commandant on 12 January 1923.   The first Coast Guard officer to attain the rank of rear admiral, he remained Commandant until 1924.   Initially, the Coast Guard was primarily concerned with its regular peacetime duties which came under three classifications—the saving of life and property at sea; protection of the revenues and prevention of smuggling; and military readiness.   The advent of prohibition changed none of these, nor did it add other duties; it merely placed a greater emphasis on the prevention of smuggling.   But, like the other agencies, the Coast Guard did not foresee the great flood of seaborne liquor which was to follow.

The Coast Guard was, and is now, the smallest of the armed services of the United States.   Originally the Revenue Marine, it had its beginnings in 1790 when the Tariff Act of 4 August 1790 authorized the construction of 10 revenue cutters to be used in the protection of the customs. This was deemed necessary, for there was increasing activity in smuggling of all sorts of goods, and the young nation was being deprived of legal duties on imports which were desperately needed by the Treasury Department.

This service for enforcing the collection of the customs was organized by Alexander Hamilton, first Secretary of the Treasury.   The cutters were built, and were manned by efficient seamen, many of whom had been officers and men in the Revolutionary Navy which had been disbanded.

The Revenue Marine, or Revenue Cutter Service as it was later called, continued as an entity until 1915 when it was combined with another service of long standing. This was the Lifesaving Service which had been operated under the Treasury, and the combined organization received a new name—"United States Coast Guard."

It may be said that a lifesaving service had its beginning in 1785, when the Massachusetts Humane Society was founded. This society built small houses of refuge along the coast, but lifeboats were not connected with them until 1807. It was still another 40 years before the U.S. Government showed an interest in this type of service.

Congress appropriated $10,000 in 1848 for eight small boathouses to be placed along the New Jersey shore. These were the first lifesaving stations in America under Government operation. They proved their value for rescue operations in short order, and in 1849 other stations were established on Long Island. Gradually, such stations became generally installed along our shores, and their history is full of heroism in saving life and property, often under the worst possible conditions.

Thus, when this service was merged with the Revenue Cutter Service in 1915, and these became the Coast Guard, there was a very extensive, efficient, and growing organization operating under the Treasury Department, well equipped for rescue duties in coastal areas as well as in the broad Atlantic and Pacific.

Operations of the Coast Guard were conducted in areas known as Coast Guard Districts, each under a District Commander with his own District organization. Thus, when prohibition began, the Coast Guard had available a well-established service with about 15 armed first-class seagoing cutters capable of cruising at sea for extended periods, a similar number of second-class cutters, and a small fleet of harbor cutters and smaller launches engaged in enforcing navigation and anchorage laws. There was also a large fleet of surfboats and other small craft attached to the lifesaving stations which later came to be known as lifeboat stations. All of these were concerned with the saving of life and property at sea, as well as protection of the revenues and the prevention of smuggling. It was believed that the smaller vessels could keep a sharp lookout for shoreline and harbor violations, and that the cutters could take care of matters at sea.

In the days that immediately followed inauguration of the dry era there was little liquor traffic along our shores. The Coast Guard was alert to the possibilities, and there were some seizures of small craft found loaded with liquor both by the Coast Guard and by the prohibition and customs agents. It took time for the rum runners and bootleggers to get organized, and it was almost 2 years before Rum Row became established.

In the fiscal year which ended 30 June 1921, 18 months after the dry law went into effect, the Coast Guard assisted vessels valued at $66 million as well as over 14,000 persons, saving or rescuing from peril 1,621 of these. Coast guardsmen boarded 18,000 vessels in their routine duties, and destroyed 19 derelicts. In the stormy season the seagoing cutters *Ossipee, Androscoggin, Gresham, Acushnet, Seneca, Manning, Seminole,* and *Yamacraw* cruised off the coasts to render such assistance as might be needed by vessels in distress. The Bering Sea and North Pacific patrols continued as usual and the Alaska patrol was conducted by cutters *Bear, Unalga, Algonquin,* and *Bothwell.* The Annual Report of the U.S. Treasury Department for that fiscal year pointed out that enforcement of the prohibition law increased the regular customs activities, and that seizure of contraband liquor by customs officers continued in increasing quantities; Coast Guard activity relating to liquor smuggling was not even mentioned. In that first year and a half, such activity was largely incidental and assumed no important proportions.

But things were beginning to take shape. In the spring of 1921, Capt. Bill McCoy ran 1,500 cases of liquor in to Savannah with his schooner *Henry L. Marshall.* On completion of this trip another captain took command and McCoy bought a second schooner—*Arethusa*—which he renamed *Tomoka.* In late May 1921, McCoy stood in off the coast of Long Island in *Tomoka,* anchored, and contacted bootleggers, representatives of whom he had talked with at Nassau. Word of his arrival spread rapidly and so did his cargo of 1,500 cases of whiskey. It was all sold within a few days—to anyone who had the price—and he departed. Bill McCoy had set a pattern.

In July, strange ships were reported off Atlantic City, N.J., and they were believed to be dealing in illicit liquor; 152 cases of whiskey, identified as having come from the Bahamas, were seized at Atlantic City. Presence of the vessels offshore alerted the enforcement agencies.

In those days, legal territorial waters were within the 3-mile limit; U.S. jurisdiction ceased at that point, and international waters began. Vessels with their liquor cargoes could come pretty well in, and seizures of foreign vessels outside the 3-mile limit could not be made legally and without possible international complications. American vessels outside that limit and, in fact, anywhere other than in foreign territorial waters, nevertheless, were subject to seizure. American rum runners merely changed their vessels to foreign registry, usually under "nominee ownership." Thus, they achieved a certain immunity.

The mysterious steamers and schooners reported off the New Jersey coast were ships without lights at night, and they hid their identity by day. The illicit nature of their visit was evident. Nor was activity all off the New Jersey shores. The British steamship *Arethusa* was reported supplying customers off New Bedford, Mass.

The schooner *Jenny T,* laden with 300 cases of liquor from the Bahamas, had the intestinal fortitude to sail into New Haven Harbor, Connecticut, and tie up at a pier at Lighthouse Point—a remote amusement resort—on 23 July. There, under cover of darkness, she began unloading her $50,000 cargo. Prohibition agents were tipped off. At dawn the next morning, they converged on the scene while unloading was still in progress, seized the vessel and arrested 18 persons, including 3 prominent residents of New Haven.

At just about this time cutter *Seneca,* Comdr. Aaron L. Gamble, USCG, left New York under orders to search the waters off the coast for "floating bars"—the mysterious vessels lying offshore. Two of these had been identified as the two-masted schooners *Henry L. Marshall* and *Pocomoke. Seneca* had been directed particularly to look for *Henry L. Marshall,* a former Gloucester fisherman owned by Bill McCoy and then under British registry. It was known that motorboats had made purchases while the schooner lay offshore.

One afternoon soon afterward, *Seneca* sighted *Marshall* running under her auxiliary engine, and started in pursuit. It was seen that men in the schooner were throwing overboard some of their cased cargo. As the cutter drew near, a motorboat was put over the side of the rum runner; the captain and mate entered it and sped away toward Atlantic City.

On orders from the cutter, *Marshall* finally hove to about 4 miles off Atlantic City. Commander Gamble and some of his men went on board and examined the vessel. She was found to have a cargo of 1,500 cases of liquor from the Bahamas. There were two manifests, one saying that *Marshall* was in ballast, and the other stating that she was conveying 1,500 cases to Halifax. Commander Gamble promptly placed a prize crew of seven men on board the schooner, radioed a message to the Coast Guard district office at New York, and towed the ship to quarantine in New York Harbor. This was the first seizure by the Coast Guard of a large rum runner in what might be termed American waters, and the first to be involved in international controversy.

Men from the U.S. marshal's office were there on her arrival. Federal officials questioned the members of the crew, and announced that they had evidence of a gigantic rum-running plot involving many persons along the Atlantic coast. As a result of this questioning, several raids were conducted soon afterward at Atlantic City. The vessel was detained by the U.S. marshal, who put armed guards on board. Seizure outside the 3-mile limit was justified by the Federal authorities by what they termed was evidence of a conspiracy to violate the customs laws and the Volstead Act. *Marshall* was formally taken into custody on 13 August under the Maritime Act of 1799.

Four days later, Britain protested the seizure, claiming she could not recognize jurisdiction by the United States over the high seas beyond the 3-mile limit fixed by international law for many years, and that the seizure was made 12 miles offshore. On 27 August 1921, warrants for the arrest of Bill McCoy and two others of Miami, Fla., were sworn out by the assistant U.S. attorney at Jersey City. More than a year later, the court held the seizure legal. The decision was appealed. Then on 20 June 1923, Judge Charles M. Hough in the U.S. Circuit Court of Appeals also upheld the seizure, condemnation, and forfeiture of the ship. The case went to the U.S. Supreme Court 3 month later but a review was denied. This was the first of many "international incidents" of this type which were to follow over the years.

The pattern set by Bill McCoy in *Tomoka* caught on rapidly. It took only a few months for numerous rum ships, with their thousands of cases of liquor, to be strung out from Maine to Florida, with concentrations off Boston, New York, Norfolk, and Savannah. Vessels also penetrated the Gulf of Mexico, lying chiefly off Galveston, New Orleans, Mobile, and Tampa. Those off New York, however, became the principal "Rum Row" because of the proximity of the huge market in the big metropolis. Most of the vessels lay just outside the 3-mile limit and waited to sell to all comers, of which there were legion.

Prohibition agents and customs officers were increasingly busy with their raids and with examinations of vessels at piers and in harbor waters. Already, the courts were full of cases involving bribery, extortion, and violation of the prohibition law. The Coast Guard was not out in force against rum runners along the coasts in these early days, for it concerned itself with its primary duties; but the cruising cutters kept a watch for anything suspicious inside the 3-mile limit and occasionally brought smugglers to book.

The 152-foot second-class cutter *Acushnet* was quite active at this time. She was cruising off Nantucket on 11 October 1921, keeping a lookout for rum runners. A two-masted schooner was sighted and *Acushnet* became suspicious of her movements. The cutter chased her from off No Man's Land to a point 15 miles south of Nantucket; on overhauling her she was discovered to be the British schooner *J. B. Young* of Lunenburg, Nova Scotia, with 1,300 cases of whiskey. The master said, on being questioned, that he was bound from St. Pierre to Nassau. The schooner, being outside the 3-mile limit, was allowed to proceed since the cutter had no jurisdiction, but *Acushnet* warned the master to keep away from the coast and escorted the vessel to a point well offshore to the south. There the schooner was kept under surveillance for some time to be sure no boats came out from shore to relieve her of part of her cargo. But when *Acushnet* departed, *J. B. Young* sailed northward again and spent 15 and 16 October at Vineyard Haven Harbor where business proved satisfactory.

The master left the ship 4 days later, promising to return, but he did not do so. The first mate and his four French sailors became alarmed when the skipper did not return; since they did not know how to navigate the vessel, they asked assistance. *J. B. Young* was taken in to Stapleton, Staten Island, with 300 cases of whiskey still in her hold. She was promptly seized by customs agents. But evidence that the vessel had unloaded liquor inside territorial waters apparently was lacking for she and her cargo were released 3 months later on orders of the Secretary of the Treasury.

Only a short time before, agents had seized at quarantine the former steam yacht *John Gully*, said to have been used by Bill McCoy's brother Benjamin and two other men in the biggest smuggling operation up to that time. They were arrested at Miami a few weeks later. *J. B. Young* was said to belong also to this "syndicate."

Not long afterward, *Acushnet* was cruising outside New Bedford, Mass., when she met the Cape Verde packet schooner *Romance* coming in from Cape Verde Islands. The cutter escorted her to an anchorage in the Acushnet River off the town. There, officers searched the vessel and found 250 cases of Scotch whiskey. The captain, owner, and 1 of her 10 passengers were arrested, and the vessel was seized. Liquor was on the ship's manifest, but apparently it had been put there after *Romance* had been sighted by the cutter.

As *Acushnet* steamed toward Boston in late December 1921, she sighted the British two-masted schooner *Golden West,* a former fisherman from Nova Scotia—one which Captain Lauriat of *Acushnet* recognized. News of the ship's departure from St. Pierre had reached Boston and the Coast Guard had kept a watch for her. *Golden West* was anchored close to shore in Massachusetts Bay, and Captain Lauriat decided to investigate. The schooner's captain showed by his manifest that he was bound from St. Pierre to Nassau with a large number of steel drums—sufficient to hold 15,000 gallons of alcohol. He claimed to have had trouble with his sails. The boarding party found only 8,000 gallons, indicating that nearly as much had been disposed of. The vessel was seized and towed to Boston, and the captain was arrested.

Earlier in the year, the British two-masted schooner *Messenger of Peace* had stranded on Ocracoke Bar on the outer island chain of the North Carolina coast—near where the colorful pirate Blackbeard (Edward Teach) had been killed in 1718. Coast guardsmen from the Ocracoke Lifeboat Station gave necessary aid, but remarks made by crew members aroused suspicion and the vessel was searched. No liquor was found, however. The schooner had been owned originally by a minister who used her in his work. He sold her, and the new owner retained the name.

Strangely enough, *Messenger of Peace,* sailing north from Nassau 4 months later, stranded again on the same spot when her master decided to put in to Ocracoke for water and provisions. The stranded vessel was observed by the Coast Guard and a boat put out from the Ocracoke station. The vessel was floated, boarded, and searched again; this time she had a cargo of more than 2,000 cases of liquor. The schooner and her crew were immediately taken into custody, but later released.

And so the year 1921 ended with a notable increase in the number of rum vessels along the Atlantic coast, and a somewhat greater vigilance by Coast Guard units—harbingers of things to come. As the new year began, prohibition headquarters compiled a list of 20 American and foreign ships which were suspected of smuggling.

The mere presence of a rum-laden vessel inside the 3-mile limit was not at this time necessarily cause for seizure. The cutters made sure, however, that the vessel disposed of no liquor. The little ocean-going steam tug *Harbinger,* with 300 cases of Black and White Scotch whiskey, had steamed from St. Johns, Newfoundland for Nassau on 24 December 1921, according to her papers. As she proceeded down the coast she put into port about every 2 days to replenish her supply of coal. She stopped in at Boston, escorted by *Acushnet*. Then, with *Acushnet* close behind her, she put in to Newport, R.I., for more supplies on 24 January. The cutter tied up at Commercial Wharf, with *Harbinger* lying outside her. Needing repairs, the liquor-laden tug steamed on through Long Island Sound, this time escorted by cutter *Gresham,* into New York Harbor and to a shipyard on Staten Island, where customs officials took over the task of seeing that she disposed of none of her cargo.

After overhaul, *Harbinger* moved to Perth Amboy, N.J., under heavy guard. Upon tying up, a large number of men boarded the tug from a motorboat to carry away the cases. Many cases had been unpacked and some bottles placed in the afterhold, despite the guards. The tug was seized by Government officials. An aftermath of this was the arrest shortly afterward of a former U.S. marshal for New Jersey on charges of conspiracy to smuggle goods into the United States, violation of the Volstead Act, and offering a $1,000 bribe to the deputy collector of customs to allow *Harbinger* to land her liquor. The vessel was not as innocent and well-meaning as she had appeared at first. There were many such instances.

Meanwhile, things were happening northeast of Boston, around Cape Ann. Customs officers had received a tip that a schooner had left Nassau bound for Salem with a cargo of whiskey and gin valued at $70,000. Eight customs officers and 10 policemen took up stations on the shore at Salem to watch for the craft or for suspicious smaller boats. As they approached they found seven automobiles and two trucks lined up expectantly and waiting patiently. On arrival of the officers, there was great activity, and all but one truck sped away immediately. Then the officers sighted the motorboat *Wilkin II* of Gloucester coming confidently into Salem Harbor with eight men on board, and signaling to the shore.

She swung in to Collins Cove and promptly grounded on a mud flat. Considering this a real break, the officers took three rowboats and put out to her. The men from *Wilkin II* scurried over the flats to elude the officers and all but one escaped. The exception, who had jumped overboard, stopped in his tracks when he saw an agent draw his revolver; he proved to be a crew member from the Nassau schooner. On being arrested, he said that the motorboat had been loaded from his ship, identified later as *Grace & Ruby*. About 1,350 burlap packages of 6 bottles each of American bonded whiskey were seized in *Wilkin II*.

The Coast Guard was notified, and cutter *Ossipee* was sent to search for and pursue the schooner from Nassau. That night, *Ossipee* pursued an unidentified auxiliary schooner off Cape Ann, believed to be liquor-laden, but apparently the schooner eluded the cutter.

However, early the next morning cutter *Tampa,* Capt. William J. Wheeler, discovered the British schooner *Grace & Ruby* riding placidly off Baker's Island in Salem Bay, and decided to check her. Her bows were covered with burlap, obscuring her name, and her stern had been painted over. Captain Wheeler hailed the ship and asked her name, which her master gave readily enough. The captain then told the master that he was under detention.

Instantly, the engine of the former fisherman was started and the schooner attempted to speed away. Springing into action, coast guardsmen fired a shot across her bow but she kept going. Solid shot then brought her to. A boarding party of three went on board and started to lower the sails. The crew tried to prevent this, but the sight of a drawn revolver ended the trouble. The cargo was found to be whiskey and gin worth about $150,000. This was undoubtedly the schooner which had supplied *Wilkin II*. *Tampa* brought the vessel into Boston where she and her crew were turned over to the proper authorities.

The case against *Grace & Ruby* took the form of a civil libel. The Department of Justice directed that she be libeled for violation of the customs laws by illegal landing of "merchandise." There was the question whether liquor constituted merchandise, and if the ship could be seized legally outside the 3-mile limit. If not, then the Government had no case. But months later, Federal Judge James M. Morton, in ruling on the case at Boston, handed down a decision upholding the seizure of *Grace & Ruby* 6 miles offshore.

"The high seas are the authority of no nation," the decision stated. "They are free to the vessels of all countries. But this does not mean that a nation is powerless against vessels offending against its laws which remain just outside the 3-mile limit. The mere fact that the *Grace & Ruby* was beyond the 3-mile limit does not in itself make the seizure unlawful and establish a lack of jurisdiction." The court held that the schooner had participated in an act of lawbreaking that reached inside the territorial waters. The *New York Times* commented editorially that it was "rather a doubtful case of constructive or extended violation," and made the point that had *Grace & Ruby's* own boat been seized, liability would have been established. The decision held.

Schooners of Canadian (British) registry were becoming an almost common sight in the coastal waters by early 1922, and ships whose papers named St. Pierre or Nassau were immediately suspect. The Coast Guard found itself more and more involved in attempting to stem the rising tide of liquor running, but there had been no effort to expand personnel or floating equipment to meet these new demands.

The effect of this new liquor traffic on the Bahamas is interesting. The Bahamas imported around 50,000 quarts of liquor in 1917—just enough for their own consumption. By the early part of 1922, Nassau had become transformed. Instead of a quiet tropical village it had become something like an American mining settlement in the days of the gold rush. Rum ships filled the harbor, and liquor buyers from the United States with fat wallets, together with their associated thugs and gunmen, swarmed through the town. Spotters for hijacking gangs sought information about cargoes, departures, and destinations. There were feuds, quarrels, knifings, and gunplay in dark alleys, carousing and fighting in bars, and sailors roaming the streets with more money than they had ever dreamed of. The natives sold these characters all the liquor they wanted, in whatever form, helped them load their cargoes, and disregarded the unsavory situation unless one of their number were involved. By the end of 1922 the Bahamas were importing 10 million quarts a year and receipts from liquor revenues were at an annual rate of over a million pounds. Nassau enjoyed its prosperity, if not its source.

St. Pierre et Miquelon was getting along pretty well, too. This port had the advantage of a good harbor and reasonably good facilities, but at this time the town definitely ranked after Nassau. The situation there was about the same, only on a smaller scale.

Despite the vigilance of customs and prohibition agents, and the activities of the Coast Guard with its normal equipment, personnel, and regular duties, the amount of liquor coming into the United States from the sea was steadily increasing. If the flow were to be stopped or even slowed up, additional measures obviously would have to be taken. But the Coast Guard was not then ready to assume the official task of fully preventing this new type of smuggling. It had too few vessels; those it did have had inadequate speed to cope with the motorboats which took the liquor in and which were becoming speedier by the month. The 3-mile limit posed a serious problem, for the rum ships were free under international law to lie just outside that limit without molestation; only when they ventured closer could the Coast Guard take legal action. The fast motorboats which took the liquor in were subject to seizure, but most had little difficulty in eluding or outdistancing the few cutters in a position to give chase or intercept them.

About the first recommendation to augment the Coast Guard's facilities came from Col. William Hayward, U.S. district attorney at New York who, on return from Florida in early February 1922, suggested to Roy A. Haynes, then Federal Prohibition Commissioner, that the Coast Guard be given a seaplane. He felt that observation from a seaplane could be made for a distance of 65 miles over the water in clear weather, and that when a suspected craft was sighted a landing could be made alongside and a guard placed on board if necessary. This was deemed impracticable at the time, and nothing was done; but this recommendation was the beginning of an effort to give the Coast Guard better facilities for the task before it.

Much more was expected of the Coast Guard than it was possible to render without additional funds, floating equipment, and personnel. This was a very frustrating situation to coast guardsmen who were trying to do a conscientious job. The drys did not appreciate the problem, and the wets cared little. The service had several 100-foot former Navy submarine chasers at stations along the coast with neither funds nor personnel to operate them. However, nine of these were lent to the Prohibition Bureau which was in a position to man and maintain them. The Coast Guard continued its best efforts with what it had.

A pattern seemed to be developing among the courts in certain areas in which there was a readiness to be very lenient toward alleged violators, and minor technicalities often swung the verdict in favor of them. The courts released many more than they convicted.

Cutters on patrol kept alert for suspected ships, as did the shore stations. Many times, of course, suspicions proved ill-founded or definite evidence was lacking, but they had to be followed up. For instance, Samuel Holdzkom, in charge of the Coast Guard station at Longport on Absecon Island, and his men were watching the two-masted schooner *Comanche*. From their station a few miles southwest of Atlantic City, they had signaled the schooner at sunset as she crossed the bar between Longport and Ocean City, but the signal had been ignored. Holdzkom watched through his glasses and became suspicious. The coast guardsmen quickly embarked in their power boat and gave chase. As they were approaching, the crew of the schooner, knowing capture was inevitable, were seen throwing case after case and several bags overboard. Overhauling the schooner in the back thoroughfare, Holdzkom ordered her to stop, which she did at a shot across her bow. The coast guardsmen boarded the vessel with their revolvers drawn, searched the ship, and found no liquor on board; it had all gone over the side. But the ship was seized, the captain and crew were arrested, and all were later released.

A former subchaser named *Fidus* was proceeding leisurely up New York Harbor from quarantine one fine morning. Customs inspectors were headed down looking for her, and they boarded her for inspection.

They found the skipper, a former Navy ensign in an old uniform, together with a motley crew; there was no liquor, but there were plenty of signs that there had been some. The skipper came up with a pretty good story. He told of having been boarded by pirates 14 miles off Montauk Point, bound and gagged at revolver point, and robbed of 230 cases of Haig and Haig valued at $23,000. Crew members discounted the pirate story and said *Fidus* had disposed of her cargo outside the 3-mile limit off Montauk, at which time they saw no pirates and no attack.

The 60-foot motorboat *Krazy Kat II,* with $10,000 worth of whiskey, and the lives of her three men, became imperiled when she lost her bearings in a choppy sea and ran aground on the Jones Inlet Bar off Freeport, Long Island. She sent up rocket signals, and residents notified the Coast Guard. The crew of Station 88, near Freeport, reached the scene and found the vessel leaking badly; incidentally, they discovered in the hold 100 cases and 25 burlap bags of whiskey which had been loaded from another ship off Sandy Hook. The men were treated for exposure and customs officers took them to Manhattan. Such incidents, of which there were many, kept the Coast Guard units, prohibition agents, and customs officers alert and busy.

The larger ships, mostly two-masted schooners but also some small steamers, normally maintained their immunity outside the territorial waters and, in these earlier days, sold to all comers. Many had large tanks in their holds filled with alcohol. A contact boat would come alongside, give orders for Scotch, Bourbon, or Rye, together with the name of the brand desired. The offshore crew would then break out the bottles of the size, shape, and other characteristics of the brand desired, place them in wire trays, and lower the trays into the tank of alcohol. When the bottles were filled, they were hauled on deck, and coloring and flavoring were added to the proper bottles. The appropriate labels and other markings would then be affixed, the bottles sealed, placed in their own particular straw jackets, and sewn into burlap sacks. On exchange of money, these would then be lowered into the customer's boat, often with a deliberate dunking in the sea so that markings of salt water would give visual evidence that the product was "right off the boat."

Most of the liquor from rum runners in the bootleg trade was not "legitimate." Much of it was cut, and cut again. The amount of impure beverage sold by the bootleggers under forged labels and purporting to be British or American bonded whiskey was estimated at this time to be 75 percent of the total smuggled in.

The small contact boats were the usual run of motorboats of all descriptions. The boats had to operate inside the 3-mile limit and were, of course, vulnerable to capture. To go 3 miles to sea for a load was usually no inconvenience. These smaller craft made trip after trip, usually landing their cargoes successfully. Some got caught; that was an occupational hazard! The cutters and other boats of the antiliquor forces were not fast, and initially there had been little need for rum runners to use speedboats. They had done very well with what they had.

Yet, the advantages of greater speed became evident to the inshore rum runners and gradually faster craft came into use. By the late summer and early fall of 1922 many shipyards were building fast motorboats with special features. The intent was obvious. But the shipyards violated no law in building them, nor did the owners break any rules by merely owning them.

The rum runner knew the advantages of the 3-mile limit; antismuggling forces knew only too well its disadvantages. More and more, it was felt that if the limit could be pushed farther out, vessels lying outside would find the weather more of a problem, and certainly the small craft from shore would find their trips more difficult and time-consuming. Furthermore, Coast Guard vessels would have more searoom and chances of intercepting small craft might be greater. Some small boats might hesitate to go out 12 miles except in good weather. Though a small boat would be liable to capture for a longer time, it also would have more room for maneuvering, and a distance of 12 miles is a lot of sea space, especially in fog.

Things had come to such a pass that international cooperation was sought late in July 1922. There was an exchange between the United States and the British Governments on the question of rum running. Since most of the larger rum runners were American ships which had transferred to British registry for convenience and protection, the United States proposed that the two governments enter into a reciprocal arrangement whereby the authorities of each would be empowered to search vessels outside the territorial waters up to a distance of 12 miles from shore. Britain balked at giving U.S. "revenue officers" the right to search British ships outside the 3-mile limit. This ushered in extended negotiations not only with Britain but also with other foreign countries; these eventually succeeded, but the 3-mile limit stood for another year and a half.

Meanwhile, the subchasers which the Coast Guard had lent to the Prohibition Bureau were seizing a good number of rum runners, and customs agents were active. For instance, a small but speedy motorboat had been observed making a run into New York every Wednesday night for many weeks. Customs agents in their subchaser spotted this craft one night in Gravesend Bay and gave chase. As the customs men drew near, a rum runner in the motorboat, *Seabird,* took a shot at his pursuers, and this was followed by an exchange of 20 shots. One of these killed the owner of the boat, who was running in 30 cases of whiskey taken from a ship 7 miles offshore.

Liquor running on the Delaware River was growing to substantial proportions. Choice brands were being brought in by small but swift boats manned by crews as fearless as the pirates that used to sail the Spanish Main. This inspired the collector of the Port of Philadelphia in August 1922 to appeal to Secretary of the Treasury Mellon for a "fast cutter" to combat smugglers coming into Philadelphia. New Orleans, also, was becoming one of the big supply centers; "dry navy" concentrations were being set up in that vicinity. And "Rum Row," now pretty well established with many vessels lying offshore just out of bounds off New York, became a part of life.

Liquor continued to flow into New York City in great streams. The bulk of the rum running operations in late 1922 was on Long Island; Federal agents who traversed "every foot of the coast" frankly admitted that the contraband goods were being landed, transferred to waiting motor trucks, and taken into New York City. Prohibition Commissioner Roy Haynes declared that hundreds of vessels were anchored outside the 3-mile limit all along the coasts, and that off the Jersey shore alone there were 60 foreign ships and hundreds of small craft. Contact boats swarmed out to them and dickered as in any market place. Certainly, the force of agents was not sufficient to discourage the traffic, and it began to dawn that the methods used were something less than effective. The search for the solution to the problem at this time was chiefly in the field of international law rather than in the augmentation of the anti-liquor forces and their floating equipment.

It should be remembered that saving life and property at sea was still the chief function of the Coast Guard, and that suppression of liquor traffic was still incidental. There were many occasions when the two functions combined into a single operation. The French schooner *Salvatrice* of St. Pierre had been off Nantucket disposing of her wares in early December. She had been blown out to sea in the heavy gales and badly storm-beaten while her skipper and two others were ashore. Both anchors had been lost, she had sprung a leak, fresh water was gone, and her mate had both hands frostbitten. Watched for along the Cape Cod shores for several days as a suspected rum ship, she turned up in distress near the Boston schooner *Star* which had been caught after a chase. Both vessels, taken almost together off Sandwich, Mass., were well stocked with liquor. They were taken under armed guard into Boston by *Acushnet,* which pumped *Salvatrice* all day to prevent her sinking. This vessel was again seized more than 2 years later, off Eastern Point, Gloucester, with a load of alcohol by *CG–170.*

Northeast gales with sleet and snow raged along the New England coast as the new year approached. Two rum-laden schooners crashed ashore in the storm; one, *Jennie Bell,* grounded not far from Sandy Hook, and the other, *Madonna V,* stranded 9 miles west of Montauk Point. *Jennie Bell's* crew leaped into shoal water, got ashore, and escaped. The Coast Guard at Sandy Hook notified the Customs Service which sent its *Hanson* to the scene; she picked up 70 jettisoned cases of the schooner's 510-case cargo. *Madonna V*, with 2,000 cases, was pounded to pieces in the heavy surf. Members of the nearby Coast Guard station launched boats but could make no headway against the wind and sea, and finally put the old tried and true breeches buoy into action. They took off all of the crew who, in view of the vessel's cargo. were held and later sent to New York.

In this same fierce northeast gale, the two-masted British rum schooner *Annie L. Spindler* of Yarmouth, Nova Scotia, became a total wreck. She was sighted early in the morning by coast guardsmen at the Race Point Lifeboat Station at the tip of Cape Cod, 10 minutes before she went aground on the nearby rocks. She was flying distress signals and her eight men were lashed to the rigging. This vessel crashed aground through heavy surf and promptly began to break up. Coast guardsmen could not launch their boats in the heavy seas and so they shot a line across the ship and brought all ashore by breeches buoy. The victims, exhausted and ill from exposure, were treated at the station. During and after the wreck, crowds which grew to hundreds waited on shore hoping to salvage part of her cargo!

Enforcement agencies by this time knew that their methods were meeting with little success; liquor was entering the country in an ever-rising flood, and they were casting about for new ways to meet the emergency. After New Years of 1923, there was perhaps the first suggestion that the U.S. Navy be called upon to fight the Atlantic coast rum runners. Following complaints by members of the National Congress of Mothers who resided along the coast, the legislative department of that organization wrote President Harding on 13 January urging the use of the Navy for that purpose. The proposal was seriously considered but no action was taken.

In this first phase of the Rum War at Sea, the Coast Guard had hardly a semblance of the necessary manpower and floating equipment to handle the situation. The law was openly flaunted; the vessels of Rum Row were easily visible from shore only a little over 3 miles away, and the Coast Guard was then little more than a nuisance to them. The vessels displayed conspicuously signs advertising their wares and inviting all comers to load up. And virtually all comers did; traffic between Rum Row and the shore was heavy. Because enforcement agencies were not adequately organized or properly equipped, this traffic met only spasmodic interference. The traffic was so highly profitable that the risk seemed almost insignificant. This phase lasted as long as did the 3-mile limit.

As time went on, it became evident that all was not well among the supply ships. By mid-February, there had been many tales, official and unofficial, of piracy in Rum Row. Some were confirmed. One of these was the story of the auxiliary schooner *P. J. McLaughlin*. She was lying at anchor off Seabright, N.J., when the man on the midnight watch noticed the approaching outline of a trawler without lights. He notified his captain who called out: "Watch out, you're running us down." A voice from the other ship replied: "Watch out, we're coming aboard!" The trawler quietly tied up alongside and 20 armed highwaymen of the sea swept over the side. The like number of men in the schooner, realizing their helplessness, offered no resistance. Some were thrown into the hold, others were locked in their cabins, all were securely bound. The trawler's men then calmly transferred to their ship the entire cargo of 4,200 cases of liquor, and quietly departed.

A mystery surrounded the 70-ton schooner *Victor*, a seasoned and previously seized rum runner. She was found 12 miles south of Ambrose Lightship adrift, deserted, stripped of her sails and rigging, and with lifeboat missing. Below in her cabin the tables were set for dinner with freshly cooked food. Had she, too, been a victim of pirates? Men of the Coast Guard tug *Hudson* who inspected her could only guess.

On 11 March, the Yarmouth, Nova Scotia, schooner *Eddie James* sailed dejectedly into Halifax Harbor. Some days earlier, she had left Halifax for the Jersey coast with 600 cases of liquor. She had anchored to dispose of her cargo and some had been delivered. Not long afterward, at dusk, a launch from a large and powerfully built steamer drew alongside, and five sturdy men armed to the teeth came over the side brandishing their pistols. They fired a volley, hitting and wounding the supercargo. Two of the pirates then held the crew at bay while the others removed the entire remaining cargo, and took $8,000 in cash for good measure. The pirates then escaped, taking with them the wounded man. *Eddie James* headed back to Halifax.

Grim evidence of foul play appeared soon afterward. A fog hung heavy over Vineyard Sound, and coast guardsmen of the Gay Head Lifeboat Station heard the faint sounds of whistles and bells coming over the water. As the fog lifted momentarily, they saw a steamer which was awash. When the men started to launch their boats to go to her assistance, the vessel rolled over, her boilers exploded, and she went down. This steamer was the 150-foot *John Dwight* out of Newport. The men made an extensive search but found no trace of the crew. It was presumed at the time that the crew had left in their own boats, but these could not be found. The next day, eight bodies with life preservers were discovered floating in Vineyard Sound amid barrels of bottled ale. The bodies were all cut and mutilated, giving rise to the theory that the men might have had a battle with pirates or a fight among themselves. The answers to this riddle and what caused *John Dwight* to sink were never known.

Piracy had become the worst foe of the rum runners—far more to be dreaded than the almost pitiful fleet of antismuggling craft. On shore, the hijackers were the pirates' counterpart. Some of the pirates were known as the "go-through-guys" who waited until a ship had sold most of her liquor and amassed a fair amount of cash; then they boarded the ship and took the cash—their prime interest rather than the liquor. Often the pirates crippled the ship's motors to prevent pursuit.

Many authorities became very vocal, demanding greater efforts at enforcement. Seemingly disdainful of legal difficulties of an international nature, Deets Picket, a temperance official, stated in Washington, D.C.: "The thing to do, and the only thing to do, is to detail U.S. destroyers to round up these ships, bring them into port, confiscate the ships and their cargoes, and jail every man found on them." More and more, the Navy came up for consideration as a means of stemming the flood.

In early April, President Harding recognized a widespread impression that the Administration was pursuing a perfunctory policy as to enforcement. Those familiar with the situation knew that the agencies were doing their best with what they had, but the President felt the idea should be dispelled. He was determined to bring about better cooperation between Government departments and the enforcement units. One official urged the President to employ 50 Navy submarine chasers for pursuing rum runners within territorial waters; they would be manned by petty officers and placed under the Coast Guard for a short time. Navy officials generally were opposed to using their war craft in the civil work of enforcement.

Nevertheless, Harding looked with some favor on the use of a part of the Navy for the purpose. Prohibition Commissioner Haynes proposed employing eagle boats and similar Navy craft then lying idle. Secretary of the Navy Edwin Denby. had received a number of requests to use naval craft and had rejected them, pointing out that there was nothing in the original powers granted the Navy to authorize its use for the enforcement of criminal statutes. But this *was* in the official thinking. Senator Dial of North Carolina said: "It is worse than a farce—it is an outrage that, with the Shipping Board having something like 1,000 ships to say nothing of the Navy, the Coast Guard, and other Government agencies, these rum runners should be able to carry on this illicit trade." But the solution to the problem involved much more than just ships in number.

While these matters where being discussed pro and con, and indecision reigned supreme, the situation continued unchanged at sea. Britain had again refused a mutual search agreement, while expressing a wish to cooperate in other ways. Coast Guard vessels remained alert for violations. Cutter *Manhattan* was inward bound for New York when, off Fire Island, she sighted the two-masted British schooner *Patricia M. Beman* without lights. Lt. Comdr. M. J. Ryan decided to board her for examination. He found all sails set and the schooner dragging anchor; the vessel was deserted. There was evidence of a fierce battle having taken place on deck; bullet holes were numerous, and rifle cartridge shells were scattered about the deck. Below, the clothes of crewmen were lying all around, indicating that the men had not given much advance thought to their departure. No whiskey was found, but there were many burlap wrappers and empty cases. Papers on board showed that between 12 January and 27 March the ship had disposed of 3,918 packages of liquor. It was theorized that there had been a fight with pirates, in which the latter had won, and that the bodies of the crewmen had been thrown overboard. *Manhattan* could only tow the ship to the barge office at New York.

One group of men worked out an entirely legal plan. They purchased a large yacht which they anchored outside the 3-mile limit. The yacht was complete with band and waiters in uniform. Boats ran to and from the beach carrying passengers for their drinks—truly a "floating bar." As cutters passed, those on board waved friendly greetings which were returned. No law was being broken.

One vessel, known at times as the "Queen of Rum Row," was the 217-foot steamer *Yankton*. While she avoided involvement with the Coast Guard, her story illustrates the nature and some of the vicissitudes of life in the rum fleet.

Built in Scotland nearly 30 years earlier as a luxurious British steam yacht under another name, and erroneously reputed to have been once owned by Sarah Bernhardt, she became an American yacht and was sold to the U.S. Navy at the beginning of the Spanish-American War. Her name became *Yankton*. During her "hitch" in the Navy she served as a gunboat in that war, as fleet tender, and as an admiral's yacht with the fleet; she went around the world with the Great White Fleet in 1908 as an auxiliary, was at Vera Cruz in the 1914 crisis, and escorted convoys in the Mediterranean in World War I. Having outlived her usefulness to the Navy, she was sold in 1921.

Yankton turned up at Nassau where she was libeled and sold by order of the British Admiralty Court. She was again seized and sold within a few weeks. In January 1923 her Nassau skipper recruited a new crew at Havana—a motley lot of Englishmen, Cubans, Italians, Mexicans, Portuguese, Spaniards, and Venezuelans. Their appearance was that of a crew of buccaneers handed down from the old days of piracy. A $500,000 cargo of 8,000 cases of grain alcohol and some bales of Cuban tobacco was placed in the vessel ostensibly for a quick trip to St. Pierre.

The ship proceeded northward, well offshore, stopping periodically for sales to small craft before reaching Rum Row. From time to time small speedboats came out to *Yankton* and took cases in relatively small lots.

While anchored within sight of Ambrose Channel Lightship, there arrived on board a man who described himself as a representative of New York bootlegging interests. After a conversation with the supercargo, the master was ordered to take his ship to Providence, R.I., where part of his remaining cargo would be removed. This man departed, and the steamer proceeded eastward well off the southern shore of Long Island. When southward of Montauk Point she was hailed by two large motor launches. The men said they represented the Providence consignees, and presented apparently satisfactory credentials. About 2,000 cases of alcohol and 2,000 pounds of Cuban tobacco were forthwith unloaded into the motorboats which sped off toward the northeast, and *Yankton* put about. The consignees ashore never did receive their shipment!

The vessel steamed slowly back to Rum Row with the remainder of her cargo but with a greatly diminished supply of coal and sea biscuits. Upon her arrival two tugs drew alongside and tied up. Very suddenly, the crew of *Yankton* were completely overwhelmed as 40 fully armed men swept over the gunwales brandishing their guns; they held the whole crew at bay. After receiving gun point assurances that they would meet with no interference, this boarding party of hijackers calmly removed most of the liquor which remained in the ship. The tugs then steamed away unmolested, and another double-crossing incident was closed.

For nearly 5 weeks *Yankton* stayed on Rum Row, and the remaining liquor was gradually disposed of. The supercargo left the steamer with the last shipment, notifying the master that he would return with supplies, fuel, and pay for the crew.

The bunkers were about empty and the provisions almost gone; they waited many anxious days for the supercargo who never returned. The coal was used up and the crew faced starvation. Becoming desperate, the master decided to take his vessel in to New York. To obtain fuel for the fires, the crew fell to with axes and chopped up the interior woodwork and the fine teakwood decks. Steam was raised and *Yankton* with the assistance of a favorable tide, anchored at quarantine on 23 May 1923. The master signaled for customs officers to come on board, and thus she gave herself up. Papers on board provided the Federal authorities with highly valuable information.

But *Yankton* rode again, and finally ran aground on Nix's Mate in Boston Harbor in a January snowstorm.

While this vessel was waiting for the supercargo, Palmer Canfield, Federal Prohibition Director for the State of New York, and other officials embarked in cutter *Manhattan* in mid-April for a trip of inspection along Rum Row. Out of this came a very significant proposal. In his report to Commissioner Haynes, Canfield advocated the use of seaplanes, a land force equipped with fast motorcars, and a *fleet of ships operated by the United States Coast Guard*. He felt that the Coast Guard should take up more active detection of liquor smuggling since the prevention of smuggling was a duty of that service. Unless more aggressive action were taken promptly to put an end to liquor smuggling, the illegal importation of other contraband articles would assume serious proportions.

This proposition was temporarily sidetracked, but the Administration drafted a plan to employ naval vessels and personnel. President Harding had asked for a formal ruling by the Department of Justice on his legal authority to proclaim the existence of a national emergency and order out the armed forces to break up liquor smuggling. Cabinet members and Naval officers questioned whether the President had the power to transfer vessels and personnel from the Navy for duty under the Treasury Department, but here were the seeds of an eventual realization.

In September, Attorney General Daugherty handed his opinion on utilizing the Navy to President Coolidge, who had succeeded to the Presidency on the death of President Harding. It stated that there was no constitutional authority for the use of the Navy in enforcing the prohibition law except under emergency, and even in emergency it would have to be expressly authorized by Congress. The opinion added that apparently no emergency existed, and went on to say:

"There have been no unlawful obstructions of the functions of the courts or restraint of their processes, or of the Coast Guard, the Division of Customs, the prohibition unit, nor of the marshals and their deputies of the Department of Justice."

Such obstructions would be necessary in declaring an emergency. President Coolidge accepted this decision and looked for other means of meeting the situation.

The Coast Guard decided on a new approach—to starve out the ships beyond the 3 mile limit. Many ships remained for extended periods and ran out of supplies, as had *Yankton*. These were usually replenished by small craft from shore, and this became quite an operation. The legal aspects of seizure of these small craft were uncertain, to say the least. However, if these boats could be legally considered engaged in foreign commerce without a license, they could be seized for violation of law. It was worth testing. Cutter *Seminole* steamed along Rum Row, seized several of these boats, and turned them over to cutter *Manhattan* which took them to the Barge Office at New York, inviting a test in court to determine the legality of this procedure as a means of harassing the rum fleet.

It took some time for a ruling, but in a decision handed down in December 1923 by Judge Learned Hand, it was held that an American vessel which carried provisions to a foreign ship in the rum running trade was liable to seizure and confiscation. This ruling applied specifically to the case of the American steamer *Alex Clark* which had been seized 15 miles offshore by a cutter in May of that year while carrying provisions to a British liquor ship. The vessel was licensed and enrolled for coastwise trade (the definition of coastwise trade specified that a vessel's destination must be a port in the United States) and although so licensed she steamed from New York to a vessel of British registry on the high seas, and there delivered to her certain merchandise. The decision held.

As concern about better methods of enforcement grew, it was natural for the Coast Guard to undertake a more active campaign against the "rummies." In early June, additional cutters and eight 30-knot speedboats with 1-pounders were assigned to the waters of Rum Row. The cutters *Seneca, Seminole, Manhattan,* and *Gresham,* armed with 4-inch rifles and 6-pounders, took over surveillance of the 25-vessel rum fleet; they adopted the policy of using solid shot where blanks fired across a bow were ineffective in halting vessels for search, and when rum runners opened fire on Coast Guard craft.

Only a few days later *Seminole* sighted three fast motorboats in foggy weather and gave chase off Atlantic Highlands. The three boats went into the fog in different directions, but she followed *Bertha Bell,* which put on speed. *Seminole* fired a blank shot across her bows, which failed to stop her, but solid shot was effective. *Bertha Bell* was seized and her crew arrested.

Several rum ships lying off Cape May included the French 3,500-ton *Mulhouse* with 25,000 cases. Her skipper had the temerity to visit the Townsend's Inlet Coast Guard Station, 24 miles north of Cape May, and offer the officer in charge $2 a case to turn his back and let bootleggers land this contraband on the lonely stretch of beach. The answer was an emphatic "No!" Attempts at bribery were frequent; those which succeeded were fortunately very few.

Difficulties imposed by the 3-mile limit were so great and so frustrating that the State Department proposed to a number of foreign nations, including Great Britain, that an agreement be reached whereby territorial waters would be extended to 1 hours' steaming distance offshore, generally considered 12 miles. The Government was prepared to arrange this by treaty if necessary. It would put Rum Row 12 miles to sea and greatly increase the opportunity to intercept and capture the ship-to-shore rum runners. The proposal was coolly received in Britain, but a committee did keep it under consideration. The negotiations went on for many months. This apparently was the first formal step in an effort which, eventually, ended in success.

At the same time the Treasury Department foresaw the need for more funds if the Coast Guard were to be more aggressive in the fight on smuggling, and greater aggressiveness was now recognized as a "must." The Secretary of the Treasury wrote in his Annual Report of 30 June 1923:

"With a view to lessening the smuggling of liquor into this country, it is recommended that the appropriation for the Coast Guard be increased by $28,500,000 for the next fiscal year. This will enable the department to purchase 20 additional seagoing cutters, to purchase or construct 203 motor boats of the cabin cruiser type, and 91 small motor boats to be used at Coast Guard stations, and to increase the personnel of officers and enlisted men of the Coast Guard by 3,535. The seagoing Coast Guard cutters will serve as bases for the large fleet of motor boats intended to be used in patrolling inlets and the entrances to harbors, and will watch 'rum vessels' lying off the coasts and follow them as occasion requires. It is hoped that with such equipment the smuggling of liquor may be reduced to a minimum."

Soon after the death on 2 August of President Harding and elevation of Calvin Coolidge to Chief Executive, Secretary of State Charles Evans Hughes received a reply from the British Government on the 12-mile limit proposal, including objections, to which Hughes immediately replied. It was evident that some British authorities had reacted favorably, while others doubted the utility of the proposed change. Similar negotiations were conducted with several other foreign countries.

Meanwhile, pirating remained very serious. The Nova Scotia schooner *J. Scott Hankenson* was lying 15 miles off Rockport, Mass., waiting to dispose of her cargo. The motorboat *Grayhound,* a previous customer, came alongside with apparently two men who boarded *Hankenson.* One whipped out a gun and summarily shot the captain in the back. This was the signal for seven more heavily armed men to climb over the side. Not satisfied with shooting the skipper, they shot the cook when he moved to defend himself, and the crew were confined to the forecastle. The pirates helped themselves to all the liquor which remained, and departed with cash variously reported as between $35 and $20,000! The wounded captain and cook were treated at a Gloucester hospital, and the pirates were later arrested at Gloucester.

The Canadian schooner *Lucille B* of Digby, with 1,000 cases, was similarly attacked soon afterward off Boston by 15 armed pirates in 3 boats who seized her entire cargo, while the captain had gone ashore to do business in Boston. The crew, hopelessly outnumbered, had to help load the pirate craft at gunpoint. The captain failed to return, and *Lucille B* proceeded back to Nova Scotia. In this case, it was strongly suspected that the captain perpetrated a double-cross and cooperated with the pirates!

Such events brought still greater pressure on the Federal Government. The Coast Guard sought unsuccessfully for a ruling on its authority to suppress such pirating. Plans for expanding the enforcement machinery became fairly ambitious. A carefully devised program contemplated practically doubling the strength of the Coast Guard and "the placing of a prohibition agent in every brewery." While the specific changes under consideration for the Coast Guard had not, at this time, been placed before Secretary Mellon, those in charge of the service had calculated that about $20 million would have to be appropriated by Congress to carry them out. The Secretary's Annual Report recommendation for substantial expansion of the Coast Guard was beginning to take root.

Progress was also being made toward satisfactory international agreements. British legal experts sent a draft of a liquor search treaty to Secretary Hughes written from their standpoint. There was a hint that the final version might specify "an hour's steam distance from shore" as an acceptable change from the 3-mile limit. Two weeks later, final agreement appeared imminent and President Coolidge was soon in a position to submit to the Senate for ratification a satisfactory treaty with Great Britain.

Perhaps the most important capture of 1923 was that of Bill McCoy's British two-masted schooner *Tomoka* one November night off Seabright, N.J. Agents in cooperation with the Coast Guard put into effect without warning the principal of search and seizure beyond the 3-mile limit, realizing the likelihood of legal complications. The cutter *Seneca* arrived near *Tomoka* at daybreak and found the schooner riding placidly at anchor. The ship was first boarded by agents, and as soon as they were on board a fist fight developed in which all hands took part. The agents, though badly beaten up, were able to search her and found 200 cases of whiskey remaining from an original cargo of 4,200. Then *Tomoka* got underway with the agents on board. *Seneca* ordered her to stop. When she disregarded this, the cutter sent two shots screaming across her bows with the desired result. She was then boarded by a larger group of coast guardsmen from *Seneca* and seized. As might have been expected, Britain later protested the seizure, since the proposed treaty extending territorial waters had not been placed in effect. The seizure was held valid, and *Tomoka* was auctioned off 2 years later.

In the first few weeks of 1924 developments were under way which would materially change the complexion of the fight against the rum runners. Not only were "twelve mile" treaties with Britain and other nations imminent, but President Coolidge had given his approval to the recommendation that $28,500,000 be appropriated by Congress for expanding the Coast Guard. According to plan, about $20 million of this would be used for specially designed craft—20 cruising cutters, 200 cabin cruising motorboats, and 100 small speedboats. It was thought that these vessels would put a cordon of blockaders around the Atlantic and Gulf coasts which would be fully effective. The rest of the funds would be used for maintenance and personnel. Commissioned officers would be increased from 209 to 353; warrant officers from 396 to 716; and enlisted personnel from 4,051 to 7,122.

Plans for floating equipment, however, became somewhat modified. President Coolidge asked the Director of the Budget to ascertain whether the Shipping Board and the Navy Department had any suitable vessels which the Government might purchase for use by the Coast Guard. If this were the case, then acquisition of larger vessels would be expedited, probably at considerable saving to the Government. The Shipping Board and Navy would be relieved of some vessels not then in use, and the Government would pay for them.

After almost 3 years of virtual futility in stemming the flood of liquor from the sea with wholly inadequate facilities, the Coast Guard faced the new year of 1924 on the threshold of a great expansion. This was to change the Coast Guard from a small organization, known chiefly to the mariner, to a well-known service of mature size. The second phase in the war against the rum runners was about to begin.

CHAPTER IV

Destroyers for
the Coast Guard

As the Coast Guard entered the year 1924, it was in a position to look ahead with some optimism in anticipation of better floating equipment and augmented personnel. Despite best efforts of the enforcement authorities, liquor smuggling was still on the increase, and rum fleets operating in waters adjacent to the American coasts numbered 158 vessels.

The smugglers also had an inshore fleet of several hundred motorboats and small vessels capable of speeds up to 18 knots; a few much faster. By this time, most of these were directed from New York City. One New York syndicate is said to have owned and operated a fleet of about 100 large and small craft. And the smugglers had a "bribery fund" which was used freely.

Shipments of liquor from Europe since the beginning of 1922 had risen to almost fantastic figures. The Coast Guard reported that rum runners had jettisoned 20,000 cases while under fire. One Coast Guard estimate was that 100,000 cases were coming in each month from Great Britain, Canada, France, Germany, Spain, Havana, Santiago, Jamaica, and the Bahamas. Smuggling was also being done on the Pacific coast, but it was minor in comparison with what was transpiring in the Atlantic.

Even the smaller Rum Row off the Massachusetts coast was fairly active. In mid-February of 1924, four British and two French vessels comprised this fleet. These were anchored well at sea, 18 miles south by east of Cape Ann. Cutter *Tampa* and the Coast Guard motorboat *Pioneer* were with them, cruising through the Row and standing by to prevent traffic with the shore. Several boats went out to the fleet, but departed on sighting these vessels.

Remembering always that the Coast Guard had its regular duties to carry out efficiently, its 29 steam cutters and small boats of the shore establishment were by no means a formidable barrier to the operations of the "rummies." Up to this time, the Coast Guard had captured 149 vessels, mostly small craft, and had seized 30,847 cases of liquor. The Service estimated that it had been able to intercept only about 5 percent of the liquor entering the United States from the sea. But with enlargement, which now seemed almost certain, its abilities in the fight against smuggling would be vastly improved.

In his efforts to expand the Coast Guard, President Coolidge learned that some naval vessels were available. He was thus able to raise his sights on floating equipment, and lower them on the needed appropriation. On 1 February 1924 he forwarded to Congress supplemental estimates of appropriations amounting to $13,853,989 for increasing the equipment and personnel of the Coast Guard. Of this, $12,194,900 was for reconditioning and equipping 20 destroyers and 2 mine-sweepers or other suitable vessels to be obtained from the Navy Department, together with the construction and equipment of 223 "cabin cruiser" type motorboats and 100 smaller motorboats. The rest was for additional operating expenses brought about by the enlargement of the program. The President also recommended the appointment of additional temporary commissioned and warrant officers.

Meanwhile routine seizures continued. The ship-to-shore fleet was continually getting new boats, and to elude pursuers speeds had become increased so that 30 percent were able to turn up 25 knots. The courage, skill, and audacity of their operators were notably on the increase.

Speaking of audacity, the skipper of the British rum ship *Istar* had plenty. *Istar* liked the Virginia Capes region and lay 15 miles offshore with a cargo of Scotch and English whiskey; this had been purchased overseas at about $15 a case and was sold here for $35. This converted yacht was under the watchful eyes of two Coast Guard cutters. Just one more voyage, and she would have netted her captain-owner a million dollar profit. Her captain landed at Cape Henry in a small yawl which he abandoned on the beach. He then went to Norfolk carrying about a quarter of a million dollars in American currency. This he exchanged at a bank for English pounds sterling and drafts crediting him with the equivalent in English money.

He frankly told the Norfolk bankers that he hoped to make one more trip with a full cargo, after which he would retire with a million dollars made in the transport of liquor. *Istar* had made less than half a dozen voyages. The captain returned to his vessel in a ship chandler's launch generously provided for the purpose, carrying with him his English money and drafts.

Congress, by act approved 2 April 1924, appropriated the funds requested for the Coast Guard, and shortly afterward authorized the additional personnel. Steps were taken immediately to put the provisions of the law into effect, and the law enforcement program was pushed toward completion. The whole undertaking was one of great magnitude.

It was a task for which the service had no precedent, and details of the program had to be worked out in an orderly and systematic manner. Thus, overhaul and repair of the destroyers, construction of the smaller craft, enlistment and training of additional personnel and procurement of officers naturally were to take a considerable amount of time. Coast Guard officers drew up plans for the acquisition of some 300 large and small vessels properly equipped, and for the procurement and recruiting of nearly 5,000 more officers and men. One-year enlistments were allowed, with a brief training period at Philadelphia.

The Commandant appointed a board of five officers, under leadership of Comdr. John Q. Walton, to select the 20 destroyers for the Coast Guard. This board reported for duty to the commanding officer of the Philadelphia Navy Yard on 15 April 1924. A special Navy Yard force opened up the boilers of the destroyers, lifted the turbine casings, removed the condenser heads, and disassembled pumps and other auxiliary machinery for inspection by the board. After many days of diligent inspection and examination, the first six destroyers were selected—*Jouett, Cassin, Beale, Downes, Patterson,* and *McDougal.* These were towed around the back channel to the wharves near the shops so that work would commence promptly.

Capt. Harry G. Hamlet, who had been in command of cutter *Mojave* at Honolulu, and Capt. Carl M. Green arrived at Philadelphia shortly afterward as the senior Coast Guard officers in charge of the operation.

The board continued its work of selection. It was decided to overhaul 18 destroyers at Philadelphia and 2 at the New York Navy Yard. As work on each of the original six destroyers was completed and the ship placed in commission, another destroyer took its place. As work progressed it was necessary for Headquarters to select the officers and crews for the destroyer fleet, and Captain Hamlet set up a Receiving Unit at the Philadelphia Navy Yard. After the selections had been completed, the board was dissolved. Officers were assigned as inspectors and engineer officers for the various destroyers.

The engineer officers, chief watertenders and chief machinists mates took a 4-week course in oil burning and the operation of destroyer power plants at the Navy Yard Oil School. The commanding officers and executive officers attended seminars held by Naval officers with experience in destroyer service.

These destroyers had been laid up for most of the period since World War I. Some were pre-World War I "broken deckers"; others were of the newer flush deck design which had proved highly effective. All had been used hard during the war and had aged before their time. Length varied from 293 feet to 315 feet, and tonnage from 742 to 1,150. All were steel vessels driven by steam turbines. They were in various stages of disrepair and a tremendous amount of work was required to put them into serviceable condition.

The destroyer fleet of World War I served chiefly in convoy escort duty and on patrol off the French coasts and in the English Channel. These were the most tempestuous waters of the North Atlantic war zone; the vessels had held the sea in all weathers, winter and summer, the year round. In those all-too-infrequent periods in port, the ships had to be fit for duty at sea on an hour's notice. They were uncomfortable vessels in any kind of sea, and were generally wet. Most, however, were good "sea boats." They had reeled off six and seven thousand miles a month per ship, equivalent to more than twice around the world in a year. Men and ships became weary and racked, but they had carried on magnificently. On cessation of hostilities these ships by the dozen became surplus, and were tied up.

This work of rehabilitation fell upon the Coast Guard; but it was carried out with a vengeance by a thousand coast guardsmen. There was censorship at the Philadelphia Navy Yard, and no civilians were allowed near the section where the fleet was being readied.

Lying at Philadelphia for an extended period had done them no good whatever. The whole summer of 1924 was spent on these first destroyers, overhauling their hulls and machinery, rehabilitating the living quarters, locating and getting on board spare parts and equipment, and finally requisitioning and obtaining the thousand and one articles of supplies needed. Lt. Comdr. John H. Cornell assigned to command *Trippe* said: "For 1 year, we struggled to get this appalling mass of junk back into shape." The winter of 1924–25 was exceptionally severe. Work on these destroyers went on day after day in close to zero weather often without a vestige of heat. Some boilers and engines were in fairly good condition, while others were in a deplorable state. New, quick-firing, long-range guns were installed; torpedo tubes and Y guns for depth charges were removed to lighten weight and remove unneeded equipment.

The destroyers which were transferred from the Navy to the Coast Guard initially numbered 20; 5 more joined in 1926. These 25 ships are listed, together with some pertinent data:

Name	Length	Tonnage	Built at	Year
Ammen............	293	742	Camden, N.J..........	1911
Beale............	293	742	Philadelphia, Pa.......	1912
Burrows..........	293	742	Camden, N.J..........	1911
Cassin............	300	1,020	Bath, Maine..........	1913
Conyngham........	310	1,090	Philadelphia, Pa.......	1916
Cummings.........	300	1,020	Bath, Maine..........	1913
*Davis............	315	1,071	Bath, Maine..........	1916
Downes...........	300	1,072	Camden, N.J..........	1915
Ericsson..........	300	1,090	Camden, N.J..........	1915
Fanning..........	293	742	Newport News, Va.....	1912
Henley...........	293	742	Quincy, Mass..........	1912
Jouett............	293	742	Bath, Maine..........	1912
McCall...........	293	742	Camden, N.J..........	1911
McDougal........	300	1,020	Bath, Maine..........	1914
Monaghan........	293	742	Newport News, Va.....	1911
Patterson..........	293	742	Philadelphia, Pa.......	1911
Paulding..........	293	742	Bath, Maine..........	1910
Porter............	310	1,090	Philadelphia, Pa.......	1916
Roe..............	293	742	Newport News, Va.....	1910
*Shaw............	315	1,110	Mare Island, Calif......	1917
Terry............	293	742	Newport News, Va.....	1910
Trippe...........	293	742	Bath, Maine..........	1911
*Tucker..........	315	1,090	Quincy, Mass..........	1916
*Wainwright......	315	1,150	Camden, N.J..........	1916
*Wilkes..........	315	1,110	Philadelphia, Pa.......	1916

*Joined in 1926.

In the late summer of 1924, *Henley* went to sea with an inexperienced and untrained crew—the first of the destroyers to be commissioned. Outside of a half dozen old-time Coast Guard men, the crew were enlisted and shipped directly from the recruiting office to the ship. They might have been shoe salesmen or clerks one week; the next week they were on board a destroyer with the rating of apprentice seaman or fireman third class. Great were the difficulties of running a specialized ship with an inexperienced crew. Other destroyers, longer in preparation, had a larger proportion of trained men.

When the other destroyers became available, intensive efforts were made to combat the rum runners by scouting, long-range sweeps, and picketing each night when close to shore. Sixty days at sea was normal, with perhaps an occasional few hours in port to satisfy logistical requirements. There were, of course, problems involved in destroyer duty that were not common to those in the conventional cutter. After duty in the destroyers, some officers went on assignment to Headquarters in Washington to give first-hand information on problems and solutions;

the study of these proved valuable and greatly increased the effectiveness of the destroyer force.

The restoration of the destroyers and the subsequent efforts in the suppression of rum running had a profound effect on the history of the Coast Guard. Previously the service had been one completely engrossed in its relatively limited field of activities. Suddenly, the service was faced by a challenge which devolved upon the younger officers who not only found themselves in command of a different type of vessel but in an effort entirely different from anything in the past. The great surge of spirit that accompanied this has carried on through later years and influenced the alertness and progressiveness of the present day Coast Guard officer.

While the work of readying the destroyers was under way, the Coast Guard continued as before in its operations against the rum runners. Cutters cruised the coasts, kept Rum Row under surveillance, and attempted to intercept and seize the contact boats between rum ships and shore. Many captures were routine without special significance or unusual circumstances, but now and then an important event broke the routine.

Seneca, cruising off Long Beach, sighted motorboat *K–13091* near a Rum Row ship of British registry 10 miles offshore, and signaled the motorboat to stop. This was ignored. *Seneca* sent a shot screaming across her bows. The small craft opened fire with small arms, and about 60 shots whined over the heads of the coast guardsmen. *Seneca* directed her gunfire closer to the motorboat, and when her shots fell too close for comfort, the boat halted. She was searched, and while no liquor was found, her two men were arrested and charged in court with impeding Coast Guard officers in the performance of their duty.

Seizure of motorboat *Lynx II* involved tragedy. This boat was sighted off Roamer Shoals Light by Boatswain Edward Butler in his patrol boat just before daybreak. Opening up his engine, he gave chase. As he called through a megaphone, and fired a revolver shot across the bow to no avail, *Lynx II* plunged ahead. Determined to stop the craft, the patrol boat resorted to rifle fire and many shots scored. One made a direct hit on the fuel tank and *Lynx II* stopped. Captain Pedro was found dead on the cabin deck, hit in face and knee. One bullet had exploded two bottles of liquor he had had in his coat pockets. The other men surrendered themselves, their boat, and their 500 cases of liquor.

Success in the long negotiations over a 12-mile agreement was announced on 5 May 1924 after the King of England had signed the treaty; it had already been approved by the Dominion legislatures. On 22 May President Coolidge issued a formal proclamation putting the treaty into immediate effect. Similar treaties were signed with Germany and Sweden.

The "twelve-mile treaty," as it was called, did not mean that the limit was strictly 12 miles from shore; it was "an hour's steaming distance"—

merely 12 miles on the average. It provided that a vessel loaded with contraband could be seized if found in contact with any American craft so powered that it could reach the nearest land of the United States coast within a period of 1 hour from the point of contact. The actual operation of the boat over this course by the seizing authority was essential as legal evidence to support the case. This meant that faster ships must remain 15 to 18 miles out at sea while carrying contraband if that indicated an hour's steaming distance for them; but it meant much greater distance than before for the small boats running the contraband in from the big ships and consequently greater vulnerability. Many of the large rum ships lay 30 or 40 miles out because many contact boats were very fast. Otherwise, the new limit did not seem to bother the ship to shore runners who, by this time, were becoming more professional in their operations, with better and faster boats, and more experience.

The larger vessels often maintained their offshore stations for as much as 4 months, and continued to do a landoffice business. However, they became more scattered. The fleet still consisted chiefly of run-down tramp freighters, some obviously on parole from the scrap heap, and old cargo schooners and converted fishing vessels. Some would be occasionally in close proximity, perhaps for company or to exchange information. Sometimes, during smooth weather, one vessel would transfer cargo to another prior to departing the area. Weather was a bigger factor than before; in heavy weather rum running was virtually at a standstill.

With the ships spread over a much wider area, it was more difficult for the contact boats to locate their supply ships. This brought about more use of planes by the syndicates, chiefly for spotting and locating particular rum vessels so that at night small boats could go out to the exact location.

A brief account of one patrol will serve to illustrate the experience of the cutters before the Coast Guard had the benefit of an expanded fleet, and just as work on the conversion of destroyers got underway. *Seminole,* Comdr. Philip H. Scott, left Stapleton on 17 May 1924 for patrol off Montauk Point. After passing Ambrose Channel Lightship she sighted an inbound speedboat which veered off toward the Highlands as if to avoid observation. Taking an intercepting course, *Seminole* fired two blank shots which served only to increase the boat's speed. There were many boats in the vicinity and the speedboat went among them, making it inadvisable for *Seminole* to continue fire for fear of hitting others. The speedboat made False Hook Channel, got behind a tow of garbage scows, and escaped.

Seminole resumed course for Montauk Point, examining two fishermen off Fire Island. One rum vessel lay 4 miles off Jones Inlet, but no suspect vessels were sighted along the Long Island shore. On reaching Montauk Point at dawn, the cutter stood toward the rum fleet, checked names and positions of the vessels, noted general inactivity on the Row, and stood in to New London to have witnesses present for the hearing in the case of a sloop, *Sadie A. Nickerson,* which *Seminole* had captured earlier.

The cutter then steamed to a point off Block Island, boarding and examining all suspicious boats encountered. Many anchored rum ships were encountered 15 to 20 miles southeast of Block Island; *Seminole* cruised and drifted among them until daylight on the 20th, when she identified 11 schooners and 3 steamers in the fleet, 10 of them well-known in the area. Several fishermen were boarded and examined but no liquor was found except in the sloop *LaFelice.* Some, however, showed by splinters and aromas in their holds that they had been carrying cargoes more costly than fish.

Returning to Block Island area, the cutter seized the gas screw *Fosstena* for violation of customs and navigation laws; *Fosstena* apparently had been prevented from loading by *Acushnet* which was standing by the British schooner *Richard B. Silver.*

At New London, *Seminole* got word of an attempt to coal one of the rum runners. Accordingly, she returned to the fleet off Montauk where, in foggy weather, there was some activity. *LaFelice* was sent in to New London in charge of Lt. Rae B. Hall with a prize crew. Her master was drunk enough to disclose his plan of operation and even his rendezvous, but he would not disclose his recognition signal which would have helped to catch his co-conspirators.

Several of the "mackerel vessels" were examined; only one had mackerel. Another, *Naomi Bruce* of New Bedford, fled toward the mainland, and after an hour's chase was brought to with a shell after a blank had produced no effect. On examination, no liquor was found for she had fled before loading. Two of the three men in this boat were taken on board *Seminole* for search, and Commander Scott sent to the boat an officer and armed crew who, with her own engineer, pursued another motorboat seen leaving a nearby harbor.

Seminole then steamed eastward and met *Naomi Bruce.* She had succeeded in overhauling the other boat after an hour's chase; the boat turned out to be *Aquidneck* of Newport. The Coast Guard found no evidence to warrant seizure, despite splinters from cases and the smell of alcohol. After a sound warning, *Naomi Bruce* was allowed to return to New Bedford.

That afternoon as *Seminole* headed for New London, a motorboat was sighted running out toward the rum fleet. After a zigzag pursuit, solid shot stopped the boat. She was the yacht *Rivalen* with liquor and three men on board; all were seized. *Seminole* returned to New York.

In many respects, this cruise had been successful, but it demonstrated weaknesses inherent in the methods necessary with inadequate floating equipment. Capt. W. V. E. Jacobs, commander of the New York Division, was prompted to call the attention of Headquarters to the need for constant supervision over *each unit* of the rum fleet.

Vessels which had been large, luxurious yachts were sometimes used as contact boats. The steam yacht *Little Sovereign,* in its earlier and happier days, had received special comment in the magazine *Yachting* as a shining example of a fine, luxurious modern yacht. She eventually fell into the hands of the rum runners and her name was shortened to *Sovereign.* Later this was contracted to *Vereign.*

Under command of Capt. John Wilson (later identified through finger-prints as having risen from a naval reserve ensign to lieutenant commander in World War I), *Vereign* sailed out of Newport with a crew of 13. Off Montauk, she took on a load of 1,200 cases of champagne, whiskey, and alcohol valued at $100,000. When she was so full of cases that only the engine room and pilot house were clear, she started back. About 8 miles southeast of Block Island she was sighted by *Seminole,* which approached her closely and ordered her to stop. A shot was fired across her bow; Wilson, defiant, put on speed and attempted to run. Scott ordered his gunners to fire solid shot, but these failed to find their mark. Two explosive shells followed, the first of which exploded over the pilot house carrying away the ventilator; the second made a direct hit on the pilot house. Fragments fanned out through the forward end where the skipper was at the wheel. The three men in the pilot house were variously wounded. *Vereign* hove to and surrendered.

The rum runners called for a doctor, and Lt. Rae B. Hall and a boarding party were sent by Scott to *Vereign.* Hall found that one man had been hit in the thigh, and the skipper had had his thumb nearly shot off. The wounded were treated on board *Seminole.* A prize crew was placed in *Vereign,* and the ship was taken in to New London.

About the time *Henley* was making her first patrols, *Seneca* ran alongside the slowly drifting Norwegian steamer *Sagatind,* 40 miles offshore. *Seneca* took the situation in hand and fired three 3-pound shots across her bow, anticipating sudden flight. But there was no response from *Sagatind.* The cutter hove to and a boarding party went to the silent ship to discover a most sordid condition. They found 43,000 cases of liquor left from an original 100,000 cases, $26,000 in cash, and the deck still piled high with cases. All of *Sagatind*'s crew were stupefied from drink except three whose jaws were broken; one man had a broken leg; many had black eyes. All were herded from the forecastle to the deck, cursing and staggering. The master said fights in the crew had been daily routine since the ship had cleared from Antwerp for St. Pierre. At first he had tried to prevent the fights, but had given up on reaching Rum Row. *Sagatind* was the largest rum runner captured up to that time.

Almost a year later, libels placed against *Sagatind* and her cargo were dismissed on failure of the Government to prove that the vessel was importing liquor rather than merely transporting it. Under the Volstead Act, no forefeiture followed seizure of liquor in transportation unless there was a conviction of the persons responsible for it, and there had been no personal convictions in this case.

Pirates and "go-through-guys" were still operating in the Row. The French steamer *Mulhouse,* a shabby vessel of about 1,000 tons, had made various trips to Rum Row, and in late June of 1924 she was anchored off the New Jersey coast to dispense her wares. She had thousands of cases of liquor reputed to have been worth about $500,000. *Mulhouse* was tempting. After a week at anchor, a boat drew alongside and 30 pirates swarmed on board, brandishing guns and knives. Saying they would shoot to kill, they rounded up the crew and imprisoned them in the forecastle under guard.

The pirates then calmly relieved the ship of her cargo, loading it into several schooners. It was not done hurriedly; it occupied 3 days during which the pirates held an orgy, and sold to all comers at bargain prices. Brandy, whiskey, champagne, and wines were whisked away to the New York market. When the cargo was gone the pirates departed.

No alarm had been given and there was no chase. *Gresham* was in the vicinity several times during this period, but noticed nothing amiss. Men from nearby rum ships released the steamer's crew the morning after the pirates left, and the vessel departed for France.

Up to mid-1924, the Coast Guard had very few junior officers in the ranks of ensign to lieutenant. With the advent of the destroyers, this presented a serious problem. In order to procure such officers for destroyer duty the Coast Guard Academy class of 1925 was graduated in September of 1924; thus about 200 officers were temporarily commissioned. As the destroyers became available for duty these new officers were utilized as watch standers. Even so, there was no surplus; in many of the vessels the executive officer stood the morning watch and the first dog watch, and the two junior officers stood the remaining watches in turn. The need for additional junior officers continued, and even the class of 1927 was graduated a few months early.

With the new treaty in force, the seizure of the smugglers involved to a fine point the position of the seizure or contact. The navigator not only had to be personally sure of his position, but able to defend his work and prove to a sometimes skeptical court how he determined the position. Attorneys for the smugglers were smart, well-paid lawyers. They began studying navigation and called in experts in the field. Some cases went into the intricacies of compass compensation to embarrass or weaken the testimony of the navigator. And the speed of the captured vessel in determining "one hour's steaming distance" was extremely difficult to prove to the satisfaction of a doubting court.

Not only was the Coast Guard thwarted by lawyers and courts, but other legal officials often proved difficult. Lt. Comdr. W. H. Shea, commanding officer of *Acushnet,* had written in an operations report of 30 April 1924 regarding seizure of motorboats *G–408, 744–E,* and *L–885:* "The boat was seized, and it was the intention of the commanding officer to charge the boat and men with violation of R. S. Nos. 4377, 4337, and 4197. The case was taken up with the U.S. Commissioner at New Bedford, Mass., who decided after many hours of consultation and discussion that the complaint could not be legally drawn against numbered boats under the above Revised Statutes, as those statutes provided only for licensed and enrolled vessels and in his opinion, a numbered vessel was not a licensed vessel. Article 1, of Customs Regulations, 1908, specifically states that vessels of less than 5 tons cannot be licensed." All too often, it seemed to the Coast Guard officers that courts seized at any technicality to find in favor of the lawbreakers.

It is said that in one court, a Coast Guard witness was asked what he had found in a seized motorboat. "One hundred cases," replied the witness, to which the judge said: "I thought this was a matter of liquor. There is no law against carrying cases. Case is dismissed!"

By mid-1924 there were about five big liquor rings handling most of the business in New York. The large syndicates sold to smaller rings which they often controlled and these, in turn, disposed of the liquor to others. They bought the liquor in Europe or elsewhere far in advance. Many ships were chartered through their own agents; cargoes were delivered, and the ships themselves handled them. In many instances, the syndicates hired small speedboats to go out and bring in the liquor. Sometimes they maintained a fleet of small craft themselves, as well as a complete hauling service with motor cars, trucks, and moving vans, and men to operate them. These worked mostly between outer Long Island and New York City.

The combine of outlaws was highly organized. Its intelligence was more and more transmitted between rum running forces afloat and those ashore by radio dispatches in codes and ciphers and, when extreme secrecy was needed, by couriers. Liaison between New York and Europe was fairly well established. The average contact boat around the end of 1924 could carry 230 cases. The profit to the carrier was about $5 a case, a compensation of around $1,250 for 4 hours of work. If the runner were caught, high-priced lawyers made it difficult to convict him. If the boat were seized, the Government had to sell it at auction, and generally the boat owner bought it back. One successful trip paid the entire bill and the odds in favor of a successful trip were tremendous.

Meanwhile, work was progressing on rehabilitation of the destroyers at Philadelphia; some were in better shape than others, and these were ready for duty earlier. *Henley* had been the first to go into commission. *Jouett* was next. Winding her way up through The Race and into New London under cover of darkness, *Jouett,* Lt. Comdr. R. L. Jack, was the first of four destroyers to arrive there in the fall after protracted tests at sea following conversion. *Cassin, Downes,* and *Beale* followed, unaccompanied by publicity of any sort.

This fleet of destroyers was placed under the command of Comdr. W. H. Munter. As these vessels became available, they were sent to sea patrolling Rum Row, watching the supply ships to prevent if possible contact with boats from shore, and generally keeping things under surveillance. This relatively small destroyer force had not been in action for many weeks before the east side of the State Pier at New London was procured under lease as a permanent base for those vessels and the section based patrol boats.

According to an article published in the New London *Evening Day* on 31 December 1924, vessels of the New London Base had captured that year a total of 65 ships, 290 men, and liquor worth about $1,500,000. The various agencies working the waterways around New London—the Coast Guard and its embryonic destroyer fleet, New York Customs, marine patrol and the local customshouse—had confiscated 30,000 cases of assorted liquors. As a matter of interest and record, seizures of rum runners by the New London forces during 1924 were:

Acadien, trawler, by *Redwing*
Acoma, yacht, by *Seminole*
Admiral Schley, launch, by Customs
Amerold, barge, by *Seminole*
Amriald, schooner, by *Tampa*
Anna, sloop, by *Cassin*
Aquidneck, schooner, by *Tampa*
Bonito, sloop, by *Cassin*
Com-An-Go, by Customs
Dick, speedboat, by *Tampa*
Edith Louise, sloop, by *Downes*
Elizabeth Wilson, sloop, by *Jouett*
Fantensa, yacht, by *Acushnet* and Customs
Fosstena, sloop, by *Seminole*
467–J, launch, by *Redwing*
Gemma, trawler, by *Seminole*
Hattie, sloop, by marine patrol
Hercules, sloop, by *Cassin*
Independence, sloop, by marine patrol
J. Duffy, schooner, by *Downes*
Jenney T., sloop, by *Seneca*
John Leonard, schooner, by *Jouett*
J–1013, barge, by *Seminole*
J–1151, motorboat by Customs
K–6160, speedboat, by *Seminole*

K–13645, motorboat, by *Downes*
K–13686, motorboat, by *Seminole*
LaFelice, sloop, by *Seminole*
Lorraine Rita, tug, by marine patrol
Madonna della Grasia, launch, by *Jouett*
Marguerite, yacht, by *Jouett*
Mary, yacht, by *CG–233*
Mickey, barge, by marine patrol
9404, barge, by *Seminole*
Nora, sloop, by Customs
North Star, schooner, by *Tampa*
173–O, motorboat, by *Seminole*
179–J, motorboat, by *Seminole*
Over The Top, schooner, by *Tampa*
Pacific, sloop, by *Seminole*
Pal, sloop, by marine patrol
Petrolla 10, launch, by *Downes*
Pocomoke, schooner, by *Jouett*
Rivalen, yacht, by *Seminole*
Rosalind, sloop, by Customs
Sadie A. Nickerson, sloop, marine patrol
Sadie A. Nickerson, sloop, by *Seminole*

Sadina, steamer, by Customs	*Underwriter,* tug, by *Cassin*
Sioux, yacht, by marine patrol	*Underwriter,* tug, by *Cassin*
Tattina, launch, by *Cassin*	*Vereign,* yacht, by *Seminole*
Theodore, yacht, by marine patrol	*Virginia,* sloop, by *Seminole*
Theodore, yacht, by marine patrol	*Warbug,* speedboat, by *Downes*
Uncle Sam, yacht, by *Tampa*	*Wilkes-Barre,* steamer, by New
Underwriter, tug, by *Jouett*	Haven police
Underwriter, tug, by *Cassin*	*William Malloney,* tug, by *Tampa*

The rum runners were not to be discouraged. Some were seized time after time. This list shows that tug *Underwriter* was brought in four times in 1 year. Each time she was released on bond by the court and was immediately back on the job. This sort of thing was terribly discouraging to the officers and men of the Coast Guard. It happened so frequently as to have a definite effect on morale.

As the destroyers went to sea, all hands realized that the problem was new and that they must learn as they went along. They had to learn the ways of the rum runners and the supply ships, the techniques of pursuit and arrest, and presentation of their cases in court. Most of these destroyer crews were green, with a few experienced officers and chiefs. One technique that figured largely in their activity was that of keeping their ship afloat and themselves alive in the winter weather of the North Atlantic.

By late winter and early spring the Coast Guard had most of its newly acquired destroyers in commission. One by one, they arrived at their assigned bases. To augment this fleet a large number of the newly built 75-foot patrol boats, the "six-bitters," were reporting for inshore and offshore duty. They were rugged, seaworthy craft powered with twin Sterling engines of 200 horsepower, and were to perform excellent service despite the fact that their top speed left much to be desired in the rum chasing business. The 36-foot patrol boats for inshore and harbor work were also being delivered.

As this fleet was building up, the available destroyers operated much as had the cutters. They took cruises of several days each through Rum Row, observed and identified the various ships, watched for contact boats, and made seizures and arrests as opportunities were offered. After one of these cruises, Lt. Cmdr. M. J. Ryan, commanding officer of destroyer *Patterson,* mentioned the general belief that under the existing system of patrol no large-scale smuggling could be done by motorboats, and that the 75-footers made it extremely hazardous for them. He mentioned a new development, however, by which the runners were succeeding in getting quantities of liquor to port.

Vessels in the New York Harbor entrance were not boarded. Coasting steamers, trawlers, sailing vessels, tows, all entered and proceeded to their docks without a visit from Coast Guard or customs officials—a wide open opportunity. There was a class of small steamers and tugs which met the liquor vessels far offshore where transfer of cargo could be accomplished unobserved. They could carry 10,000 cases in without being suspected. Landing the cargo in port was a minor problem. Ryan felt it imperative that some Government agency board every entering vessel that was not required to clear through customs or quarantine.

In his Annual Report for the fiscal year 1925, Secretary Mellon appealed for further floating equipment for the Coast Guard. Despite the 20 destroyers, the 75-footers and other patrol boats, he said that the fleet should be provided with 10 new first-class cruising cutters, 25 more patrol boats for offshore duty, 6 vessels of the mine-sweeper class, and 5 more destroyers. He said that results being accomplished by the Coast Guard had fully justified the temporary enlargement of the service, but that further resources of personnel would be required and that enlargement of the service should proceed on permanent lines.

At the time of the report, all of the vessels authorized by Congress had been placed in service except a few patrol boats. Recruiting of additional personnel had been successful, and numberless other essential details had been attended to—a job of stupendous proportions for a service the size of the Coast Guard. The Secretary said: "I cannot speak too highly in expressing my commendation of the Coast Guard for the work thus done, for the expedition and smoothness with which it has gone forward, and for the actual concrete results brought about in the prevention of smuggling. There is a marked diminution in this illicit enterprise."

With this additional floating equipment on duty, the plan finally adopted called for locating and continuously picketing or trailing every contraband laden vessel off the coasts, and for utilizing all available facilities to intercept and seize shore based contact boats which might manage to slip through. Although sometimes thwarted by loss of contact or delay in locating new arrivals, the plan proved quite successful.

New measures brought about new counter-measures, and somewhat different tactics were becoming evident in the rum fleet. In the earlier days, most contact boats had been fairly small craft, many operated by amateurs. Now the professionals, largely controlled by the syndicates, had taken over. The boats were larger, faster, and of greatly increased capacity. Sometimes they had to run as much as 50 miles to sea to get their loads. There was danger in every foot of water. The Coast Guard vessels were more numerous and were shooting oftener, but the rum runners' greatest fear was still the hijacker which infested the Row.

The transactions at sea had been for cash, but the hijackers and "go-through-guys" had changed that. While some cash was still passed, the usual method which had been adopted was rather ingenious. The rum ships wanted no great amount of money lying around to tempt the pirates. Most sales were arranged by the syndicates, which now controlled just about everything in the illicit trade. A card was taken—often a playing card—and torn into two or more pieces. Or sometimes dollar bills torn in two served the same purpose. One-half was held on board the rum ship and the other half ashore. Each card had its own pattern and commanded a certain number of cases. The parts were always matched up to identify the buyer and, if satisfactory, he simply took his load. Payments were made ashore between the interested parties.

With the additional vessels functioning, the Coast Guard charted Rum Row with all the accuracy and persistency of a defending force under wartime conditions. Maps at the operations bases showed by colored pins the position and name of each rum ship, her capacity, and the type of contraband. Arrivals and departures were carefully recorded each day. Individual skippers had known habits and preferences for certain areas, and these were understood and noted. Instead of the previous informal campaign, the Coast Guard now waged a well-planned and systematic offense with floating equipment which at least approached adequacy in the areas of greatest activity.

Wherever a rum ship lay, a Coast Guard cutter, destroyer, or 75-footer took up a position nearby. The rum ship might be anchored well outside the treaty limits, and was herself immune from molestation; not so the contact boats which came out to her and made her business profitable, and which could be trailed and intercepted on return. Though contact boat traffic became far less, many runners succeeded in slipping through; the torrent of liquor flowing ashore became at most a stream. The rum fleet was not by any means routed; it became widely scattered, its trade became somewhat disorganized, and most of its supplies were cut off. Though the rummies persisted for many years, the fleet suffered from all the vicissitudes of a real war fleet under heavy pressure at sea with home ports far distant.

This ended the second phase of the Rum War at Sea, and the third and final, but the longest, phase began.

CHAPTER V

Tricks and

Tactics

WHEN THE DESTROYERS and "six-bitters" were available in force, the Coast Guard's effort to prevent smuggling of liquor from the sea reached its peak; from mid-1925 until the end of prohibition, this effort was held at about the same level with no let-up. While the war against the rum runners has been recounted chronologically up to this point, it is practicable now to consider activities in certain broad areas in which chronology will not be strictly followed.

At first it was largely a matter of speeds between the rum runners and the Coast Guard vessels, in which the rum runners came off best. This advantage of speed was held for years; even when the 75-footers and the speedy 38-foot boats became available to the Coast Guard, the rum runners still held the advantage when there was a chase. The contact boats had the advantage of maneuverability over the destroyers which could turn up over 30 knots. Many contact boats which were owned by the syndicates were constructed in yards where Coast Guard contracts also had been let. The bosses discovered the exact speeds of the new craft being built for their adversaries, and they changed their speed plans accordingly.

Therefore, if speed alone were relied upon, the Coast Guard would have been continually "behind the 8-ball." The Coast Guard searched for ways and means of overcoming the handicap, and this resulted in certain tactics and tricks which often proved very successful. It became more and more a battle of wits, in which the rum runners also used tricks and tactics to throw the Coast Guard off balance, to evade capture in a chase, to hide or destroy evidence, and to produce misleading intelligence. The Coast Guard was not at all backward in productive countermoves.

Many tricks were simple, others were real operations. A very simple one occurred when Comdr. A. J. Ahern, skipper of *Seminole,* discovered motor dory *K–12126* lying alongside the British rum ship *Thorndyke.* On seeing the cutter lower her launch, the three men in the dory abandoned their craft and climbed on board *Thorndyke*. When the coast guardsmen reached the dory they counted 20 cases of liquor there, then attempted to board the larger vessel to capture the three men. However, they were met with hostile action and, being greatly outnumbered, they withdrew. They took the dory with them, leaving the bottleggers stranded.

When the destroyers and smaller vessels went to sea to picket and scout the vessels of Rum Row, many of the latter shifted position constantly, thus adding difficulties for the Coast Guard vessels watching them. Despite the rum runners' intelligence activities which had become well developed, this complicated the problem for contact boats in locating their sources of supply.

The rum runners in ship to shore traffic tried innumerable methods of throwing the Coast Guard off. One time, a radio distress signal was received by coastal stations which indicated that Frying Pan Shoals Lightship off the North Carolina coast was in trouble. The lightship carried no radio. Rescue craft reached the lightship promptly, but found that nothing was wrong. Rum ships made this broadcast to concentrate Coast Guard activity in the lightship's vicinity. *Manning* had been on station with the large rum vessels, and it was believed that the message would draw her away, and divert the attention of others. With the entrance to the bay unguarded for the time being, contact boats ran their loads into the Cape Fear River without interference.

One hoax worked for a while. Perhaps 10 or a dozen small craft would proceed to the offshore rum ships in a body; the slowest and least useful boat would take on only a few cases while the others took full consignments. This boat would be a decoy if a cutter came upon the scene. In that event it would go near the cutter and attract its attention, thus practically compelling it to give chase in a direction away from the others. When the chase got under way the loaded boats would head at top speed for the harbor and, in most cases, successfully land their cargoes. The Coast Guard eventually caught on, but even so it was a maneuver difficult to deal with.

One method employed to avoid capture with necessary evidence was used innumerable times, but it was not especially satisfactory to the smugglers. *Gresham* was keeping a close check on the 28 vessels which comprised the rum fleet, when she sighted the seagoing tug *Albatross* moored alongside the Norweigian steamship *Strudsholm*. The cutter started immediately for the tug, which promptly cast off and sped toward the open sea. Thus began a 50-mile zigzag chase which lasted for 4 hours.

As the chase progressed, those on board the cutter observed the crew of the tug throwing case after case overboard—apparently certain of capture and determined to have no contraband on board at the time. At one point *Gresham* stopped to recover two cases of Scotch to hold as evidence, and then continued the chase. Finally, *Gresham* closed the distance and fired several shots across the tug's bow; one went close over the pilot house and the effect was instantaneous. The tug stopped and waited for *Gresham* to come up. The vessel was boarded and searched, but all liquor had been disposed of. The captain was arrested and put in the cutter's brig because of his belligerent attitude on arrest and disregard of the order to stop. A prize crew was placed on board, and *Albatross* was taken in.

This procedure of throwing the liquor overboard while being chased was frequently employed especially when small craft were speeding shoreward from the rum fleet. This happened often enough to make beachcombing an interesting and sometimes lucrative passtime in certain sections. Many of the cargoes which went overboard consisted of cases with strong manila lines that connected and supported the cases; the lines often led to partially submerged buoys. The rum runners knew where the cases were left, and could go out the next day in broad daylight and retrieve them.

Another somewhat allied method used sparingly in the earlier days was to place the contraband on rafts and float the rafts in to shore where recipients were waiting. This was usually unsatisfactory and was soon abandoned, for the winds and tides did not always oblige, and there were more recipients than the plans called for.

Destroyers, used in picketing, had the disadvantage of not being able to make sharp, quick turns. A destroyer, having located an offshore rum runner tried to stay with her; she would circle, or lie to. This was not always simple. A fog bank during the day might enable the "black" (the Coast Guard's code name for a rum runner) to shake off a destroyer. Misty weather at night, and a smoke screen from the black's diesel exhaust, would foul a searchlight beam enough to permit escape. The destroyer could maintain contact only under fairly favorable conditions of visibility.

The rum runners developed a rather standard escape maneuver for use while being trailed. This was to run at full speed, followed as far back as possible by the destroyer. A smoke screen would blot out the runner, which would then reverse course and pass close to the destroyer, headed in the opposite direction. The destroyer would ring up full speed and, with hard over rudder, try to follow—both vessels operating without lights in violation of the Rules of the Road. The outcome of the chase was usually determined by the degree of moonlight or mist; but the escape had to be made before midnight if the liquor were to be run in and landed before daylight. To counter this, the destroyer usually tried to keep some distance from the boat she was trailing. If the black did not succeed in getting away on her first attempt there would follow much twisting and turning, and often the smoke screen came into play. These escape maneuvers frequently kept up for an hour or so either until the rum runner escaped or gave up to await another try at catching the Coast Guard napping. Had radar been available at the time it would have been of tremendous assistance.

The best method for the destroyers to use in picketing was to circle the black continuously. However, if the circle were too wide a contact boat could sneak in under cover of darkness and get a load. Destroyers usually circled at about 10 knots from dusk until dawn, and the 75-footers did likewise at somewhat lower speed. In the meantime, the searchlight was often focused on the black. To "hold" the rum ship, the destroyer had to have way on her, for when the former doused his lights and began maneuvering, the time required for a large ship to work up speed would have been prohibitive, to say nothing of the difficulty of turning quickly. If a rummy entered the contact area and was picked up by the Coast Guard for picketing and trailing, she had little chance of making contact.

It was not legal under International Rules of the Road to throw a searchlight beam onto the bridge of another ship. Lt. Comdr. J. E. Whitbeck, commanding destroyer *Ericsson,* wished to avoid this and yet keep his black in sight. Since machine guns were to be tested monthly, *Ericsson* hove to close aboard the black he was trailing and Whitbeck called to her skipper: "Look, Cap, we're going to test some machine guns tonight so please keep your lights on so we won't accidentally hit you." The black's skipper waved acknowledgment and left his lights on. Machine guns were mounted and manned on the flying bridge of the destroyer, and the searchlight was kept secured. At 10 o'clock the black doused lights and started to run. Guns promptly opened fire almost in his direction. After a few bursts the rum runner's lights came on again and she hove to, with no further attempt to elude *Ericsson.*

As has been pointed out, most of the rum runners had a much smaller turning radius than the larger cutters and destroyers. One clear November night, *Seminole* sighted and overhauled the British schooner *Thorndyke* about 70 miles southeast of Sandy Hook. *Thorndyke* was under jib, foresail and leg-of-mutton riding sail but making little headway in a diminishing wind. *Seminole* lay with engines stopped and a searchlight on the vessel. Suddenly the schooner put on power, doused sail and attempted to run away. *Thorndyke* tried to elude *Seminole* by running in circles, and for half an hour both vessels ran full speed with full left rudder. Since *Thorndyke* could turn on a smaller radius than the cutter, they were eventually running in concentric circles with *Seminole* outside and her searchlight trained on the black. This conjures up a somewhat ludicrous scene. Finally, convinced that the schooner could not lose the cutter that way, the former straightened out. On this course the cutter trailed her throughout the night, but stopped in the morning as *Thorndyke* passed over the horizon.

Rummies who were being chased by large Coast Guard vessels had a favorite method by which they took advantage of shoal water. Since the rummy drew about a fathom or less, and the larger vessels considerably more, the former would simply lead her escort toward a bar or shoal; Nantucket Shoals were particularly favored for this tactic. If the destroyer or cutter skipper were bold enough and kept the trail, the black would maneuver over a shallow bottom. The trailing vessel obviously could not follow without grounding or sanding the condensers. In this maneuver, the black usually escaped.

Tugs with tows were not especially suspect; therefore, as the rum runners had pressure put upon them, they resorted many times to this expedient. *Lorraine Rita* (formerly *Albatross*) was a tug, and in the early part of 1925 was successful in bringing liquor in from the high seas ostensibly operating as a tow boat with the liquor being transported in the vessel towed. All kinds of vessels were used if they looked innocent enough, even garbage scows owned and operated by the city of New York.

With more aggressiveness in Coast Guard operations, there was also a change in the type of contact boat. The rum runners developed a low hulled speedboat with a flattish bottom and a sharp chine line together with a pill box type of pilot house. These newer vessels were powered with a Liberty type marine conversion of the famous aircraft engine of World War I, and had two, three, or four engines. The craft were often armored. Some had pilot house armor concealed by outside paneling; others had armor plate openly bolted on the outside of the hull to protect gasoline tanks and engines. On their run in with a load, islands were made on deck by building bulwarks of liquor several cases thick to protect the crew who could not get behind the armor of the pilot house or engine room.

These craft were classified as 400-, 800-, 1,200-, or even 1,600-case boats. One of the four-engined blacks was actually run over a measured mile course with 32 tons of sand in bags loaded to give the equivalent weight of a cargo of liquor and exceeded 30 knots. As time went on, boats were built without fancy equipment to make full use of space. Sometimes the inside of the hull was protected from the weight of the load by having battens built longitudinally to keep the cargo from breaking the planking.

Some of these later boats were almost bare hulls with no facilities whatever on board; they were not long at sea. Everything was sacrificed for cargo capacity, speed, maneuverability, and endurance. The rummy personnel in these contact boats lived a rather austere existence. Even heads were sacrificed for cargo space, and buckets on deck served as substitutes. If a bucket were observed to be occupied or about to be occupied, some destroyer men considered it great sport to harass the occupant; the officer of the deck would ring up full speed and dash close aboard the black, sometimes succeeding in upsetting everything with the wash!

Despite mounting opposition by the Coast Guard, the lure of huge profits was such that the liquor interests were not easily discouraged, and they resorted to almost any means to continue the illicit trade. Picketing forced them to use highly maneuverable, fast, economical diesel vessels, so there appeared on the scene modern motor driven cargo ships. They had very fair capacity, and many were equipped not only with radio, but also radio direction finders to all appearances the same model as those the destroyers carried. Because of their size and speed, these newer vessels were more difficult to locate and picket or trail. They would arrange their rendezvous with contact boats by radio, using secret codes, and if trailed or picketed would resort to all manner of evasive tactics. Fog was probably their best friend; it facilitated departure from a destroyer's unwelcome presence. Yet, it sometimes handicapped them in making contact. Some rummies gained a reputation for skillful evasion; and many Coast Guard commanders became reputed for their skill in "holding" the blacks. It was a cat and mouse game with a touch of the ridiculous at times—a comparatively large and expensive vessel which had been built for national defense manned by close to 100 men shadowing a little black.

Contact boats naturally did not like the searchlights turned on them. Many times there were chases in the darkness, with searchlights held on the quarry. In a number of cases, the black used rifle fire to put the searchlight out of business and to wound or kill those directing the beams.

If a rum runner were being chased by one of the smaller patrol boats, a favorite scheme was to jettison whiskey cases in the wake so that they would be hit at full speed by the patrol boat, thus sustaining damage to the hull.

The Coast Guard had many colorful officers. Comdr. Philip H. Scott, who commanded *Seminole* in the earlier days of the Rum War, was one. "Phil" Scott, as he was affectionately called, was an officer with nearly 30 years of experience in the old Revenue Cutter Service and the Coast Guard. He was the kind of man one would expect to meet as a commander of a cutter. A southern gentleman with a Virginia accent, he was a beloved skipper, an expert seaman, and a terror to the rum runners. For relaxation, he studied the Latin and other classics from original texts, and 18th century books in English.

He made very effective use of captured boats, as in the case of *Naomi Bruce,* recounted in the preceding chapter. On one occasion he seized the diesel tug *Pacific,* capable of 8 knots, put on rummy's clothes and cruised around in her. He talked with the rummies, then hoisted the Coast Guard flag, and made many seizures with the tug.

On Valentine's Day of 1924, a speedboat was sighted from *Seminole* running from the rum fleet toward Jones Inlet. Scott sent a shot across

Rear Admiral Frederick C. Billard, USCG, Commandant of the United States Coast Guard, 1924–32.

President Calvin Coolidge. The great expansion in Coast Guard floating equipment and personnel to fight the Rum War resulted from his aggressiveness and foresightedness.

Captain Bill McCoy standing on the deck of his beloved *Tomoka.*

Cutter *Algonquin,* Bering Sea patrol veteran. In off-seasons she sought Pacific smugglers.

Cutter *Acushnet* **brings in** *Salvatrice.* Schooner, with 2,000 cases of alcohol, is seized and towed to Boston.

Captain Bill McCoy's *Henry L. Marshall.* Seized by cutter *Seneca* off Atlantic City.

***Seminole,* an aggressive adversary of the rum runner.** This cutter was a terror to the smuggler in the first years of prohibition.

Cutter *Seneca* steaming out to patrol area. She made many important captures between errands of mercy.

Former steam yacht *Istar* off the New Jersey coast. Her owner amassed a fortune.

Rear Admiral Harry G. Hamlet, Commandant, 1932–36. As a commander, he was in charge of readying the destroyers for the Coast Guard.

Henley, the first destroyer to join the fleet. She operated against the rum runners from 1924 until 1931.

Cutter _Gresham_, a beautiful vessel to all but the rum runner.

Beale **trails an unidentified rum schooner.** Such cat-and-mouse tactics were tedious for all hands.

Destroyer *Downes* enjoys a quiet period in port while conditioning ship and crew for the next patrol.

Captain Rae B. Hall. As a lieutenant Hall suffered a trying experience in captured *K–8940*.

Rum runner *Atalanta* alongside *Ericsson*. A halt in the operations of this chronic offender.

Captain William H. Munter. As commander, Munter was in charge of the busy Coast Guard Base at New London.

Captain John S. Baylis. As lieutenant commander, Baylis was commanding officer of *Paulding*.

CG–17 was destroyer *Paulding,* captor of many liquor craft including *Francis P. Ritchie.*

Coast Guardsmen examine *Alice* of Seattle. The pike in the skipper's hands, lower right, was used to remove liquor from secret compartments.

Paulding **searches a rum runner.** Commanding officer's view from the bridge as seizure is imminent.

Harbor cutter *Arcata* in Puget Sound.   Her skipper's tactics helped to make up for her lack of speed.

Chief Skugaid loads from *Lillehorn* of Vancouver.   Inveterate rum runners of the Pacific coast.

Commander Edward W. Holtz. Ensign Holtz effected an important and daring capture of *Hakadata*.

Commander Charles F. (Shorty) Howell, commanding officer of *Algonquin,* and star witness in the *Quadra* case.

Pacific rum runner *Coal Harbor*. Her seizure was one of the most important in Pacific waters.

CG–100, **the first of the 75-footers.** Sleek and efficient, these new craft proved able adversaries of the rummies.

The first 38-foot cabin picket boat, *CG–2385.*

The 125-foot patrol boat *Tiger* watching for a contact boat reported heading her way.

Tampa lying to on picket duty.   She and her sister ship *Mojave* saved two patrol boats in the storm of October 1925.

CG–128 with contraband seized from *K–10193*.   This capture took place in New York Harbor.

Destroyer *Cassin*, of World War I fame, heading for the open sea and her patrol area.

her bow and she stopped, headed toward the cutter, then dashed off. Solid shot proved more effective; one went through her port side and out the other, damaging only the planking and demolishing a thermos bottle a crewman had in his hand. There was no liquor on board, but the skipper had orders on the British steamship *Butetown* to deliver choice brands at $20 a case, and other evidence which justified seizure. Prisoners were taken on board *Seminole,* searched and confined, and holes in the boat were patched. Scott then armed and manned this boat and sent it out in charge of Lt. (j.g.) Carleton T. Smith to patrol. Certainly, this boat would not be suspected! Within 3 hours she captured the rum runner *K–8940* with 60 cases. The last case had hardly been taken on board the cutter when another motorboat was heard rushing in from seaward.

Lt. Rae B. Hall volunteered to operate *K–8940* and Scott gave permission. Jumping into the boat with four other armed coast guardsmen and a Coast Guard flag, Hall gave chase and overhauled the boat, which held no liquor. He then took *K–8940* on patrol in the vicinity of offlying rum vessels. It was a very fast open boat with a low canvas spray shield. The weather was intensely cold, close to zero. When near the British schooner *Cote Nord,* Hall started to chase the rum runner *Cigarette,* a boat capable of 45 knots, and a chronic offender. The pursuing craft shipped a sea which flooded the well of the fly wheel, and water from this drowned the engine, stopping it. It also drenched all the men's clothing and signals. The only garment left dry was Hall's shirt, which he removed to use in drying the engine. Finally the motor was started, but again the fly wheel drowned it and there was nothing more to use for drying.

Hall then decided to anchor. He and his men tried unsuccessfully to communicate with passing vessels. In an effort to keep warm and dry their clothing they extemporized a stove made from an empty gasoline can with oil-soaked life jackets for fuel. Later they tried to start the engine again, and this time it caught fire. The flames were extinguished, but the motor was dead. They drifted for hours.

Meanwhile, *Seminole* could not locate them; at daybreak the next morning the cutter steamed within a mile of them but did not sight them, to the great disappointment and discouragement of the five men who were now reported as missing. She found them, however, a few hours later. All five were taken to the hospital, four of them frozen but otherwise well, and Hall with burns suffered in putting out the fire in the engine.

One type of harassment used by the rummies smirched the character of those who brought them to book. Laws regarding seizure required that the vessel, tackle, apparel and furniture be taken into custody at the time of the seizure of the offending vessel. This harassment was the practice of the local representatives and the master of the captured rum runner going before a justice of the peace or some minor court with whom an "information" was filed. This asked redress from a wrong; that, for instance, "John Doe, the captain of the Coast Guard vessel *Blank,* did feloniously take away, steal, and appropriate to his own use the following articles—a sextant, charts, parallel rules, time piece used in navigation, the personal property of the affiant," and such. Newspapers frequently reported in headlines that a Coast Guard officer was accused of stealing the personal property of the crew. The public swallowed it. The men were protected legally by the U.S. attorney who would then request a change of venue to a Federal court, as the local court had no jurisdiction. Seldom did such cases come to trial as they were not pursued. The rum runners had gained their objective by defamation of character.

Effective picketing by destroyers and six-bitters caused rum runners of Atlantic City at one time to adopt a new tactic. They went out on strike! With the new hazards, they felt that compensation of $1 a case transported was not enough, and demanded $2. A New York *Times* reporter quoted one as saying: "We go out and we get the stuff and start back. We're fired on, and if we're close pressed very often the cases go overboard. If we come back empty-handed, we get no pay at all."

One night a rum runner was sneaking in to Long Island Sound when it caught fire. A patrol boat from New London happened along; the choice was to let him sink and avoid future trouble, or put out the fire. So the coast guardsmen put out the fire and towed the boat to the New London base. It was tied up at the wharf, and a few nights later began taking in water. The cargo of liquor was quickly removed and piled on the wharf and in an adjacent shed. Sailors naturally passed by and before long quite a few bottles were missing; these had found their way into town under shirts and jackets! The local scandal which resulted caused much discomfiture in Coast Guard circles until it quieted down.

The Coast Guard destroyer force followed the conventional naval organizational plan. It was divided into three divisions of six; one division was located at Boston, another at Destroyer Force Headquarters at New London, and another at State Island in New York. At the beginning of the dark of the moon or after off-shore boats had been dispersed by a gale, a sweep by a division of destroyers was made at high speed from the Virginia Capes to the Canadian border, following the coastline, the destroyers at double visibility distance apart. This usually meant an area of 100 to 120 miles offshore was searched. In patrolling under normal conditions, each destroyer of a division was assigned a definite area. Each day in the early morning a search was made of the area to locate rum runners, using either a standard Navy search plan or a specialized Coast Guard method. At night, an offshore rum runner was picketed by each destroyer; other rummies farther inshore were assigned to the six-bitters.

Not only was the Coast Guard faced with tactics of the rum runners, but often with tactics of the courts. The Coast Guard's work did not end with the seizures; it entailed amassing and presenting completely detailed evidence, and avoiding all the pitfalls and legal booby traps conjured up by bootleggers' attorneys whose regard for truth and justice was nonexistent. The unpopularity of prohibition generally and the sympathy evidenced by the public and sometimes by the courts for those engaged in its circumvention were discouraging. One Federal judge whose district included Connecticut was so biased that, regardless of the completeness and nature of evidence, conviction was virtually impossible. At one time the Coast Guard, therefore, issued instructions that no seized vessel was to be brought into the jurisdiction of his district if any alternate choice were available.

One case will illustrate the difficulty. A small American cargo vessel operating in the vicinity of Block Island and Long Island Sounds was suspected of liquor running. No liquor was found when she was boarded, but there was reason to suspect that she had concealed tanks behind false bulkheads. Boardings frequently had to be made with the vessels under way, and in this instance it was impracticable to take the careful measurements needed to determine if there were foundation for the suspicion. Later, however, this vessel was caught running without lights; she was seized, taken into New London, and tied up at the Coast Guard pier at Fort Trumbull. She was measured, the suspicion was confirmed, and concealed tanks proved to be full of illicit alcohol. The court's ruling in this case was that, inasmuch as the vessel had been originally seized for running without lights, she could be prosecuted only for that offense, regardless of anything else. The Coast Guard was directed to restore the vessel and cargo, intact, to her owners.

The 75-foot patrol boat *CG–113* was picketing the British schooner *Clemencia* on the night of 11 April 1926, 90 miles off Barnegat. Soon after midnight, the 71-foot armored rum runner *Atalanta*, powered with three high-speed motors, came up from the north with mast light and one lower light aft, but no running lights. Boatswain C. C. Cole hailed her and ordered her to come alongside. One of the three men on board asked: "Which boat is this?" Cole answered: "This is a U.S. Coast Guard boat." As *Atalanta* came up on the starboard side, Cole grasped her life rail to hold her off while a fender was placed between the two vessels.

Cole ordered a seaman to put a line on *Atalanta* while he held the rail. As the seaman stepped aft to comply, the man who claimed to be master struck Cole a stinging blow in the face; the engineer immediately started the rum runner with all engines apparently at full speed.

CG–113 promptly started in pursuit. As soon as the fleeing black had cleared *Clemencia's* bow, solid shot screamed over her superstructure as Cole opened fire with the 1-pounder. As firing commenced, lights from four small boats loomed up nearby, but *Clemencia* doused her lights. Cole's machine gun jammed, but firing continued with the 1-pounder and rifles. Fire was returned by *Atalanta;* her shots went wild. Flashes from the guns of both vessels pierced the darkness as the pursuit grew hot. After 40 minutes *Atalanta* had gained visibly, and in an hour and a half she was nearly a mile away. The chase was then abandoned. Cole and his men believed that the black had been hit during the chase since there had seemed to be an explosion in the distance.

CG–113 returned to *Clemencia's* position but found she had weighed anchor and, despite a careful search, was nowhere to be seen.

Somewhat later *CG–113* returned to her base at Atlantic City. A general call was broadcast to seize *Atalanta* wherever found. She was discovered at Atlantic Highlands, seized by the Sandy Hook Coast Guard Station, and delivered to the New York division commander. *Atalanta* was released without any maritime documents in force on payment of $530 imposed by customs for violations committed. She was taken over by her owner.

That was not the end of *Atalanta* by any means. Destroyer *Ericsson*, Lt. Comdr. Lloyd T. Chalker, was cruising 100 miles offshore 6 months later when she sighted the two-masted schooner *Julito* hove to under foresail and jib; she headed for her. A small vessel seen with the schooner sped away and *Ericsson* set off in pursuit. The boat was overtaken and examined; she proved to be *Atalanta*. No liquor was found on board, but the men were arrested and the vessel seized because she was seen leaving *Julito*, which was a foreign liquor-laden vessel, and had fled, necessitating pursuit.

The rum runners frequently resorted to bribery. This was usually unsuccessful, and on some occasions proved a boomerang. A boatswain in command of a patrol boat in New York Harbor was approached by a syndicate agent who asked if he would like to use his six-bitter to run a load of liquor in to New York from an offshore rum vessel at $8 a case. What a foolproof method of transportation! This boatswain promptly said he was not in a position to, but knew one who was, and said the agent would be contacted.

The matter was immediately reported to the Coast Guard division office, and Boatswain Pittman, in command of *CG–203*, was ordered to make contact. Pittman did, and was offered the same bribe if he would run 500 cases in to New York in his patrol boat. Pittman agreed. He informed his office and received his instructions.

CG–203 then set out, but heavy weather frustrated the first two attempts. The third try was successful. In Ambrose Channel a motorboat stopped alongside and two agents stepped on board *CG–203*, which then proceeded to a point 18 miles southeast of Sandy Hook. There she went alongside a handsome white two-masted British schooner. She was *Madeline Adams,* expensively equipped, and carrying champagne and whiskey worth $250,000. No effort was made to seize her. *CG–203* took on 500 cases and, with the agents, returned and tied up at the Battery.

At that point, the agents were arrested, and a heavy customs guard was placed about the pier and patrol boat to insure the integrity of the cargo. Because of the nature of the event, the Coast Guard would reveal no details. Reporters at the Battery saw the patrol boat bulging with liquor and the customs guards all about; they drew their own conclusions. Their imaginations ran rampant, and so did the publicity they produced which strongly implied that coast-guardsmen had turned rum runners!

The episode was reported to Washington, which ordered *Seminole* to go out and get *Madeline Adams.* She was no longer off Sandy Hook, and it took 2 days for the cutter and other craft which joined the search to locate her. *Seminole* finally discovered her 20 miles south of Fire Island; on sighting the cutter, *Madeline Adams* headed seaward at full speed, but *Seminole* overhauled her and captured vessel and crew.

During World War I many wooden cargo steamships were built of one design—as alike as peas in a pod. These were used to transport supplies to the armed forces in Europe, and if they delivered one cargo they were considered to have justified their existence. Many did better than that. After the war these ships were laid up and many were sold to American and foreign buyers. One, sold to an American oil company, was renamed *Texas Ranger;* another went to a rum running syndicate and was renamed *Holmewood* with home port Bridgetown, Barbados.

In the later years of prohibition, *Holmewood* resorted to an audacious expedient, which several times proved successful. On the last of these occasions, she loaded at St. Pierre a liquor cargo worth a half million dollars, and steamed close to New York. As she approached, she was camouflaged to look like *Texas Ranger,* and displayed a name board bearing that name. The real *Texas Ranger* was frequently seen at New York in legitimate trade, and the Coast Guard knew her well. *Holmewood,* with her new look, steamed into New York Harbor in broad daylight up through The Narrows, and to a point off Haverstraw in the Hudson River.

She was reported to the Barge Office as *Texas Ranger.* The report of her arrival was read with consternation by a Coast Guard officer who knew that vessel was in southern waters. Then Coast Guard intelligence became suspicious through radio direction finding, and alerted the New York division and customs. (This episode receives further comment in chapter VIII.) The vessel was abandoned, and the crew rowed ashore. The town police, and coast guardsmen in *CG–131* and *CG–203* and customs officials converged on the scene. Seizure was effected by the customs men, who requested an armed guard, which the Coast Guard supplied. *Holmewood* was taken down the river by the Coast Guard to another anchorage.

New tricks were continuously added to old ones. Liquor was often stored under layers of ice and fish. It was discovered that rum runners had also resorted to such things as false bottoms, secret compartments, false partitions, double holds, and other contrivances. This required coast guardsmen to look carefully beyond the obvious when stopping and examining suspicious craft.

One destroyer skipper observed a new fishing vessel inbound at the entrance of Long Island Sound with a crew which seemed suspiciously unlike fishermen. He stopped her and sent over a boarding party which found this vessel with a full load of fish. The party searched the ship down to the keel. Though they found no liquor, the skipper sensed that appearances were deceptive. The vessel was taken in to New London and tied up at Fort Trumbull. There the master was loud in his claims for damages resulting from spoiled fish.

The Coast Guard officers were in a bad spot until it was discovered that the hold seemed rather shallow for a fishing vessel. A line was passed under the keel from port to starboard and this revealed a discrepancy between the depth of the hold and the draft of the boat. Breaking through concrete in the bilges, the officers bored through wooden planking into a compartment below which was stowed with liquor. This schooner had been especially designed and constructed with a false bottom.

Another vessel attracted attention because she was deep in the water and had only a part cargo of fish; these were not fresh and of doubtful value. At New London, the fish were removed, but no signs of liquor were observed. Outside and inside measurements, however, did not check one with the other. Over the protests of the master, who claimed his vessel would sink, the examining officer caused a heavy steel pointed rod to be driven through what appeared to be the inside of the bottom of the vessel. No water entered, and after the rod had been passed in a few feet it brought up against the real bottom. The compartment was loaded with liquor.

The American fishing schooner *Marianne,* long suspected as a rum runner, was seized in April 1930. At New London she was found to have a concealed hatch. This gave onto a spacious storage room between the keel and false keelson extending from the engine room to the bow. So impressed were the officers at the base that they had a naval architect make a drawing of the whole design.

The disguised fishermen with secret compartments were all contact boats. False bottoms built inside the hull became quite easily detected by measuring. Therefore, some had a false bottom built *under* the regular hull after she had been measured by the Customs authority and her papers had been made out showing length, beam, draft, and tonnage. If suspected, the vessel was brought in for examination and measurement. If there were discrepancies, the inside of the fish bins and hull were carefully examined for signs of a flush watertight "manhole" cover or similar entrance. In one instance Lt. Roderick S. Patch noticed that a suspected vessel had short, stubby masts stepped on heavy blocks about the size for a case, and that the shrouds staying the masts had turnbuckles on one side and pelican hooks on the other. By slipping the pelican hooks the mast pivoted to one side revealing an opening which gave access to storage space for 600 cases of liquor.

The six-bitter *CG–241* was cruising northwest of Block Island. The scallop dragger *Francis P. Ritchie,* a well-known rum runner, was sighted 2 miles offshore, and the patrol boat stopped her for examination. A very thorough search was made; a line was found hanging on a panel, supported by a nail—apparently harmless enough. The nail was removed with a hammer, and three ports fell forward disclosing a false compartment under the pilot house of sufficient capacity for 300 cases. Some time after that, *Ritchie* was again seized, this time by destroyer *Paulding.* The false compartment was full but so was the whole boat!

One afternoon, *CG–288,* Chief Boatswain's Mate O. Lambert, stopped the oil screw *Alamac* of New York for examination. The master claimed to be an innocent fisherman. Lambert sensed several suspicious circumstances including no liquor, no fish, and no smell of fish. On measuring, he found that three feet of space could not be accounted for. He accompanied *Alamac* to New London for thorough examination. Coast Guard officers cut through a concrete deck in the hold of this "fisherman" and removed 1,000 bags of whiskey valued at about $80,000.

Rum runners with false compartments, false bottoms, and such devices were not confined to New York and New England waters. The Pacific coast knew them, too. The rum runner *Alice,* an ex-Navy 50-foot motor sailer that had been housed over and fitted with a mast and boom, was seized by coast guardsmen from the base at Anacortes, Wash. She had been running in liquor from nearby British Columbia. *Alice* was taken to the base where, on examination, an almost fantastic arrangement was discovered.

The method of loading and unloading this boat was unique. Built onto the outside of her hull on each side of the keel, and below water, was a 22-foot long compartment. It was just wide enough to take a sack of liquor easily. In all probability the boat was loaded in a boathouse or on a beach at low water, with the compartments dry. A cord a bit larger than marline was well secured to each sack; the sacks were placed in the opening of the compartment at the after end and then pushed forward with a 22-foot pike pole. The cords were left long enough to extend out of the opening and these were attached in order to an iron piece shaped like a condensed letter U to keep the cords in proper rotation. When the compartment was fully loaded, the cords were folded into the compartment, a thin board was then nailed over the opening, and the boat was floated on the next tide for its journey.

In unloading, it was neither necessary to have the compartments dry nor to beach the boat. Operating from a skiff astern, or in shallow water, the board was ripped off, the iron piece pulled out with a pike pole hook, and the sacks dragged out by the cords, one at a time.

In the accompanying photograph, *Alice* was being unloaded under the watchful eyes of the Coast Guard. When it was demonstrated to the master of the craft that it would be to his advantage to do the unloading, he readily agreed. He is shown at the lower right with the pike pole; the chief petty officer at the starboard stern holds the U–shaped iron piece.

With this introduction to Pacific rum running, let us look further into the situation along the west coast.

CHAPTER VI

Along the

Pacific Coast

LIQUOR SMUGGLING along the coasts of Washington, Oregon, and California never attained the volume or the big business aspects of that in the Atlantic.   Gigantic markets such as those in the heavily populated Middle Atlantic States, New York, and New England did not exist there, and so smugglers in large numbers were not attracted to it.   Yet, there was good demand chiefly in the areas centered around Puget Sound and Seattle, San Francisco, Los Angeles and San Diego, and Pacific waters were sailed by many who were willing to take the risks of rum running for the sake of large profits.   Practically all of the seaborne liquor for the Pacific coast was run in from British Columbia, mostly from conveniently located Vancouver, the Province's largest port.

The position of the Pacific coast rum runners was far less advantageous than that of their brothers in the Atlantic, due partly to the turbulent condition of waters in the latitude of San Francisco, and to the fact that good harbors are widely separated.   It required concentrations of operations in certain specific areas where Coast Guard activity could also be concentrated.   Theoretically, at least, suppression of rum traffic on the Pacific was easier than in the coastal stretches of Florida and between the Virginia Capes and New England.

The amount and nature of rum running operations on the west coast called for no destroyers, and none operated there.   The lifeboat stations were ill-equipped for any duty except lifesaving, and this continued to be their principal function.   The small cutters were notoriously inadequate, but frequently gave a good account of themselves.   Patrol boats attached to the regular Coast Guard section bases were augmented by additional patrol craft.   These and the regular cutters represented the Coast Guard's antismuggling forces on the Pacific coast.

Alice, mentioned in the preceding chapter, had a relatively short run. So did many others likewise engaged in the Strait of Georgia-Puget Sound vicinity.   Deep, sheltered waterways between numerous islands

75

together with the proximity of Vancouver to the Seattle market offered rum runners an attractive operating locality. Most of the activity here was with small craft. There was no need to employ the large ships to lie offshore and wait for the contact boats. A black just dashed in to deliver a cargo, hoping to be unobserved. To prevent this as much as possible, the Coast Guard maintained patrols, and seizures became numerous. Much liquor inevitably slipped by, but the Coast Guard was relatively as successful here as elsewhere in holding down the amount landed.

In the early days, bootlegging in Puget Sound was highly profitable. The boats at first were orthodox small craft; these gradually gave way to low-lying, fast launches with engines of 250 to 500 horsepower, and speeds varying from 20 to 35 knots, following the Atlantic pattern. Strange as it may appear, many of these boats kept regular schedules. Agents ashore kept them informed of every movement of law enforcement authorities.

The patrol of the Strait of Juan de Fuca, the Strait of Georgia, and the approaches to Puget Sound was the responsibility of the commanding officer of the base at Port Townsend. There were subsidiary bases at Anacortes and Port Angeles. An extensive patrol covered the southern shore of Juan de Fuca Strait from Port Angeles westward to Neah Bay. The patrols were reasonably effective in deterring water landings; they were carried out chiefly by 75-footers when these became available. In the later years of prohibition smuggling in the area was held to very minor proportions. Not only were the patrols concerned with preventing the smuggling of liquor, but also aliens and narcotics.

The cutter *Arcata,* like many others, did not have the proper speed to chase rum runners. She was an 85-foot harbor cutter, and when "opened up" in quiet water, could turn up only 12 knots. Despite this, she had a creditable record. Under command of Boatswain L. A. Lonsdale, by skillful and patient endeavor, she was able to make a good number of seizures, many of them involving speedy craft.

Late one afternoon *Arcata* was lying off Marrowstone Point at the entrance to Admiralty Inlet when *Searchlight,* a swift gasoline motorboat, made her way leisurely out of Puget Sound. As she passed *Arcata,* her skipper waved a greeting. Not long afterward, the cutter anchored for the night near Point No Point in a dense fog. Just before daybreak the fog lifted a trifle, and the watch reported to the skipper that a launch was anchored nearby. Lonsdale took a look and recognized *Searchlight;* with several men he put off in his boat for an examination. All the evidence he could find, however, was one or two bottles of beer. Could she have landed her cargo? The skipper decided to search the shore. Putting off into the fog in another direction he circled in and his suspicions were confirmed. He found 24 cases of liquor; then he obtained an admission from the crew that the contraband was theirs. *Search-*

light was seized.   Chance played its part here, when the two vessels anchored within a few hundred yards of each other.

In this case, and in many others, liquor smugglers were discovered by accident.   Harbor cutter *Guard,* a 67-footer, went out from Seattle to search for a family which had become marooned on Smith Island during a heavy gale.   Boatswain Greene and his crew made a thorough search and finally found them.   However, while watching the shore from *Guard* for signs of the family, Greene discovered a boat on the beach from which two men were stealthily carrying liquor.   The coast guardsmen went ashore promptly; one of the men approached Greene and said: "Here is a thousand dollars if you keep quiet about this."   The skipper's reply was: "Nothing doing."   The men were placed under arrest, with an additional charge of attempted bribery for full measure, and taken on board *Guard.*

Perhaps *Arcata*'s outstanding capture occurred in June 1924.   Her skipper had word that rum runners probably would try to bring liquor to Seattle for the Fourth of July.   *Arcata* lay in wait under cover of darkness in Mutiny Bay.   One boat came in, giving the harbor a wide berth.   Then a second was heard approaching; she ran into the harbor, heading between the cutter and the shore.   *Arcata* immediately got underway, put her searchlight on the speedboat, and a shot which she put across her bows echoed across the quiet waters.   The answer from *M–775* was a change of direction and a burst of speed.   The rum runners whipped out a rifle or pistol and bullets whistled over the heads of the coast guardsmen.   The cutter went in pursuit and began firing in earnest.   One of her shells pierced the speedboat's gasoline tank, and a terrific explosion followed.   The forward deck was raised off the boat, and bolts of flame shot through the portholes.

Drawing alongside the flaming craft, *Arcata*'s crew pulled four men from the rum runner.   Streams were played on the flames to no avail; *Arcata* towed the still burning boat to Point No Point and beached her. In the hold was the suspected cargo of contraband, but the two crewmen were doing more than just running liquor; they also had two contraband Chinese.   In this encounter, the two crewmen were injured by shot, and burned; both of the Chinese were badly burned.   All were arrested.

While the Washington coastal areas had no problem of large rum vessels lying offshore for contact boats, such vessels did transit the waters from Vancouver to the California coast.   Cutter *Haida,* a 240-foot vessel, patrolled offshore and picketed a few rum runners which occasionally laid-to.   Often these were simply decoys to keep track of and influence Coast Guard movements.   The rummies would finally move on, and *Haida* would trail them sometimes as much as 50 miles offshore. The small rum runners, perhaps 60 feet in length, would stay out sometimes as much as a week or two, tying up a patrol while riding out severe gales and tremendous seas, so that their compatriots could carry on without Coast Guard interference.

Eventually a black would decide to shake off the trailing cutter. The technique was the same as in the Atlantic. The black would let the cutter get close aboard in fog or darkness, reverse course quickly, put on power, and go back alongside the cutter in the opposite direction. Before the cutter could turn about the black was lost in fog or haze, her skipper knowing that a searchlight in that condition of visibility was practically useless in picking up a small target.

The markets for liquor at San Francisco, Los Angeles, and San Diego attracted rum running in those areas. Contact boats operated there much as they did off New York. Large rum vessels would load at Vancouver for a run south, and after delivering their wares, would return to Vancouver for a new load. Monterey Bay, about 70 miles south of San Francisco, and Half Moon Bay, somewhat nearer, were excellent for clandestine operations because of the many landing places, proximity of good roads, and relatively sparse population. Therefore, a patrol was maintained over an extensive coast line between Point Arguello and Point Arena. Weather permitting, this patrol was carried out chiefly by cutters *Shawnee* and *Cahokia,* each vessel relieving the other. These were large steel steam tugs of 151- and 158-foot lengths, respectively, with cruising speeds of about 10 knots and top speeds of about 12. These were usually rugged patrols which lasted from 5 to 7 days.

Shawnee was based at San Francisco, *Cahokia* at Eureka, 80 miles south of the Oregon line, and a third, similar cutter, *Tamaroa,* at San Pedro, south of Los Angeles. Some 75-footers operated out of the San Pedro and Alameda bases. The Pacific coast is extensive, however, and the rummies were driven to isolated spots away from these areas for landing their cargoes.

Some large rum running "mother ships" of the Pacific became quite famous. One was the British steamer *Ardenza.* Sailing from Leith, Scotland, she passed through the Panama Canal with 25,000 cases of Scotch whiskey, and steamed up the coast to Half Moon Bay. There she remained for 7 months in 1924. Contact boats from San Francisco took 18,000 cases, and carried provisions and supplies to her on return trips. It is incredible to suppose that her presence and business were not known. It was said that contact boats passed through the Golden Gate at certain hours when a particular official on duty found it profitable to be unobserving! Finally, *Ardenza* disposed of all her cargo and steamed on to Victoria, British Columbia, where she was seized for debt, sold to new owners, and taken back to Leith.

For a time, notably in 1923, several rum ships from British Columbia were lying 30 miles off San Francisco, threatening to become the nucleus of a Pacific "Rum Row." This was the closest approach to a "row" which, nevertheless, was never really established.

Many of the larger rum vessels ran down the coast from Vancouver to hover off the Mexican shores and pass their cargo to fast motorboats. Coast Guard cutters often trailed them for hundreds of miles. A favorite spot for hovering was off Ensenada, Mexico, about 90 miles south of San Diego. The large schooner *Malahat,* which ran rum between trips to Australia, and the smaller halibut-type schooner *Chief Skugard* were famous rum runners which habitually sought this area. When the smaller boats were loaded, *Chief Skugaid* usually headed for the open sea and cruised at 6 or 7 knots, with *Shawnee* trailing. Once *Shawnee* was decoyed as far south as Acapulco and Socorro Island, over 1,000 miles from San Diego. It was such decoy missions that took the cutters so far to sea that there was little chance of a seizure, and drew forces away from the coast where they could have been at least a deterrent to landing operations.

Most seizures were routine affairs, but occasionally something happened to set one apart, as in the case of *CG–811* and *A–2193.* One night the six-bitter *CG–811* was drifting off Sunset Beach and, at 1:15 a.m., heard the sound of a high-speed motor to seaward. Soon she sighted an unidentified craft only a quarter mile distant, got under way quickly, and chased it. The pursued craft, the 38-foot *A–2193,* dashed close to shore, anchored near the surf line, and launched a dory. *CG–811* displayed lights, illuminated her Coast Guard ensign, sounded her siren, flashed her searchlight on the speedboat, and started to draw alongside. At this, *A–2193* immediately started up, not bothering to take in her anchor but cutting the manila anchor line. The dory continued in to the beach and the one crew member who was rowing escaped.

As the rummy sped away, *CG–811* gave chase and blazed forth with five warning shots from a service rifle. Since the speedboat refused to heave to, *CG–811* fired into her hull with a machine gun. The refugee then headed inshore through the surf and was beached; the remainder of her crew escaped. Upon impact with the shore the boat burst into flames which totally destroyed her. *CG–811* stood by for a while, and then hastened full speed for her base to report.

The crew of the patrol boat then proceeded by automobile to the scene of the seizure and salvaged the 732 pints of contraband from the wreck.

The Coast Guard was particularly anxious to capture *Hakadata.* She was a Panamanian auxiliary schooner which had long been operating in the Ensenada vicinity. She would take up a position close to the 3-mile limit of Mexican territorial waters where she could observe approaching vessels. She had to be on guard against both the American and the Mexican police of the sea. Should a Mexican vessel approach, *Hakadata* would stand to sea to be out of Mexican waters; if an American ship arrived, she would seek the safety of Mexican territorial waters. She had for a long time evaded the vigilance of the patrol boats, and instructions had been issued to seize this vessel wherever found on the high seas.

The small Coast Guard cutter *Vaughan*, Ens. Edward W. Holtz, left San Pedro in April 1927 on regular patrol while these instructions were in force. She followed the coast line southward in the hope of discovering *Hakadata*. The next morning she stood in to Ensenada Harbor to see if any suspected vessels were moored there; none was seen and, without stopping, she went on.

Ensign Holtz knew *Hakadata's* habit of lying off Santo Tomas Point, and procceeded to that area. Owing to the slow speed of *Vaughan*, he felt that the only way capture of the vessel could be accomplished would be by a ruse or some unexpected maneuver. He knew the Mexican Government operated vessels of the same type as his. Proceeding along the coast without flying any distinguishing Coast Guard flags, Holtz hoped that, if *Hakadata* were encountered, he might be momentarily mistaken for a Mexican vessel. Shortly after noon, *Vaughan* sighted a two-masted vessel lying hove to off Santo Tomas Point. Holtz continued to a point between the suspect vessel and the shore, and there fixed his position by careful cross bearings which put him just inside the 3-mile limit.

Vaughan then increased to her full 8-knot speed and stood toward the schooner which, on closer approach, was identified as *Hakadata*. The rum ship immediately got under way and stood farther offshore. The cutter hoisted her Coast Guard ensign and by whistle signal commanded the vessel to heave to. This was ignored. A blank shot was then fired across her bow which brought the desired result. Cross bearings were taken showing the position to be 4.5 miles from the nearest land. Holtz maneuvered fairly close to *Hakadata* with the intention of boarding.

Observing that seizure was imminent, the crew of *Hakadata* went below to the engine room, set fire to the vessel, and abandoned ship in a dory; the master and his four crewmen were taken on board *Vaughan*, searched, and confined below decks. Smoke and flames poured from *Hakadata's* hold, engine room and pilot house. The ensign concluded that because of the nature of the cargo of alcohol and the location of the fire, which made explosion likely, it was not safe to risk *Vaughan* alongside.

Holtz then decided on bold action. He called for volunteers to row with him to the burning ship to try to put out the fire before the vessel exploded. Three courageous seamen promptly stepped forward. After securing all *Vaughan's* chemical fire extinguishers, the four rowed to *Hakadata* in the dory and went on board. They battened the holds and compartments to smother the flames as much as possible; then all four dropped below into the burning engine room through a pilot house hatch.

These heroic and daring coast guardsmen fought the fire for an hour and a half, after which time it was completely extinguished. The pilot house and engine had been badly damaged by fire, but the flames never managed to work forward into the hold where the alcohol was stored.

Holtz and his men then searched the ship and removed to *Vaughan* all documents, papers, and books that could be found. In the hold were 146 cases and 72 cans of alcohol; the hold and the captain's cabin were sealed. A prize crew took over *Hakadata* whose anchor cable was used as a tow line and secured to *Vaughan,* and the long tow began.

The sea was rising, and 2 hours later the tow cable parted; this and the anchor were jettisoned and a hawser was substituted. Meanwhile, cutter *Tamaroa* had been dispatched to assist. She met *Vaughan* in the evening and took over the tow, and the three vessels proceeded to San Pedro.

One of the earlier famous seizures in Pacific waters was that of the fast British twin screw steamer *Quadra.* A 175-foot vessel of 683 tons, she had left Vancouver in September 1924 with 12,000 cases of champagne and whiskey, and a crew of 30. *Quadra's* presence off the California coast was known, and several cutters had been warned to watch for her. *Shawnee,* Lt. Comdr. Charles F. (Shorty) Howell commanding, was cruising offshore looking for the rum runner *Principio,* but was also alert for signs of *Quadra.* The cutter was about 6 miles northwest of the Farallon Islands when Ens. W. S. Morse sighted a vessel on the horizon with its trisail set. *Shawnee* steamed to the westward of this vessel to cut off its escape to free waters and identified her as *Quadra.* Alongside the steamer lay a small fishing boat, *C–55,* with two men. As the cutter approached, this boat cast off; the larger vessel hoisted the British flag and steamed rapidly westward. *Shawnee* went after *Quadra* and quickly overhauled her.

Howell sounded four blasts with his whistle as a signal to stop, and she obeyed. Meanwhile *C–55,* with 50 sacks of liquor just loaded from *Quadra,* was speeding away. *Shawnee* sent a shot across her bows to stop her, and her crew were taken on board the cutter. Howell asked the master of *Quadra* to show his manifest, which was refused; he then told the master that he was under arrest and ordered him to take his vessel into port under her own power. This, too, was refused. Howell sent a boarding party of four to the steamer, and the cutter then took her and *C–55* in tow for San Francisco. The seizure of *Quadra's* $500,000 cargo was the biggest of its kind on the Pacific coast up to that time.

This case went to trial at San Francisco several months later, and 10 of the defendants were convicted. The U.S. attorney at San Francisco wrote to the Commandant: "The clean-cut, fine appearance of Capt. Charles F. Howell and his men in court, and the straightforward manner in which they testified, has reflected great credit upon the Coast

Guard and the Government." The verdict was appealed, but the U.S. Supreme Court upheld the convictions.

Some of the smaller Coast Guard cutters did not always have the best of navigational equipment; the tugs *Shawnee, Cahokia,* and *Tamaroa* had no gyrocompasses or fathometers, and depended upon radio bearings which were not too reliable, and on celestial observations when off soundings. The newer officers were not always adept at navigation outside of pilot waters. As we know, it was most important to be specific as to the exact location of a seizure, and to be able to convince a court of its accuracy. When a commanding officer was uncertain of his position, as happened on more than one occasion, one or two gave in to the temptation to make a log entry specifying a position favorable to his case. Since a log is a legal document, this was a serious offense. Fortunately, such offenses were few.

Cahokia, in command of a chief warrant officer, was cruising off the Farallon Islands one evening; for 3 days she had been watching for the three-masted schooner *Coal Harbor* of Vancouver, a well-known rum runner. *Cahokia* sighted the vessel, overhauled her after a chase, and signaled her to heave to. The master refused, saying he would let no one on board. The skipper of the cutter sent a boarding party and a boarding was effected under protest of the master. An inspection and search revealed a full cargo of assorted liquors.

The vessel was seized, and the master was ordered to take her into San Francisco under her own power. He refused, and started his vessel at full speed toward the open sea. Since he would not stop, *Cahokia* went alongside while both vessels were moving ahead, and with excellent seamanship tied up to her without damage to either ship. A prize crew was placed on board, *Coal Harbor* was towed to San Francisco, and the captain and crew were arrested.

At the time of the seizure the navigational fix was in doubt. To be legal, the position would have had to be within the 12-mile limit. When asking the Naval Radio Direction Finder Stations for a fix by radio, the commanding officer found that this fix, which put him outside the limit, did not agree with his own. At San Francisco it was charged that he had afterward adjusted the log entry to show his position as inside the limit.

When the case against *Coal Harbor* came up for trial, the U.S. district attorney undertook to prosecute on the basis of the evidence of location given by the commanding officer of *Cahokia*. It was discovered, however, that the chief warrant officer had perjured himself in his testimony. A Coast Guard trial followed in which the officer was found guilty of having altered logs and otherwise falsifying, as a result of which he was broken to chief petty officer. Unfortunate publicity set the Coast Guard back on its heels for a time in that area. *Coal Harbor* and her master and crew were finally released.

One other important Pacific seizure by the Coast Guard was that of *Federalship.* She and *Malahat* were the largest vessels in the "mother ship" fleet. But after this seizure, rum running by water on the west coast declined. In the later years of prohibition, activity there was sporadic and disorganized, and while there continued to be some, it was no problem of consequence. The Pacific coast cities got their liquor mostly from the land side.

The Coast Guard cutter *Algonquin* was one of the two principals involved in the *Federalship* case. This cutter was based at Astoria, Oreg. She was built in 1898, was 205 feet in length, and in her old age could hold 15 knots without difficulty and could cruise comfortably. In the winter months of 1926–27, *Algonquin* had been temporarily assigned to duty in the California Division to help out the three smaller cutters on regular duty there.

The *Federalship* seizure threatened to have serious international repercussions—it was one of the most important seizures, and the last of consequence, in Pacific waters. *Algonquin's* commanding officer at the time was Comdr. Charles F. Howell, formerly of *Shawnee,* but he was on leave and therefore did not personally participate. Lt. Frank D. Higbee and Lt. W. S. Shannon were the two senior deck officers; since seniority between them was not clear, they assumed a dual commanding officer-executive officer responsibility. This was the situation at the time of the incident. Had Commander Howell been in active command, his attitude and knowledge of sea law might have altered the chain of events.

Algonquin happened to have steamed northward to the Columbia River vicinity. At Vancouver, a steamer was taking on a load of liquor. She was *Federalship,* flying the Panamanian flag, and suspected by the State Department as being not of bona fide Panamanian registry. Under Panamanian Law 54, enacted 11 December 1926, a merchant vessel which had acquired Panamanian nationality lost that nationality if it was devoted to smuggling. She was a 43-year-old German iron ship known 2 or 3 years earlier as *Gertrude,* of Belgium. She was known to have made two or three trips previously, having disposed of her liquor cargoes while lying far off the California coast. Most of this had found its way through the Golden Gate in fast contact boats. Her skipper was Capt. S. S. Stone; this time she carried a crew of 20 and a cargo of 12,500 cases of Scotch whiskey reputedly worth $1 million.

Owners of *Federalship* were said to have been also the owners of *Quadra* and *Coal Harbor.* The steamer sailed from Vancouver on 22 February 1927 and headed down the coast, ostensibly bound for Buena Ventura, Colombia.

On the following day, *Algonquin* received orders to proceed to sea and to pick up and trail the steamer *Federalship. Algonquin* put to sea, and as she was cruising in fog off the Oregon coast, Lieutenant Higbee discovered the vessel. She was flying no flag at the time. When this contact was made, the vessels were about 75 miles off the mouth of the Columbia River. *Federalship* was no stranger to the Coast Guard; Captain Stone was already under indictment in a previous smuggling case. *Algonquin* decided to trail the rum runner, and followed her southward. She reported to the Division Commander each day by radio, in code, the movements of the suspect vessel. One day Captain Stone became so annoyed at being trailed that he asked *Algonquin* what she was doing, and why she was following. The cutter replied that she was doing her regular patrol duty, and continued trailing.

Federalship was shadowed to a position off the California coast, where she displayed a Panamanian flag. A radio check on this was made with Headquarters in Washington, D.C., and the Division Commander at San Francisco decided the vessel should be seized. *Cahokia* was sent out from San Francisco to assist, with orders to sink or seize the rum runner, and *Algonquin* was also ordered to seize her and bring her in.

At a point about 275 miles west-southwest of San Francisco, the two cutters made contact and followed *Federalship* for a short time. At daybreak, *Cahokia* fired one shot across *Federalship's* bows and ordered her to stop. The rum ship paid no attention. A second shot, this time from a 1-pounder, met with no response. *Algonquin,* equipped with heavier guns, steamed ahead of *Cahokia* and raised the international code flag "King" recognized throughout the world as meaning "You should stop your vessel instantly." Stone called from his bridge: "I'll not stop. How do I know but what you're a lot of bloody pirates?"

Algonquin radioed the situation to San Francisco and was directed to fire into *Federalship*—in the stern to avoid killing any crew members. Ens. Frank K. Johnson, division officer aft, received orders to load service rounds in the starboard 6-pounder. This he did, as *Federalship* once more was called upon by Lieutenant Shannon to stop. Stone again refused.

A shot from the 6-pounder hummed over the vessel. Shannon gave Stone another chance but there was no change of heart in the rum skipper. The next shot from *Algonquin* meant business. It passed just above the deck aft and hit the starboard rail and a wooden hatch cover, throwing splinters all over the stern of *Federalship*. The rummy then promptly hove to.

While *Algonquin* stood off, *Cahokia* pulled alongside *Federalship* and boarded her. Captain Stone assumed a defiant attitude, which did not lessen when he was instructed to proceed under his own power to San Francisco; he said if they wanted him there, they would have to tow him in. He and his first mate were removed to *Cahokia*, and the 18 members of the crew, comprising 6 nationalities but all claiming to be British subjects, were herded below decks. A prize crew took over.

The two cutters headed toward San Francisco with *Federalship* in tow, and these were joined later by *Shawnee* and *Smith*. The captive was anchored 2 miles off Hunter's Point in San Francisco Bay. She was then visited by a dozen customs inspectors and guards who found the cargo intact, a small arsenal of Winchester rifles, revolvers, and ammunition, and a mass of valuable documentary evidence. A cutter stood by at the anchorage which held not only *Federalship,* but the rotting hulks of *Quadra* and *Coal Harbor.*

The rum runner's cargo of 12,500 cases was removed to the U.S. appraisers stores for safekeeping. The keeping was not safe, for apparently it disappeared while in custody of customs.

The U.S. attorney claimed that the seizure had been lawful, and called for a special session of the Federal Grand Jury. Captain Stone was brought ashore by the U.S. marshal and formally placed under arrest on the previous conspiracy charge; in default of $20,000 he was remanded to jail. Others were jailed, and 63 indictments charging conspiracy to violate the customs laws of the United States were returned by the Federal Grand Jury against officials and members of the Consolidated Exporters, Ltd., owners of the vessel, and the officers and crew.

The defense claimed that *Federalship,* flying the Panamanian flag, had been seized illegally, and that the United States had committed an "act of war." They disclaimed any evidence of smuggling, asserted that *Federalship* had not once been within the 3-mile or 12-mile limit since leaving Vancouver, and that the United States exceeded its authority in seizing the vessel so far offshore.

It was declared by the U.S. attorney that, under Panama law, the ship had automatically lost her registry by engaging in rum running and was, therefore, a ship without a country operating with fraudulent papers. On this basis, seizure of *Federalship* on the high seas as a renegade pirate vessel, and not a bona fide craft of any country, was justified. The conflict became spirited and assumed the aspects of a sensational and far-reaching international controversy.

When the *Federalship* case was presented to the Federal court, it was shown that the Coast Guard had adopted a questionable policy, as the doctrine of "hot pursuit" had not been followed, and that it had no legal right to fire on the vessel so far outside territorial waters. The Coast Guard was ordered to tow the vessel to the point of seizure and to release her.

Soon afterward, *Federalship's* name was changed to *La Golondrina.* After her rum running days, this vessel was put into service towing log rafts between the logging camps in Haro Strait and Prince Rupert, British Columbia. She was still at work in 1940. At that time, Lt. Frank K. Johnson, who had fired the shot that hit the vessel at the time of seizure, was in command of cutter *Cyane.* Both *Cyane* and *La Golondrina* responded to the distress signals of the steamship *Alaska* which had stranded in British Columbia waters. Together, they succeeded in floating her.

The six-bitters assigned to west coast bases performed well on patrol, but for the most part were not involved in major events. In the Atlantic, however, the 75-footers saw plenty of action. Let us now turn our attention to that area.

CHAPTER VII

The Second Line

of Defense

IT IS PROBABLY no exaggeration to say that at one time or another liquor was landed on virtually every mile of mainland shore from the Virginia Capes to Maine. The big quantities went to the cities; but smaller quantities, especially in the earlier days, found their way to the inlets, rivers, and beaches, and into the hands of willing customers including otherwise perfectly law-abiding citizens of good repute. Small operations like these were by no means beneath the notice of the Coast Guard, but to keep a sense of proportion and place importance where it belonged, the Coast Guard turned its aggressiveness and principal attention toward the men that made rum running a real business. It was there that the antismuggling campaign paid its best dividends. Local police could handle the insignificant landings if they cared to; many did not.

The destroyers and regular cutters were primarily concerned with the larger offshore rum runners and with the contact boats found in their vicinity. Yet, many of the latter slipped through the cordon or, as we might say, the first line of defense. In such cases, the second line of defense was very important. This comprised smaller Coast Guard vessels which usually patrolled along the coasts nearer shore, and in bays, harbors, inlets, and the larger rivers.

For smaller craft, the Coast Guard had a few 110-foot World War I Navy subchasers, some slow harbor tugs and launches, and motor lifeboats and surfboats attached to lifesaving stations and built for heavy weather lifesaving only. Against these, the rum runners had specially built speedboats with one to four high-speed engines; they could literally run circles around any vessel the Coast Guard had except, perhaps, the destroyers acquired at the time. Yet, the Coast Guard was supposed to catch them. To build a formidable second line of defense, the Service laid plans for a large number of fast patrol and picket boats.

After study of rum runners' methods, two classes of small craft were indicated. The first was a patrol boat of sufficient size and seaworthiness to operate for days at a time picketing offshore rum runners and patrolling coastal waters; the second was a smaller, faster but sturdy picket boat for day runs chiefly in sheltered bays, harbors, and inlets.

The basic design for the larger class was prepared at Coast Guard Headquarters in Washington, D.C. An outside naval architect, Mr. John Trumpy of Camden, N.J., was engaged to complete the designs. Bids were received in April 1924, and during the next 14 months, 203 of these 75-footers were built at 17 yards, mostly on the east coast. These were the "six-bitters." They bore no names, but were numbered CG-100 through CG-302. The first was commissioned 21 October 1924, and the last on 18 July 1925—an amazingly good construction record.

The hull was of fairly heavy construction and of flush deck design. A substantial wheelhouse housed radio equipment. Trunk cabins extended over the engine room and after quarters, and a military mast was stepped at the forward end of the wheelhouse. The commanding officer and engineer had quarters in the after cabin, and the six other crewmen were bunked forward in the forecastle. A 1-pounder was mounted on the forward deck; a .30 caliber machine gun and small arms comprised the rest of the armament. Intended for 1-week patrols, design and equipment provided the maximum of seaworthiness and speed consistent with sea and wind conditions encountered within 20 miles from shore. Twin 200 horsepower Sterling six-cylinder gasoline engines gave a speed of 15-16 knots. The cost of each completely equipped vessel averaged about $35,000.

Construction of 103 picket boats was undertaken at the same time. These were of two types; there were 30 single cabin, open cockpit 35-footers (numbered CG-2200 through CG-2229), and 73 double cabin 36-footers (numbered CG-2300 through CG-2372). Both types had speed of 24 knots. These boats, complete, cost about $6,800 each.

The 75-footers and these picket boats were the backbone of the Coast Guard's inshore operations. Many six-bitters were used offshore to picket larger rum vessels. However, good seaboats that they were, they were not sufficiently seaworthy to remain offshore in all weathers, nor were they fast enough to give more speedy contact boats a prolonged chase.

One source of useful craft was the rum runners themselves. Their boats were fast and seaworthy enough for inshore waters, and many were suitable for offshore work under normal weather conditions. Many blacks which the Coast Guard seized were transferred to the Coast Guard, converted, and used to good advantage. In all, 649 such vessels were so transferred during the prohibition period; of these, 232 were useful in varying degrees, and 101 were used until the end of prohibition.

This fleet together with the destroyers and regular cutters comprised the Coast Guard's floating equipment for use against the rum runners from 1925 to 1930. Changes during the period were very minor. On 1 January 1928, besides the 25 destroyers listed in chapter IV, the Coast Guard fleet consisted of the following named vessels:

CRUISING CUTTERS FIRST CLASS		CRUISING CUTTERS SECOND CLASS		HARBOR CUTTERS HARBOR LAUNCHES	
	Feet		Feet		Feet
Alexander Hamilton	204	Acushnet	152	Arcata	85
Algonquin	205	Apache	185	Calumet	94
Bear	198	Cahokia	151	Chautauqua	88
Gresham	205	Carrabasset	155	Chicopee	88
Haida	240	Comanche	170	Chippewa	88
Manning	205	Kankakee	182	Chulahoma	88
Modoc	240	Kickapoo	157	Davey	92
Mojave	240	Manhattan	120	Golden Gate	110
Northland	216	Mascoutin	151	Guard	67
Ossipee	165	Morrill	145	Guthrie	88
Redwing	187	Pamlico	158	Hazel	96
Seminole	188	Pequot	166	Hudson	?
Seneca	240	Saukee	151	Leopard	94
Tallapoosa	165	Shawnee	158	Mackinac	110
Tampa	240	Snohomish	152	Raritan	103
Tuscarora	178	Tamaroa	151	Tioga	81
Unalga	190			Winnisimmet	96
Yamacraw	191			Wissahickon	96

125-FOOT PATROL BOATS

Active	Dix	Montgomery
Agassiz	Ewing	Morris
Alert	Faunce	Nemaha
Antietam	Frederick Lee	Pulaski
Bonham	General Greene	Reliance
Boutwell	Harriet Lane	Rush
Cahoone	Jackson	Tiger
Cartigan	Kimball	Travis
Crawford	Legare	Vigilant
Cuyahoga	Marion	Woodbury
Diligence	McLane	Yeaton

100-FOOT PATROL BOATS

Corwin	Forward	Naugatuck
Dallas	Gallatin	Patriot
Dexter	Mahoning	Petrel
Eagle	Nansemond	Wolcott

MISCELLANEOUS PATROL BOATS

Cook	Patrol	Swift
Cygan	Smith	Tingard

It was not until 1930 that there was further expansion of the small craft fleet. To meet increasingly difficult problems on the Great Lakes, especially around Chicago, Detroit, and Buffalo, 33 lightly constructed 34-foot V-bottom speedboats were built capable of 30 to 34 knots. To cope with the Long Island Sound problem, six new 78-foot patrol boats were developed, with speeds around 24 knots. In general appearance, they were like the six-bitters. These were numbered CG–400 through CG–405. The 38-foot picket boats, so familiar in the days of World War II, were also developed in 1930–31; 21 were built.

The boats of the inshore patrol rendered invaluable service; their list of seizures, many very important, was long. While their assignments necessarily concentrated for the most part on the contact boats, many were involved in seizures of the larger ships. It is these smaller craft, particularly the 75-foot patrol boats, to which we shall turn our attention.

As the Coast Guard campaign increased in tempo, the rum runners became more desperate and certainly were not losing their nerve. This was evident time and again. They often proved dangerous men to tangle with. An instance of this was the case of *K–11599*.

The 36-foot patrol boat *CG–2319* was patrolling off Sandy Hook in January 1925, when the motorboat *K–11599* was sighted; after a chase she was ordered to heave to for examination. The motorboat put on a burst of speed, and *CG–2319* put a shot across her bow. This went unheeded, but a rain of shots which followed stopped her. A rummy in the cockpit yelled: "You've hit one of us." The injured man was found to be bleeding heavily and was given first aid. The craft was liquor-laden.

Both boats went in to Sandy Hook. James C. Moore of *CG–2319* immediately commandeered an automobile and its driver; with the wounded man, who was in danger of bleeding to death, and his other prisoner, he started for the Long Branch Hospital. The driver suddenly stopped at a lonely cross-road and six men swarmed about the car. Moore was overpowered before he had an opportunity to fight back. Attacked with a blackjack, he fell by the roadside, shamming unconsciousness. Satisfying themselves that Moore was helpless, his assailants drove away with the wounded man and the other prisoner. By feigning unconsciousness, Moore probably saved himself from being beaten to death.

Under most weather conditions the 75-footers could carry out their assignments effectively. Nevertheless, they were not capable of remaining on picket duty fifty or a hundred miles at sea for any length of time, especially during violent storms. This was adequately demonstrated during the first year in which these craft were utilized in large numbers.

In October 1925, many of the 75-footers were on offshore picket duty from Block Island to Cape May. Among them were *CG–126, CG–128, CG–134, CG–147,* and *CG–238*. The weather had been rather boisterous, but in the evening of 9 October the wind freshened and before the night was over it had attained whole gale force of more than 70 miles an hour. The sea rose, and by daybreak it was a churning mass of huge waves. The wind and sea battered rum runners and patrol craft alike, making living in that sea extremely perilous. All five of these patrol boats got into trouble.

All day 10 October, that night and the following day, the gale and heavy seas tossed the patrol boats about like driftwood. Except for one, they were not then concerned with chasing rum runners, but only with keeping afloat and alive. Radio antennae blew away and apparatus was damaged, making communications for some impossible. Having heard nothing from several of these craft for 2 days, the Coast Guard sent cutter *Tampa* and destroyer *Cassin* out into the storm on a search.

CG–147 and *CG–238* were the luckiest. Fortunately, *CG–238's* radio remained operative, and *Tampa* succeeded in locating her off Cape Cod where she had run out of gasoline and was drifting helplessly. She had been able to avoid severe damage. *Tampa* took her in tow. Cutter *Mojave* was also in the area looking for 75-footers; she picked up *CG–147* disabled off Nantucket and towed her to her base there.

CG–126 had been picketing the rum schooner *Arcola* not far south of Block Island, when the storm broke. As the wind and sea rose, *Arcola* weighed anchor and put to sea. Dutifully, *CG–126* trailed her in the intensifying storm. The schooner proceeded in heavy seas to a point 125 miles from Montauk, with the patrol boat following and taking a terriffic beating. For 2 days *CG–126* and her men were battered in their fight for survival; never once did the men lose control of their vessel, but they became exhausted, and one engine went out of commission. It was fortunate that the radio functioned, enabling the vessel to keep in touch with destroyer *Patterson*. *CG–126* was ordered to return to Montauk Point, and succeeded in doing so on one engine, arriving gratefully at Fort Pond Bay. All were convinced that they had escaped death by a very narrow margin.

Patrolling off Nantucket, *CG–134* got caught in this gale and tried unsuccessfully to make the lee of a small island. Before daylight on 10 October the engines became disabled, the galley fire was extinguished, the radio antennae blew away, and she was taking in water. The crew got out a sea anchor which promptly carried away. Pumps were inoperative and the crew bailed by hand, making no headway against the flood. Then an unusually heavy gust of wind blew the pilothouse open. Boatswain Woolard, realizing his helplessness, took his last flare and fired it. This caught the eye of an officer on the bridge of the steamship *Republic,* which was 7 miles northeast of Nantucket Island and 4 miles east of *CG–134. Republic* altered course toward the patrol boat, drawing alongside an hour later. By that time *CG–134* was sinking, and Woolard requested that his men be taken off. These eight men of the

Coast Guard who normally were rescuers became the rescued. A boat was lowered in the vessel's lee and the completely exhausted crew were saved.

CG–128 was also lost. She was caught by the storm about 50 miles south of Nantucket. The pounding she received from the huge seas soon caused a serious leak which the pumps could not handle before they went out of commission. Bailing was then done by hand and, miraculously, the men managed to keep the ship afloat. In the vicinity was the Anchor Line steamer *Cameronia,* which discovered *CG–128's* plight and maneuvered to windward. She sent liferafts to the beleaguered men who jumped onto them, and all were taken on board. *Cameronia* then radioed that she had rescued the six crewmen, and was taking them to Glasgow! To Glasgow they went, returning shortly afterward to await new assignments.

There was a great deal of activity along the shores of Long Island, and the six-bitters and smaller patrol craft were in the thick of it. They made innumerable searches, and seizures were almost a daily occurrence. The great majority of these were of routine nature in which violence or unusual factors played no part.

These patrol craft, however, encountered incidents, some details of which set them apart from routine experience. In June 1925, *CG–282* discovered the 78-foot two-masted schooner *Mary Langdon* of Rockland, Maine, anchored 2 miles east of Nobska Light. She was a typical lumber schooner and had a large deckload of lumber. Boatswain Fish ordered her to move, which she refused to do. *CG–282* returned to Woods Hole for further orders from the base commander, who then went out and ordered the schooner into Tarpaulin Cove. Two men from the patrol boat moved lumber so as to gain access to the hold. *Mary Langdon* was deeply laden with 2,000 cases of Scotch whiskey. She was well hemmed in at Tarpaulin Cove, with *CG–237* lying practically alongside, and cutter *Redwing* offshore on her way from New London to Woods Hole. *Redwing* was called for assistance. The vessed was seized, the six crewmen were arrested, and *Redwing* towed the schooner to New Bedford.

The 75-footer *CG–290* was busy and aggressive. On one occasion, in the fall of 1930, she sighted the steam trawler *Penguin* headed eastward and being trailed by another trawler, *Helen,* running without lights. The patrol boat's skipper set course to head her off, and when 7 miles east of Race Rock signaled *Helen* to heave to. She merely put on speed for escape. A warning shot did not stop her. As *Helen* sped off into the darkness, *CG–290* manned her guns and gave chase. She opened fire with her 1-pounder and machine gun, sending a spray of shot after the fleeing trawler. *CG–289,* which was patrolling near Cerberus Shoal, was attracted by the firing, and closed in. She also opened fire, and both six-bitters continued the chase, firing until Napatree Point was reached. Several shots had found their mark; *Helen* was taking water, slowed down, and stopped in a sinking condition. *CG–290* then rescued the four men and took them prisoner before the vessel sank with her 1,000 sacks of liquor.

Three weeks later *CG–290* became victim of an attempted ramming. She was cruising near Cerberus Shoal, and discovered another boat running without lights. The patrol boat cut toward her. In the beam of her searchlight, liquor could be seen piled on the decks. A shot across her bows had no effect. Determined to stop her, the skipper fired another shot. With great audacity, the boat turned and headed at 20 knots for *CG–290*. When 25 feet away, the black sheered full right, and *CG–290* went full left at the same time; a collision resulted. The patrol boat suffered a broken wheel rope, and maneuvered with her engines; the black, identified as *High Strung* of Providence, hove to. The boat and her three men were seized.

One rum runner was notably successful in not only evading the first, but also the second line of defense. The 135-foot trawler *Hohenlinden,* of Montreal, a former Boston vessel, sailed from Halifax in August 1926 and apparently proceeded through the Coast Guard fleet and harbor police, landing with her cargo of 2,000 cases at the old Standard Oil Co. dock at Bayway, N.J. This was one of the most daring attempts to land liquor up to that time.

The Coast Guard obtained information of her presence at Bayway, and sent a party to the pier where 1,000 cases had already been unloaded. The crew fled in disorder at the approach of the coast guardsmen, who pursued and fired upon them without effect. As was often the case, the name on the stern had been altered; certain letters of the name *Hohenlinden* had been painted out to show the name *Henlin.*

The vessel was aground when seized. Three patrol boats were sent to try to float her. *CG–206* and *CG–208* tied alongside port and starboard and succeeded in freeing the ship. This old offender was towed to the Statue of Liberty, and turned over to customs authorities.

Most of the rum ships and contact boats were well-known to the Coast Guard; it was not necessary to board all vessels sighted. The Coast Guard had a regular list of suspected rum ships. One on the suspected list frequently found in Rum Row was the British three-masted auxiliary schooner *Vinces*. She had been picketed and trailed on several occasions, and had been seized in 1927 (see chapter X). But she returned to the job as did so many others which underwent the temporary inconvenience of seizure. One night 2 years later, *CG–290* was patrolling a mile north of Montauk when, through his binoculars, her skipper sighted a three-masted, bold headed schooner proceeding without lights. *CG–290* headed toward and gained on the schooner which proved to be *Vinces*. The black began circling indicating a coming attempt to ram, an ever-present danger to the patrol boats. However, when two blank shots were fired across her bow, she hove to. *Vinces* had plenty of liquor and was seized once more.

The patrol boat *CG–808* (formerly the famous rum runner *Black Duck*) was on Long Island Sound patrol one night in August 1931. When about 2 miles east of Cornfield Point Lightship she sighted the speedboat *Artemis* running dark and heading toward her stern. This was an old offender with a record of several seizures. Approaching at a high rate of speed, it was impossible to train the patrol boat's searchlight on her. The black obviously intended to ram, and as she drew close the coast guardsmen fired one pan of machine gun bullets into her. Almost immediately *Artemis* struck *CG–808* a very heavy blow on the port quarter, carrying away strips of planking and part of the guard rail, and nearly knocking the patrol boat's crew overboard. The speedboat then sheered off and laid down a heavy smoke screen.

CG–808 immediately gave chase at top speed, and the searchlight revealed a deck load of contraband. The patrol boat continued to fire with her machine gun, and several hits were scored as the chase grew hotter. *Artemis*, throwing out her smoke screen, maneuvered evasively to try to keep *CG–808* in the smoke and escape. During one of these maneuvers, she turned sharply to port; as the wheelropes and sheeves of the patrol boat had been weakened by impact from the collision, no great strain could be put upon them and *Artemis*, turning in a smaller circle, placed the pursuer in the smoke and escaped.

Apparently *Artemis* proceeded southeastward and landed her cargo about 3 miles west of Orient Point on Long Island. Shortly afterward, Comdr. John S. Baylis, then Chief of Staff of the Destroyer Force at New London, requested and was granted permission to borrow a plane, together with its pilot. Flying low over Orient Point they saw hundreds of people struggling up the bluff through sand and beach grass carrying cases or sacks of liquor. They looked for all the world like a swarm of ants carrying eggs. Several skiffs were still on the beach. But there was no *Artemis*. Baylis radioed the nearest patrol boats to seize the contraband he had seen.

It appeared almost certain that, with all the firing, some one in *Artemis* would have been hit. Two men with gunshot wounds had turned up at the hospital at Greenport, only a few miles from Orient Point. Since they might have been taken ashore in the skiffs, they were placed under guard.

Artemis was discovered in a shipyard at Port Jefferson, where she was to have her collision and gunfire damage repaired. The boat was eventually taken, but after a hiatus she was back again at her old tricks.

One night in December 1932, *CG–163* was patrolling southwest of Old Plantation Light in lower Chesapeake Bay. She sighted the 56-foot 40-knot *Matilda Barry*. When the speedboat caught sight of *CG–163*, she increased speed and immediately veered to get a nearby passenger steamer between her and the patrol boat. The latter turned up full speed and chased the rummy for several miles. The usual signals to stop went unheeded, so three warning shots were fired at the fleeing craft. Suddenly, the rum runner circled around the patrol boat at high speed, laying down a thick smoke screen which caused those in *CG–163* to suffer serious stinging of the eyes, nose, and throat. What *CG–163* did not know at the time was that one of three shots that had entered the pilot house and hull had parted the steering rope.

The master realized he could not escape; he slowed his engines, went aft, threw a dory overboard, and was either carried overboard by the painter or fell into the heavy swells. *CG–163* went alongside and put two armed men on board. Aided by her searchlight, the patrol boat picked up the master, who was calling for help; he was hauled on board, apparently lifeless. After 3 hours of artificial respiration, the man was pronounced dead. *Matilda Barry* and her men were taken to Norfolk.

The night of 9 December 1929 was cold and clear, with a light breeze from the northeast, and bathed in bright moonlight. *CG–123* was patrolling off Jones Inlet, her crew entranced by nature's beauty. Also enjoying the perfect weather was the rum boat *Mary Mother Elizabeth* running without lights 2 miles farther at sea, and heading toward Jones Inlet with 470 sacks of liquor. Boatswain Christensen of *CG–123* sighted the black, changed course to intercept, and called on her to heave to. She was boarded and searched. The master then offered Christensen a $3,000 bribe to allow the vessel to proceed and land her cargo, which the boatswain refused. Instead, he checked the vessel further, and found several papers that contained radio information, wave lengths used both by rum runners' ships and shore stations, and calls of the stations then in use. This proved highly valuable to the Coast Guard.

CG–401, a 78-footer was off Watch Hill one night when high-speed motors were heard and a motorboat without lights was sighted. The patrol boat pursued, illuminated her ensign, and fired warning shots. Since these had no effect, she fired her 1-pounder and machine gun into the vessel, scoring a number of hits. *CG–401* overtook her after a 30-minute chase and boarded her. Sacks of liquor were piled outside the deckhouse for protection; and her hold was full of contraband liquor. This was the yacht *Whispering Winds* which was later turned over to the Coast Guard and became *CG–986*.

As time went on, the rum runners developed very good intelligence. Inshore activities of the Service were fairly well known to the rum runners. Unusual activity on the part of the rummies' spies aroused suspicions one night. During the evening, the officer-in-charge of the Coast Guard station near Brenton Point, Narragansett Bay, received a telephone message from a man he knew, and whose reliability seemed to have been established. This man pretended to have information that liquor would be run into the Sakonnet River late that night, but the officer was suspicious.

The coast guardsmen went into action. The officer-in-charge of the station had suspected that the call was to draw his boat away from the actual activity. The picket boat proceeded immediately at top speed toward the Sakonnet River. When she had gone far enough to convince any watchers, she turned about and headed silently, without lights, toward the West Passage entrance. Those in the picket boat heard a powerful motorboat speeding up the bay, heading for East Passage. The picket boat put about and gave chase. After a while it was discovered that the pursued craft was running without cargo. Assuming this to be a decoy, the picket boat dashed to West Passage where a second speedboat was racing up mid-channel. The coast guardsmen followed and gained on the speedboat but she, too, was light, and this was recognized as a ruse. The natural impulse then was to rush back to East Passage or Sakonnet River; however, the skipper felt that was the obvious thing to do and, instead, headed for the extreme western shore of West Passage.

There, he discovered the rum runner *Herreshoff* moving slowly against the shoreline. *Herreshoff* speeded up on being discovered and went to mid-channel ahead of the picket boat, which illuminated her ensign and fired a rifle shot across the black's bow. *Herreshoff* merely put on more speed, and then firing began in earnest. A rain of bullets went through the armor plate around the pilot house and through cases of liquor piled inside for added protection.

The picket boat trailed the black closely; the latter turned her searchlight on the picket boat to blind the helmsman, and cases were thrown into the wake in the hope of disabling the Coast Guard boat. A well-placed rifle shot put the rum runner's searchlight out of business, and the case-dumping stopped. After a long chase, the black neared the head of the bay where she would be forced to stop. As it was about to pass the Rhode Island Yacht Club, *Herreshoff* was run ashore, and the crew leaped out and escaped. The coast guardsmen did not dare to fire for fear of hitting bystanders. The boat and her liquor were taken into custody.

An important seizure was made by *CG–234*, Boatswain Austin H. Troy, early in January 1925. In the course of her patrol, *CG–234* went into Huntington Bay where she found the Italian 618-ton four-masted auxiliary schooner *Arco Felice II*, of Naples. She was flying no colors, and a ship's boat was tied astern. Troy boarded her. He found that her papers were not in order, and he asked what *Arco Felice II* was doing in Huntington Bay. He was told that the vessel had put in 3 days before in a leaking condition; the only purpose was to pump the ship. The boarding party investigated. They found very little water, but a modest amount of liquor. The holds appeared to have been recently cleaned. When the crew were mustered, two members on the list did not answer; the "captain" said they were at Huntington on liberty. Troy asked for the log book and was told there was none, but a search revealed three hidden in a chest along with other papers including two crew lists, one with 12 names, the other with 10. Also found were two revolvers, an automatic pistol, and a shotgun. All of these were taken on board *CG–234*. *Arco Felice II* was seized. Cutter *Redwing* later towed the ship to New York, and she lay rotting off Governors Island for 2 years. The jury verdict was against all the defendants who were fined and sentenced to about 2 years at the Atlanta penitentiary.

The Coast Guard was, of course, concerned not only with rum running but also with the smuggling of narcotics and diamonds, and the landing of undesirable aliens. It was said that a pilot previously had taken *Arco Felice II* into Long Island Sound, where 50 Portuguese had unloaded a cargo of liquor; the veracity of this may be questioned, but Lt. Comdr. C. S. Root of Coast Guard Intelligence uncovered evidence that the schooner had landed aliens on previous trips.

The schooner *John R. Manta* of Providence, R.I., was a marked vessel. At one time an order had been given to all patrol boats by the base commander at New London to trail her to Providence if found. In May 1929 this vessel was at sea bound from Brava, Cape Verde Islands, to Providence with 29 passengers. At Nantucket Shoals she ventured into shallow water and ran aground, where she remained for 2 days. Two fishing vessels discovered her, helped free her from the sand, and towed her into Vineyard Haven Harbor. There she remained at anchor for 24 hours. Several Coast Guard patrol boats at Vineyard Haven identified her but did not board her. She then got under way and, under cover of darkness, landed four aliens on Nobska Point at Falmouth.

Meanwhile, *CG–231*, in command of Boatswain Ulrich F. Engman, had gone out from New London on patrol. She cruised to East Greenwich Harbor in Narragansett Bay, where she identified suspected rum boats *Astrid* and *Idle Hour* lying empty, boarded *Anna Elizabeth* and found no violations, and patrolled East Greenwich Harbor entrance to watch for an expected rum boat. The next morning she stood out of Greenwich Bay and down West Passage. There, she sighted *John R. Manta* standing in. Engman signaled her to stop, which she did readily enough, put two men on board, and informed his base commander, requesting orders. *CG–231* then went alongside again, and Engman went on board to examine the vessel.

He asked for the master. It seemed that the former master had departed from the ship at Brava and left another in command—a former cabin boy—who did not speak English, was not an American citizen, and was under age. The Boatswain asked for the ship's papers and, as no manifest could be produced, he seized the vessel. He mustered the

29 passengers, and these checked with the immigration list; he mustered the crew and found it 5 men short. A search of the vessel produced three bottles of liquor and an insignificant cargo. There were, however, 12 violations including no American citizen officer on board, no change of master in registry, no entries in the log book, no passenger list, and a gun belonging to a passenger with no permit to carry. Since the vessel was approaching Providence, and the customs officer would soon be on board to examine, the after part of the schooner was not thoroughly searched.

Leaving coast guardsmen on board *John R. Manta,* Boatswain Engman returned to *CG–231* to report to his base commander and the customs and immigration officers. The guard left in *John R. Manta* was to allow no one to board or leave the ship pending arrival of the customs officer. On turning over jurisdiction to the collector of customs, Engman was requested to stay with the vessel as there were no customs guards available.

Immigration and customs officers arrived; they and coast guardsmen searched the schooner for possible aliens. With Boatswain Engman they took the acting master into the cabin and exacted from him under oath a confession that he had aliens on board. A hatch beneath linoleum on the deck was discovered leading down to the stern shear where 11 aliens were found, all in an exhausted condition. The aliens were taken to the State pier in *CG–231,* thence by police to their station for safekeeping. *CG–231* then returned to *John R. Manta,* put two guards on board, and stayed alongside all night. The passengers were detained by the immigration officers. It developed that the aliens had paid $250 each and the passengers $50 to $75 each for transportation, and that eight crewmen who had signed on at Providence at $25 a month, had paid $150 to $250 for the return trip from Brava to Providence!

Early the next morning destroyer *Roe* arrived, and her commanding officer made a careful investigation. He and Engman then interviewed the U.S. attorney at his office following which the district attorney arrested the captain, mate, and one of the passengers, charging them with conspiracy to smuggle aliens into the United States. *CG–231* furnished a guard to the police station. The commanding officer of *Roe* ordered Engman to stand by *John R. Manta* until relieved. *CG–231* remained alongside guarding the schooner and her 16 crew members until the case was disposed of 3 weeks later.

The U.S. deputy marshal libeled *John R. Manta* and the immigration officer arrested her crewmen. The patrol boat was released and proceeded immediately to New London. That day the Commandant wrote Boatswain Engman a letter of commendation.

The Portuguese Consul at Providence later wrote a letter to the Commandant in which he said:

"The 31 men composing the crew and passengers on board the *John R. Manta* unanimously report that while handled during the period of their detention by the *CG–231* under command of Ulrich Frank Engman for several weeks, riding at anchor at the port of Providence, after a long and stormy voyage from the Cape Verde Islands and in extremely trying conditions of discomfort with unequivocal enforcement of orders from his superior officers, that said enforcement was nevertheless made by both the commander and men of Coast Guard cutter *231* in such a way that they request their greatest appreciation and thanks to be registered in their official report before the Consul of their country. Both Mr. Engman and his men were able to perform their assigned duties faithfully in the most courteous manner."

In another type of operation, Boatswain W. A. Woods, commanding *CG–187*, showed ingenuity and persistence. He was patrolling Gardiner's Bay near the eastern end of Long Island one morning in May 1926. A two-masted schooner was observed at anchor a half mile west of the Threemile Harbor entrance and 300 yards off Sammy's Beach. As *CG–187* proceeded toward the vessel, a large oyster boat was seen to leave the schooner's side and head for the entrance of Threemile Harbor. Woods could not intercept her before she reached the entrance, and so he proceeded toward the schooner. When about three-quarters of a mile from the vessel, a small motorboat with several men was also seen leaving, and heading for the beach. As the boat touched the beach he counted 10 men leaving the boat and walking toward 2 automobiles, where they stood waiting developments. Another motorboat was observed going to the westward toward Sag Harbor. *CG–187* went alongside the schooner, *Helen G. McLean* of LaHave, Nova Scotia, the decks of which were covered with cases of liquor.

For a skipper who wanted to make the most of a situation, Boatswain Woods faced a real challenge. He was alongside the schooner, an oyster boat was just inside the harbor entrance, one motorboat was heading for Sag Harbor, and another was at the beach.

Woods was equal to the occasion. He chose a landing party of three and instructed them to seize the oyster boat; they took the dory and landed on the beach. These men commandeered an automobile, drove around the beach and harbor, and succeeded in seizing at the pier the oyster boat *Pinta,* 3 prisoners, and 500 cases of liquor.

Leaving two men with machine guns in charge of the schooner, *CG–187* with three men left then chased the Sag Harbor boat *Sterling,* overhauled her, and fired one shot across her bow at which she hove to. This boat was promptly seized and her two men arrested. Woods took *Sterling* under escort back to the schooner and ordered one of his prisoners to take him into Threemile Harbor, but this was refused. Leaving *CG–187* alongside *Helen G. McLean* with the two prisoners under guard, Woods took *Sterling* into the harbor and found that the landing party had taken care of *Pinta*. He then returned to the schooner and seized that vessel. He called it a good day's work, even though the 10 men on Sammy's Beach had escaped. For this exploit, Woods received commendation from the Commandant.

CG–238 had been fortunate in the gale of October 1925; she had been picked up by *Tampa* and towed to shelter, and she had survived the ordeal. She was less fortunate in the great gale of February 1927. The wind howled out of the northeast blowing snow squalls before it, and whipping up mountainous seas. *CG–238* had been patrolling off the ocean side of Cape Cod, and the little vessel was taking a severe buffeting. When 4 miles east of Cape Cod (Highland) Light, her engines went dead and she was in real trouble. She attempted to anchor, but the force of wind and sea was too great, and her anchors would not hold. She radioed a call for assistance which alerted the Coast Guard to her plight. But before anything could be done, *CG–238* foundered in the seething mass of beach surf on the Cape Cod outer shore, and all of her crew were lost.

On receipt of the radio call, several Coast Guard vessels were sent to assist *CG–238*. The broken deck destroyer *Paulding,* under command of Lt. Comdr. John S. Baylis, a superb seaman, was anchored in President Roads in Boston Harbor. She was riding out the gale which, even there, was difficult in a crowded anchorage. Baylis received orders to proceed to the patrol boat's assistance. *Paulding* immediately got under way at 7:25 p.m. She steamed through the North Channel into the teeth of the gale, but found it necessary to reduce speed from 18 to 12 knots as she was taking green seas over her bow. On reaching Boston Lightship she changed course for Cape Cod, and steamed in the trough riding and rolling easily.

The wind and seas increased and, by the time *Paulding* was within 10 miles of Cape Cod, speed was again reduced. The vessel was taking a terrific pounding, and Baylis decided the attempt at rescue not only would be impracticable, but extremely foolhardy. It was now a matter of saving his own ship and her personnel. He did not know that *CG–238* had already foundered.

Paulding worked offshore with wind and sea on her starboard bow. Green seas rolling over bow and fantail simultaneously shook her and pounded her into what seemed to be a stone wall. First the dory lashed on deck was carried away piece by piece. All the next day the seas wreaked havoc; they roared over the decks and spray froze as it hit. Getting about the decks was extremely hazardous. Water worked into the ship and everything and everybody became soaked. No cooking could be done. Seasickness was general. Gasoline drums on the deck aft broke loose and went overboard. The anchor davit was bent flat to the deck; the Jack staff and stanchions were broken; tops of several ventilators were carried away. The sounding machine was smashed;

the wherry cradles and the wherry were broken, and the motor dory was torn from its cradle and stove in, and the after steering wheel was badly bent.

This all had to have a fitting climax; during the dark hours of the second night, the starboard guy of the No. 1 stack carried away, and with every roll to port the stack went farther and farther toward the port rail. Frantic efforts were made to get a tackle on the guy to save the stack. The vessel was put on the port tack to get her rolling deeper to starboard and thus give the men working in darkness and spray and on slippery decks a better chance of success. Then the port guy went and the stack fell over to starboard, breaking the motor sailer davit and sending the motor sailer overboard.

Live steam now endangered the men; water coming on board struck the hot boiler raising clouds of steam and threatening a boiler explosion. One man was washed or slipped overboard but fortunately was rescued. The stack hole was finally secured by a tarpaulin. A fore stay had to be rigged to stack No. 2, as the other stacks were beginning to work badly. Meanwhile, the fallen stack was being cut away, and went overboard.

Just before midnight of the second night, when things were secured about the decks, Baylis deemed it unsafe to head into the gale any longer; *Paulding* was by this time 100 miles east of Boston Lightship. He waited for water sufficiently tranquil in which to turn about. His chance came, and *Paulding* proceeded at full speed with helm hard over. The run back to Boston before the gale at 18 knots was a welcome relief from the pounding of the preceding 24 hours.

After reaching Boston Baylis, in reporting on his experience during the worst gale in 30 years, said *Paulding* had taken the hardest beating he had ever seen a vessel go through. Several of the officers and men were commended by Rear Admiral Billard, the Commandant, and six enlisted men were advanced in rating as a result of their heroic actions and devotion to duty.

Boatswain Alexander C. Cornell presented the base at New London with a Christmas present on 25 December 1930, in the form of his tenth seizure. *CG–290*, of which he was in command, was patrolling off Montauk Point on Christmas Eve in a troublesome but moderate northwest gale which had kicked up a heavy sea. At midnight the six-bitter entered Fort Pond Bay, which is exposed to northwesterly winds, and found a rough sea. Cornell stood over to the yacht club landing and put his searchlight on the pier as he approached.

The searchlight beam revealed a great deal of activity on the dock and on an offshore rum runner from which liquor was being loaded on cars. Startled and apprehensive as the beam flashed on them, the crew of the rum vessel jumped off the ship and ran up the dock. Cornell decided to investigate.

At that time, however, a dark object was seen leaving the pier, and the searchlight showed it to be a still larger offshore rum carrier heavily loaded. Cornell kicked his engines ahead and gave chase. He fired three blank 1-pounder shots as a warning; the black put on speed and threw out a heavy smoke screen. *CG-290* then fired three 1-pounder shells at the stern, all of which scored hits. The black hove to and surrendered.

This runner was 100-foot *Audrey B.*, of Nova Scotia, with 2,800 cases of liquor. Boatswain Cornell went alongside, but the sea was heavy and great difficulty was experienced in transferring coast guardsmen from *CG-290* to the black, and the prisoners from *Audrey B.* to the patrol boat. In the process, both vessels received some damage.

The patrol boat took the black in tow, but the wind and sea made it impossible to handle her. As *Audrey B.* drifted to within 100 yards of the beach, the boarding party succeeded in starting her engines, and she stood out under her own power. Despite the gale and heavy sea, both vessels made New London early on Christmas morning.

Before daybreak one July morning in 1929, the notorious rum runner *Idle Hour* was standing up Sakonnet River at the east of Narragansett Bay with a load of liquor. She was moving very slowly without lights. At the same time *CG-290*, with Boatswain Cornell in command, was standing down river. She sighted *Idle Hour* which, apparently, had also seen her. The rum boat worked close to the shadows of the shore and lay to, hoping that the patrol boat had not seen her and would proceed down the river.

When Cornell put his searchlight on her she got under way in a burst of speed. *CG-290* whistled and hailed her to no avail, and went after her in hot pursuit. The patrol boat came up very close on her starboard bow and fired a blank shot which went unheeded. *Idle Hour* could turn up 30 knots, and Cornell knew his best was 13. With a warning to the gunner to put bullets close aboard without actually hitting the boat, the machine gun was brought into play with a burst of fire. Cornell still hoped she would heave to without endangering the lives of those on board.

The interesting aspect of this is not whether the black was captured, but where the bullets went. *Idle Hour* received several machine gun hits. Both vessels were proceeding northward up the Sakonnet River, with *CG-290* on the starboard bow of *Idle Hour,* and dropping astern due to slower speed. The direction of firing was obviously within the quadrant west to north.

When firing commenced, the vessels were 1 mile down river from Fogland Point, a half-mile-long point jutting out from the river's eastern shore. It was at all times to starboard of the craft and, as they proceeded up the river, the angle to starboard constantly increased.

The owner of a summer house at Fogland Point discovered later that his house had been struck by a bullet. Knowing of the earlier encounter between *CG–290* and *Idle Hour,* this man decided that it was a Coast Guard bullet. He entered a protest with his U.S. Senator, who took the matter up with the Coast Guard Commandant, and the latter ordered an investigation.

Lt. Comdr. Clarence H. Dench conducted a thorough investigation at the scene; Boatswain Cornell attended and was cross-examined by the complainant. The investigating officer went on board *CG–290* and had her re-run the course followed in pursuit of *Idle Hour.* The skipper showed that the line of fire was clear of shore and other vessels, and that when firing commenced, Fogland Point was northeast of *CG–290.*

It was conceded that the shot could have come from *CG–290,* but as bursts of machine gun fire were being discharged at the rum runner, it seemed strange that one isolated shot of a burst should have found its way to the house. Boatswain Cornell was cleared of any culpable inefficiency or carelessness in directing his fire at *Idle Hour.* These conclusions seemed fair enough, but the Commandant issued instructions to the end that patrol boats operating in the vicinity of Sakonnet River exercise the utmost care so that there would be no possibility of any projectile striking persons or buildings on shore. It was an ever-present danger when pursuing rum runners in restricted waters, and a handicap to the Coast Guard which was fully recognized by the rummies.

The small 793–ton British freighter *Greypoint,* temporarily re-named *Economy,* was a well-known rum vessel, and the Coast Guard had been warned to watch for her. This troublesome ship could carry a good-sized cargo of liquor, and her capture was greatly desired.

On the night of 3 July 1927 Ens. Charles L. Duke was on duty and went out with two men in the 36-foot picket boat *CG–2327* to check up on the patrol covering The Narrows in New York Harbor. He looked over suspected boats in Gravesend Bay, and watched for any extra activity because of the coming holiday. The night was pitch black, the stars were blotted out by thick clouds, and a strong wind kicked up a heavy chop in the harbor.

As *CG–2327* patrolled, Duke noticed the new German liner *New York* anchored for customs inspection off quarantine with its lights outlining it sharply against the Brooklyn shore. A smaller steamer went behind her, but did not stop and continued up the harbor creeping along the Bay Ridge shore, with only two lights burning dimly. Ensign Duke's hunch that all was not well proved a good one. He headed at 22 knots for the steamer and came up in her wake close enough to make out the name *Economy.* She was salt-covered, dingy and dirty, and looked her part. From the uncertain course the freighter was taking past Bay Ridge and then across to the Jersey side, Duke was sure the pilot did not know the harbor.

CG–2327 ran alongside and then forward of her bridge; cupping his hands, Duke called for *Greypoint* to heave to, but she plowed on defiantly. Again he called, and the master replied: "I'm going to dock at Greenville. If you want me, you can find me there. I don't intend to stop now." The steamer did not slacken speed. *CG–2327,* poking her nose into every wave, raised showers of spray which drenched the three men. Ensign Duke plunged on until he was opposite the freighter's bow, where he fired two warning shots from his revolver to no avail. The ensign, soaking wet, stood up at the bow while the steersman drew close to the vessel; then he reached out, grabbed the freighter's rail, and swung on board.

Ensign Duke did not know how many men or weapons he would face, but he knew his own defenseless position with only a flashlight, and three bullets left in his revolver. From *Greypoint's* deck, in a grand exhibition of bravado, he called to those in the small boat saying: "If I'm not out of that pilot house in 2 minutes you turn the machine gun on them." There was none.

In the light of his flashlight he groped his way to the deckhouse. There he was stopped by a burly seaman whom he cracked on the head with his revolver butt. He then went up the ladder to the pilot house swinging his flashlight on six men huddled in corners. Finding the master, Duke put his revolver to his ribs, asking why the ship reeked with the smell of alcohol. He ordered the master to reverse his engines and turn the vessel about, but the captain refused. The ensign then turned the ship about himself, running her aground on Robbins Reef in 10 feet of water. There was a spot where the crew could not land!

This amazing officer herded the men together and forced them below decks. Then he called to his shipmates in *CG–2327* and told them to get help while he held the ship; they set out across the harbor to the Barge Office. The harbor cutter *Calumet* arrived at about 2 o'clock in the morning, but could not get close because of shoal water. *CG–122* went aground on the flats. *CG–143* nearly grounded, but help finally arrived after daybreak. Duke departed 4 hours later, leaving a guard to watch the 22 prisoners, and reported at Stapleton headquarters.

High officers of the Coast Guard hailed Ensign Duke's almost single-handed feat as perhaps the most heroic exploit in the war against the rum runners up to that time.

The six-bitters and small craft operating the inshore patrols as well as those which operated offshore, proved their worth in the cause against smuggling, as did the cutters and destroyers. Cooperation between all was noteworthy and vitally necessary if the tide of liquor from the sea were to be appreciably slowed down. And it was effectively diminished. One of the extremely important factors in this cooperation was that of communications. It will be interesting to explore this field, and see how it was developed and applied to the problems of the Rum War.

CHAPTER VIII

Aids to

Information

THE MORE THE COAST GUARD knew about the rum runners, the better it was able to cope with its problems. The smugglers adopted a more systematic approach, especially when the destroyers and six-bitters joined the antirum forces, and developed a very good intelligence to help them evade their adversaries. Radio communication played an important part. Recognizing the urgency of obtaining better information on rum runners' methods and activities, the Coast Guard organized an efficient intelligence service, and also made great progress in improving communications. While these were two separate fields, they were very closely related in the search for methods of outsmarting the rummies, and often blended together.

The rum runners discovered the value of radio quite early in the game. Radio became useful to the syndicates when the offshore rum vessels began sending daily code messages through a commercial radio station addressed to their representatives at Montreal. Being in their own special code, these messages meant nothing to the radio station operators; they were just meaningless conglomerations of letters, usually in groups of 10. But they contained highly important information for the "insiders"—the day's liquor sales, the daily receipts, the quantity of contraband remaining on board, requisitions for provisions, and the exact location of the vessel. This information was then telephoned from Montreal to New York to keep the representatives there fully informed.

Naval radio direction finder stations inadvertently became very useful to the rum ships. Any vessel could call these stations for bearings; two gave a reasonably accurate fix. Especially in thick or foggy weather, the rum ships equipped with radio would request their bearings by international code. The stations would then furnish them usually without knowing the identity of the vessel.

More and more rum ships became radio-equipped, and after a while the Naval stations noticed repeated requests for bearings evidently from the same ships in about the same positions. Were they assisting the rum fleet? For a while they had instructions to disregard requests from suspicious vessels. This seemed to pass up an opportunity, however, and stations were later instructed to take bearings on any rum vessels requesting them; the bearings were transmitted by special Navy code to the Coast Guard cutter assigned to the area. This proved extremely helpful.

One-way radio from ship to shore served the rummies well, but there was need also for the managers ashore to communicate with their vessels. This was less simple. Some messages were sent in code through usual channels, often warning the recipient of the approach of "hostile" craft.

The use of radio by the rum runners in keeping their managers informed of their liquor sales and inventories meant far longer stays on Rum Row. The managers sent new loads of contraband and provisions to the rum ships, thus making it unnecessary for many ships to be absent for several weeks in order to replenish their stocks.

As radio use increased and shore direction finder stations proved useful to the Coast Guard, it became evident that direction finding equipment in the larger Coast Guard vessels themselves would prove valuable. The first Coast Guard use of the shipborne radio direction finder (then called radiocompass) had been as recent as 1919, and its beginning is interesting.

Cutter *Androscoggin* was on International Ice Patrol and was about to be relieved by cutter *Tallapoosa*. Visibility was extremely poor. J. A. McCarron, electrician first class, in *Androscoggin*, improvised a loop antenna which he held in position by hand, and through the directional properties of this loop, used in conjunction with the radio receiver, he determined the direction from which the signals from *Tallapoosa* were coming, thus effecting quick contact. In 1921, a Navy type direction finder was installed in *Tampa,* and other installations followed. With this equipment, cutters could pick up radio transmissions from the rum ships and determine lines of bearing. Two cutters working together at proper distances could establish fixes.

It became expedient for the syndicates to set up their own radio stations ashore. These were, of course, clandestine, but their existence was known to the Coast Guard.

In 1924, Coast Guard communications became more important and better organized; the Chief of the Communications Section at that time was Lt. E. M. Webster; Lt. Frank M. Meals was designated Assistant Communications Officer at Headquarters in Washington, D.C., and the Section took a new lease on life.

The expanded fleet gave the Coast Guard its first experience in handling the communications of a large force. With the great increase in vessels and personnel, it was necessary to obtain radio operators as quickly as possible. This meant enlisting men who had seen only Navy, or Army, or commercial service. The result was a nonuniform group with widely varying conceptions of procedure. The experience gained at this time probably did more than anything else to emphasize the necessity for careful and thorough training of radio operators in Navy procedure. A program of intensive training was established, and it was never relinquished.

The destroyers and cutters were, of course, equipped with radio. As the six-bitters were placed in commission they, too, were provided with radio, but special equipment had to be developed and produced for the smaller vessels.

During 1925–27 11 steel 100-foot patrol boats and 32 steel 125-footers were built and placed in service. Direction finders of a special type were needed for these vessels. They were developed and first installed in the 125–footer *McLane*. Similar equipment was soon placed in the others. As usual with new devices, experimentation resulted in great improvements, and in 1928–29 better equipment replaced that of the earlier type.

Until 1924, Coast Guard-operated radio shore stations were unnecessary, as existing facilities were adequate. But need for a more far-reaching radio communications service than the Navy or commercial facilities provided became very evident. Therefore, a shore radio station was established at the Rockaway Point Coast Guard Station on Long Island. This proved so successful that additional units were soon established at Nahant, Mass.; New London, Conn.; Cape May, N.J.; Cape Henry, Va.; Fernandina and Fort Lauderdale, Fla.; Mobile, Ala.; San Francisco and San Pedro, Calif.; and Port Angeles and Anacortes, Wash.

To obtain greatly needed information about rum runners, their operations, and their intentions, the Coast Guard relied also upon other sources. Many people were completely out of sympathy with the rummies and some of these became "informers." Naturally, they ran considerable risk which was doubtless calculated. They were informing against ruthless foes. Many proved very reliable and useful; others were not consistently reliable, and their records qualified their usefulness. Sometimes, informers were working with the rummies, and these were promptly relegated to their proper classification.

Good information was often received from informers about "mother ships" from foreign ports where liquor was taken on board, such as names, types, and quantity of contraband, time of departure, and destinations. American consuls at various Canadian and European ports tended to be helpful.

There was the case of "Mr. X". No one knew who he was, where he telephoned from, or how he obtained his knowledge, but he talked frequently with Capt. E. D. Jones at New York. He gave names and descriptions of rum boats, and told where they would be at certain times. His information never failed. A great many seizures were made as a result of his cooperation.

The contact boat *Accuracy* was in the habit of running liquor into Cotuit Harbor, on the southern Cape Cod shore. One informer from that area gave a story of this boat and its operators in great detail, including a sketch of the Cotuit Harbor area and pertinent locations which would have done credit to a professional topographer!

Rummies used light planes to scout the sea area and to check on the positions of Coast Guard and rum ships. One amphibian appeared to be transporting illicit cargo. It had a habit of going out in the daytime and returning a bit before dark, disappearing always at the same point. Boats from Woods Hole were then stationed strategically where they took bearings on the plane as it disappeared. It was determined that it landed at a spot back of Providence. The area was scouted and the "landing field" was located; it was the only large field heavily turfed in a group of fields given over to truck farming. The careless ground keepers had left the landing markers up! The shore enforcement agency was notified, and that ended the practice.

After the rum runners were largely taken over by the syndicates and radio-equipped, they would receive clandestine radio messages designating a rendezvous, the name of the contact boat, the specific cargo to be transferred, and other details. The rum ship would move to the spot, meet the contact boat, and transact its business.

The rummies' shore radio stations finally went "underground," operating sometimes under the guise of "hams," but more often operated outside the "color of the law." These stations were moved frequently so as to evade prosecution by the Federal Communications Commission. If one of these stations went off the air one night as a result of being knocked off by the FCC, a replacement station would be on the air the next night using the same code. Under the circumstances of the Rum War, radio communications by both the Coast Guard and the rum runners were necessarily in code. Before late 1924 the Coast Guard's coded messages were in accordance with U.S. Navy code books; but the increased code communication by the Coast Guard brought about well-founded concern by Navy officials lest their codes become compromised by excessive Coast Guard use.

Lt. Frank M. Meals, who had been both a telegraph operator and a radioman with a good background of commercial and Government communications, was given the task, along with his other duties, of preparing a suitable code for use strictly by the Coast Guard. He was on familiar ground, for he had previously worked on codes and ciphers and their solutions. He teamed up with Mr. Robert T. Brown, a civilian employee at Headquarters, and sought the friendly help and criticism of the Army's Chief Cryptanalyst, Maj. William F. Friedman, and his wife. Mrs. Friedman later became the Coast Guard's cryptanalyst. Meals and Brown finally produced the Coast Guard's first official code book.

Radar was unknown, of course, in the 1920s and while the direction finders were very helpful, the far more efficient high frequency direction finders were still to be developed. In the earlier days, the only way the Coast Guard could locate an offshore smuggling vessel was to cruise until it was sighted. The development of direction finders made locating the rummies far simpler.

Some people ashore occasionally found cause to complain to the Radio Division of the Department of Commerce, or to their power companies, about dot and dash interference with their radio programs. On investigation, this was found to have been caused by the unlicensed operation of a radio station somewhere in the vicinity. The Department of Commerce Radio Division could not do much about it, for at that time their radio inspectors were limited by legal authority "to inspect *licensed* stations (only) at reasonable hours." A further handicap was a ruling that "inspectors have no police or investigative authority." Since the rummy stations were unlicensed, the inspectors had no authority to inspect them at all; thus the stations could operate free from molestation. The Coast Guard, however, decided to seek ways and means of meeting the problem.

Comdr. Charles S. Root at Coast Guard Headquarters, the officer then most concerned with such matters, felt that these unlicensed stations were connected with smuggling operations. Aside from the fact that the rummies were known to be using radio, there was little to go on. From time to time, Coast Guard radiomen had copied radio signals which they believed were transmitted by the rum runners. These signals were studied carefully. Coast Guard radio work of an intelligence nature was necessarily secret, and the whole story as it related to the Rum War cannot be told, even now.

New communications developments by the rum runners or the Coast Guard always engendered new means of combatting them, just as in war new weapons bring about new countermeasures. The liquor smuggler in 1927 had at his command, both on ship and ashore, the newly developed and very efficient high frequency radio communication equipment. This could operate with a fair degree of secrecy over great distances with very low power.

Lieutenant Meals was assigned in 1929 to command the six-bitter *CG–210*. This patrol boat had been fitted out ostensibly to conduct certain experimental radio work, but actually the purpose was to intercept and record certain radio traffic for the purpose of detecting and identifying persons, ships and stations engaged in illicit operations.

It was not known where the illicit stations were, or what radio frequencies were being used. All of their transmissions were in code or cipher which would have to be solved. It was assumed that the illegal stations were using a radio frequency which would attract the least attention and cause the least interference; high frequency bands seemed the most likely.   *CG–210* was equipped with receivers covering a very wide frequency range, and Meals, his crew, and his vessel went to work.

They began intercepting, recording, and decoding radio traffic definitely not of legal nature.   To bring the culprit to book, it was necessary to identify him, be able to prove the case, and take legal steps against him.   This was not easy.   On board *CG–210* an operator put on earphones and picked up countless radio signals from all over the world.   Who were the persons transmitting these signals?   Where were they located?   Was their business legal?   Proper radio stations of all nationalities had regular, assigned and published call letters for identity, and the published call books listed ownership, nationality, frequency, power, and in the case of land stations, their locality.   The illegal stations were not listed anywhere, and there was no way of discovering who they were except by the coded traffic they put out on the air.   To the listener the signals were usually meaningless.

Until the very early 1930s there were no adequate high frequency direction finders for locating rummy ships and stations.   About the only means of judging the probable location of a radio station was the strength of its signal.   If the strength increased as *CG–210* moved along, it was probable that she was heading toward it; if it decreased, she was likely heading away.

This was obviously unsatisfactory, and a better method of direction finding was imperative.   The use of high frequency equipment by the rum runners became so general that the Coast Guard was forced to develop means of locating the stations.   The Coast Guard had to experiment with and develop its own equipment.   Much credit for this new and highly specialized development should be given to Lieutenant Meals who had been placed in charge of the Coast Guard's field activities relating to these matters.

Much experimentation followed, but progress was slow.   To meet the challenge, Lt. E. M. Webster, Chief of the Communications System at Headquarters, assigned Radio Electrician Clyde T. Solt to assist Lieutenant Meals.   This made a good team.   Solt was an expert on radio direction finders, and succeeded in developing suitable equipment. Before long, several rum runners' shore radio stations had been located, and good radio bearings on offshore rum vessels were obtained.

In this connection, the Coast Guard invented in 1930 an interesting incidental means of detecting clandestine radio communications ashore. A small portable direction finder, concealed in a conventional leather suitcase, could be used in public without revealing its nature.   When the clandestine signal was received at right angles to the sides of the suitcase, it was emitted by a small concealed loudspeaker unit.   Many radio sets in houses or buildings were detected by this means.

Though the locations of the shore stations could be detected, what could be done?   No one seemed to have legal authority to take any action against them. The basic violation of law was operation without a license. Under rules of the Department of Commerce, only if a man were actually caught *in the act* of operating an unlicensed station could he be convicted; even then it would have to be proved that his signals reached beyond the borders of the State in which the station was located.

Convictions under these conditions were difficult. Police of Inwood, Long Island, raided an unlicensed radio station presumably operated for the benefit of rum runners. They found and arrested one man there who had in his possession a code allegedly used in illegal operations. The only charge against this man which the police could make stick was violation of a fire ordinance in the installation of his radio equipment. The man was fined $10 and released; the next day he was back in business operating at a new location. In another instance, prohibition agents and Department of Commerce inspectors raided three rummy radio stations in the New York area. The operators were released on payment of nominal fines, and resumed operations after moving their equipment.

This was an impossible situation. There was much desk pounding in Washington, and at meetings with representatives of the Department of Justice, Department of Commerce, and Treasury Department, it was agreed that all would work cooperatively to the end that trial-proof cases of violation of radio laws, conspiracy, and smuggling might be built up and successfully prosecuted. The Coast Guard would locate the rum runners' stations, intercept and decode their traffic, and act in an advisory capacity in station raids; the Justice Department and customs agents would do the shore investigative work; and the Department of Commerce would take an active part in preparing the radio violation cases. It was further agreed that illegal stations would be raided only when the case was virtually fool-proof.

First under this agreement was the well-publicized Travers case. *CG–210* succeeded in locating an unlicensed radio station at New Bedford, Mass.; operators in the patrol boat had recorded considerable radio traffic between this station and the rum ships. Prohibition agents did the investigative work on shore. Justice Department agents applied to the U.S. commissioner at New Bedford for arrest warrants, without success; finally they were obtained from the commissioner at Boston. The station was then raided and Joseph Travers was arrested while the tubes of his transmitter were still hot from use. Set connections, however, had just been broken, putting the transmitter out of operation.

Coast-guardsmen present quickly put the set back into operation and worked with *Nova V.*, the offshore rummy with whom Travers had been communicating. Radio operators have individual characteristics in sending, easily recognized by receivers who know them, just as voices over the telephone can be recognized by people familiar with them. This is known as "fist." When the coast guardsman began sending, the operator in *Nova V* quickly became suspicious of the change in

111

"fist" and shut down—typical reaction where the operator was engaged in illegal activity. A jury found Travers guilty, but he was soon back again at his old tricks.

Another rummy radio station was raided in Brooklyn. This likewise had been located by *CG–210* and agents working ashore. In spotting the station there had been an error of 8 inches! These 8 inches were important; the error placed the station on the wrong side of a separating brick wall between row houses, and so the wrong house was raided. It contained only a large quantity of "home brew." But the operator had been seen through a window in the act of working his set. The agents proceeded over the roof and down a fire escape, and seized the operator and his equipment.

Convictions for violation of the radio laws could often be obtained with relative ease. Convictions for conspiracy, however, were difficult and involved, and required revelation of methods used by enforcement agencies which would have defeated the whole program. Efforts to build up conspiracy cases involved the offshore vessels, the radioman ashore, their "higher ups," and information gained through interception of the radio messages. Proof was required of an agreement between individuals to commit an illegal act, and of an overt act such as actual smuggling or the use of an illegal radio station.

To prove the case the defense attorney, the judge, and the jury would require a demonstration and proof of the messages, detailed explanation of the method of decoding, and proof that certain individuals had sent and received. The jury might or might not understand what it was all about. One thing was certain: that win or lose, the methods would be revealed to the lawbreaker and his attorney, who would immediately set about to improve his codes and ciphers, making future detections and convictions more difficult. And the Coast Guard simply could not afford to reveal its methods.

Coast Guard Headquarters soon became convinced that radio-conspiracy trials were not the answer to the problem. *CG–210* had succeeded in obtaining usable information and reliable bearings on offshore rum runners. It was far more important to track down those vessels and prevent their successful operation, than to sit at trials which ended in nominal fines and suspended sentences.

CG–210 resumed its offshore work. Lieutenant Meals became commander of a new and special Coast Guard unit at New York. His new area of operations covered the coastal area from Maine to the Florida line. This unit, for utmost freedom of action, operated directly under the supervision of Headquarters. To augment its work, four additional 75-foot patrol boats with competent personnel were assigned to the unit and fitted out in a manner similar to that of *CG–210*.

Since the prime purpose of this unit was the interception, decoding, and dissemination of usable information concerning the rum runners' activities, a decode section was established. Up to this point the Coast Guard's cryptanalysis had been done by Mrs. Friedman at Headquarters, and by Lieutenant Meals in *CG–210*. Under the expanded system, more cryptanalysts were needed—men endowed with a gnawing curiosity, who were geniuses for detail and gluttons for work. Several Coast Guard radio-men with these qualifications were assigned as cryptanalysts, and this work became increasingly effective.

The campaign against the unlawful shore radio stations had produced such meager punitive results that it was decided to leave the stations alone and let them transmit. With cryptanalysis being carried on successfully, the best results were obtained by gaining usable information from the rummies themselves, and the unit concentrated on that. Thereafter, the Coast Guard had better success by taking bearings on the offshore vessels, picketing them, and making seizures on the basis of intercepted information.

One of England's best cryptanalysts was reputed to have set up some of the methods used by the smugglers. The latter, who used both straight code and cipher, changed their codes now and then, causing the Coast Guard to begin all over again on the new codes. But, having broken a code, the Coast Guard gathered a tremendous amount of useful information. Rum runners would become careless occasionally. Once an offshore boat, after getting a message in a new code, came back in the clear and stated: "We came out without the new papers; give it to us in the old." Since the new transmission had been taken down, and the old code was known, the radioman who caught the transmission passed the information along and the new code was quickly broken. By watching the movement of ships, weather and other data, together with intercepted dispatches, it was possible to determine code names for boats, positions, and other words that supplied a certain amount of valuable information.

Not only did interception of coded messages give greatly needed information; it provided some unimportant but very interesting sidelights. For instance, one Coast Guard vessel had rigged up an automobile inner tube between two davits, thus making a giant sling-shot. Some sailors with original minds placed garbage in this sling-shot and showered the Canadian rum runner she was picketing. A coded radio message was picked up from this rummy telling of the incident, and insisting that the Canadian Government file a strong protest to the U.S. Government. The rum ship's crew were understandably irate, and such practice was officially discouraged.

During 1931–33, the new unit intercepted and copied an immense amount of radio traffic, some immediately usable, some merely informative. From this traffic, it was learned that many rummies dealt not only in liquor, but also in Swiss watches, French perfume, contraceptives, firearms, and ammunition for Cuban revolutionists, and aliens. Reliable and usable information was turned over to the interested Government agencies. These activities involved not only foreign ships but many U.S. vessels which might have passed as harmless.

One case illustrative of the valuable work done by this unit was that of the Bull Line freighter *Arlyn*. The rummy group supplying *Arlyn* used a troublesome code transmission which the Coast Guard had been copying and its cryptanalysts had been trying to break for months. Finally, the code was broken, and the accumulated traffic was decoded. It was learned that some time previously the steamer *Arlyn* had contacted the Canadian schooner *John Manning* to take on board a load of illegal liquor. The result was one of the largest vessel seizures during the Coast Guard's antismuggling campaign.

Reconstruction of the event through the decoded messages showed that a shore radio station had, on 24 February 1931, sent this message to *John Manning:* "Go to 25 miles east by south from Winter Quarter Lightvessel to meet a Bull Line ship at 11:00 p.m. there. It will have full running lights. When you meet sing out if all the *Manning's* are aboard how much goods the ship got aboard."

Arlyn was the contacting vessel; in the course of going alongside the schooner she inflicted sufficient damage to cause *John Manning* to sink shortly afterward. In the meantime, *Arlyn* removed thousands of cases of liquor, and took off the entire *Manning* crew. She then brought them unsuspected into a U.S. port without clearing customs or immigration. The liquor was landed, and the crew of *John Manning* scattered undetected to places unknown.

These details were given by the Coast Guard to the customs agent in charge of smuggling investigations at New York who, accordingly, carried our further investigation. This took time, but as a result the Bull Line steamship *Arlyn* was seized in New York by customs authorities on 14 November 1932. With this information the agent built up the entire case upon which a conviction was obtained. The owners of *Arlyn* paid a fine of $10,000 to obtain the release of the vessel; the master of *Arlyn* and three other individuals were sentenced to 1 year and a day in the penitentiary, and were fined $1,000 each for their part in the conspiracy to smuggle liquor into the United States. This was an outstanding example of what could be accomplished through the use of intercepted rum runners' radio traffic.

Another example was the case of *Maurice Tracy*. On 7 and 8 April 1932, the unit decoded messages from an offshore rum runner, saying that she was then alongside a collier and loading her with liquor. The name of the collier, its destination, and the loading position were unknown. Therefore, the unit advised the Coast Guard and customs agents in the various Atlantic ports to be on watch for all colliers arriving within the next few days, and search them. Two such vessels, *Maurice Tracy* and *Eastern Temple,* arrived at New York on 8 April. Both were boarded by the Coast Guard and customs guards who remained throughout the discharge of cargo. *Eastern Temple* was given a clean bill of health, but after the cargo of coal was discharged from *Maurice Tracy,* a large quantity of liquor was found cleverly concealed in a special compartment.

The master could not say who put the liquor on board *Tracy,* and claimed no one was more surprised than he when customs officers and coast guardsmen came on board and found the liquor. The attitude of the crewmen was one of bewilderment and disbelief that liquor could have been on board. But the liquor was there and it was confiscated. When the case came up later in court, the vessel sending the intercepted radio messages was not identified, but the messages were sufficiently conclusive to satisfy the court, and the usual penalties were imposed.

In early November 1932, the patrol boat *CG–214,* aided by a radio electrician at the New York office, intercepted messages from the Canadian rum runner *Amacita* to the effect that she would land liquor in Buzzards Bay. On the basis of this information, *CG–214* and patrol boats from Woods Hole waited until *Amacita* had entered the bay. They then closed in and seized her with a full load of liquor. Operators at the New York office copied the radio transmissions from *Amacita,* and knew of the seizure the moment it happened; the rum runner's last transmission was: "The Coast Guard is here." It was a good haul, and the penalty finally assessed was $107,661.

For some time the unit had been puzzled by radio transmissions of a particular rummy group. This group "talked" a great deal on the air, but seldom were the transmissions of importance. There was one peculiar characteristic; every week or so their transmissions would consist merely of a short dash sent every 15 minutes. The meaning was obscure, until it was reasoned that it could indicate the rummies were "working," and that up to the time of the dash everything was all right; if no dash there was trouble. Efforts to obtain a bearing on this dash were unsuccessful for a long time.

Finally, one of the unit six-bitters obtained a bearing on the signal— 180° from Sandy Hook. A fast boat from the Staten Island Base ran this bearing to a point off Cape May without success. It was then noticed that the reciprocal of this bearing ran straight up the Hudson River! Perhaps the vessel searched for had entered the Hudson. Considering this possibility, the proper authorities were notified to institute a search up the river. The rummies caught wind of something, and a unit operator who had been assigned to copy this particular group of rum runners intercepted a coded message saying: "Heave your anchor immediately and get under way. Stand up river toward Albany." This information was promptly passed to Customs and Coast Guard units and patrol boats *CG–203* and *CG–131* were dispatched up the Hudson to locate the smuggler. The unit operator continued to intercept messages from the same source, including: "Anchor, take off men in life boat, hide boat if possible, come ashore on New York side, try not to attract any attention, and call—when you come ashore." Next followed a discussion about changing the ship's name and the names and nationalities the officers and men were to assume. The last message intercepted was: "Don't change name. All off and raise anchor lights. Get off! Get off!"

This vessel was *Holmewood,* alias *Texas Ranger,* seizure of which, on this occasion, has been recounted in the chapter on Tricks and Tactics. The work of the unit was directly responsible for detecting and locating this vessel, and starting the move which resulted in her capture.

Boatswain John M. Gray, who did the decode work on this group of rummies, worked night and day for months before he solved the code. The unit, and all individuals concerned, received commendation from Admiral Hamlet, who had succeeded Admiral Billard as Commandant in 1932.

These few examples demonstrate the value of this activity in detecting, locating, and bringing to book the rum runners who, themselves, had resorted to radio in code and their own type of intelligence. It is evident that the work of these units greatly increased the efficiency and effectiveness of the Coast Guard's war against the smugglers, especially in its concluding years.

CHAPTER IX

In Southern

Waters

OUR ATTENTION thus far has been turned chiefly toward the waters from the Virginia Capes to New England with particular emphasis on the seas off New York, and toward those of the Pacific coast. Little has been said of the waters off Florida and in the Gulf of Mexico. Activities in these areas did not compare in intensity with those further north. Nevertheless, New Orleans and the Florida resort areas provided most attractive markets, and plenty of rum runners were quick to seize the opportunities offered. The relative proximity of two major sources of liquor—the Bahamas and Cuba—made these opportunities very enticing and devoid of some of the problems faced by the large vessels of Rum Row.

The ports of Bimini and Nassau in the Bahamas, and Havana in Cuba, were handy and well equipped to supply any needs of those who wished to run rum into the southern markets. New Orleans, Galveston, Mobile, Key West, Miami, Fort Lauderdale, Jacksonville, Savannah, and numerous others were very thirsty ports; they cooperated to the best of their ability in having their thirsts assuaged.

Not over 180 miles from Miami was the great liquor port of Nassau; only 60 miles away lay the lesser but handier port of Bimini. Havana was scarcely more than 100 miles from Key West. In the initial stages before the rum runners became well organized, any enterprising Florida citizen who happened to have a motorboat could make a comfortable run over to Bimini, load up, and return to deliver his cargo into eagerly waiting hands. Much was landed at night on Miami Beach which was then hardly more than a bare stretch of sand. Along the whole coast of Florida, including the keys, was a multitude of good hiding places for the smaller rum running vessels. Later, fast blacks needed only a very few hours in transit from the supply source to the market.

Organization of the southern rum runners was slow to develop in the early days of prohibition. But gradually the operations fell into a pattern and became organized like those farther north. It will be recalled that Capt. Bill McCoy's first trip in *Henry L. Marshall* was from Nassau to Savannah, where he landed a large cargo of liquor in 1921. From then on, southern activity increased, organization grew, and rum running profits rose by leaps and bounds. Gangsterism flourished.

Here, as in other areas, the Coast Guard was at a considerable disadvantage in the initial period of prohibition. While there were some seizures, they had little effect upon the vast quantity of liquor landed. With the coming of the six-bitters, however, all that changed, and an aggressive Coast Guard cut down the flow appreciably though it could not stop it.

In the first 2 or 3 years, large rum ships which loaded at Nassau and headed for Rum Row often stopped at various points off the Florida coast and discharged small lots to all comers, mostly slow boats. Later, when fast craft became available, the run from Nassau or Bimini was no great problem, and the larger supply ships served no real purpose off Florida. However, they were important in the Gulf, for the markets there were much farther removed from the source. Many "mother ships" of the Gulf obtained their loads from Belize, Honduras, as well as from Nassau and Havana. As the Coast Guard stepped up its campaign, cutters and six-bitters picketed and trailed these larger rum runners, much as in northern waters. Except for one or two brief periods, destroyers were not sent to the waters of the Deep South.

Eventually, control of the supply ships, contact boats, and fast runners from Bimini and Havana fell inevitably into underworld hands. By 1925, a rum row in the Gulf had become quite firmly established. Among others, an English syndicate had set up shop with a fleet of six schooners and one converted yacht; these operated partly off Florida but chiefly in the Gulf. It became necessary for the Coast Guard to establish an expanded base at Key West in order to be at all effective in the surrounding waters.

Rum running was, for the most part, a man's game, but there were some women in the business. Grace Lithgoe, an American citizen from California, was a slender, black-haired woman, gay in nature, and fond of money. In the very earliest phase of prohibition, she had gone to Nassau and set up her own wholesale liquor business. Soon she became known as the "Queen of the Bootleggers." For several years she did a thriving business. She was a contemporary of Bill McCoy's, and was several times his guest on board *Tomoka* during trips to waters off New York. After the first few years of liquor prosperity at Nassau, the volume of business fell off drastically as a $5 per case revenue tax was imposed on all liquor going through customs there. Grace Lithgoe's business declined and she finally closed her office.

Gloria de Cesares was a beautiful woman of 29, reputedly the daughter of a French father and a Russian mother, born and educated in England,

and married to an Argentinian. She was a keen and accomplished horsewoman and navigator. The British five masted steam auxiliary schooner *General Serret* had made one trip across the Atlantic, presumably with contraband cargo, and was then laid up at Antwerp. After a series of legal difficulties in Europe, she was purchased by Madam de Cesares for 115,000 francs, or sixty-five hundred American dollars of that time.

General Serret had taken on the look of a pirate ship. Gloria transferred her to the newly founded "Gloria Steamship Company," which she intended to run personally. The vessel then got under way for the happy hunting ground with 10,000 cases of whiskey, but put into Dover Harbor ostensibly due to engine trouble. Something else was wrong, however. The master complained that he was short of money and stores, and he and his crew objected to the supercargo who had been shipped with them.

The stop at Dover automatically ended her voyage. The ship and cargo were seized by British authorities, sent to the Thames, and held by British customs officials pending payment of duties. The cargo never did get to America. The ambitious plans of Madam de Cesares never fully materialized.

Spanish Marie's plans did, however, and for a long time she led the Coast Guard a merry chase. Spanish Marie, operating from Havana, became notorious. She established and ruthlessly ruled a little rum running empire. Her greatest activity was in the later years. She was a formidable female admiral of the fastest flotilla of contact boats in the business. About 6 feet tall, well proportioned, and attractive, she was an astute business woman of iron determination, and exclusively Latin in temperament. This rum running woman was a fickle and dangerous person, with morals as free as the four winds. Her colleagues and passing fancies were rum runners, and she became the chief controlling factor in the illicit trade from Havana to Key West. Spanish Marie gradually amassed a fleet of 15 speedboats which she controlled and directed, all of which were capable of 20 to 30 knots. This fleet operated all along the Florida Keys and extended its operations even to Palm Beach during the tourist season.

Especially in her earlier days, she made it very tough for the coast guardsmen who tried to intercept her motorboats. She even adopted a convoy system at times, in which three loaded motorboats sailed together, accompanied by a fourth which carried no liquor but was "armed to the teeth." With better patrols, the Coast Guard began to make it hard for Spanish Marie. It succeeded in obtaining certain intelligence, and patrol boats in the area were kept fairly well informed of the anticipated movements of her boats. Then she countered by equipping her boats with radio and installing an unlicensed radio transmitting station at Key West for communication with them. She used an ingenious code of seemingly harmless Spanish words and phrases. However, the radio station was finally located and the Coast Guard broke the code. Transmissions were allowed to continue for they gave the Coast Guard valuable and almost continuous information.

Southern waters were not only infested by the rum runners of Spanish Marie and many others, but also by alien smugglers who found the keys and islands of Florida and the bayous of Louisiana most convenient allies. Unfortunately, the Coast Guard could not keep all of these coastal spots under continuous surveillance. However, it made a real effort to keep an eye on all suspected vessels. At one time these two types of smuggling, sometimes done by the same people, became so serious that the Commandant, Admiral Billard, went to the area to make a special personal study of conditions there. But alien smuggling is another story.

Early captures of rum ships followed very much the pattern in northern waters, and were usually of a routine nature. Some episodes, however, were unusual in various details. When seizures were made, it was necessary to be alert to tricks of all sorts, for rum runners were a vindictive lot. On one occasion *CG–249*, later to become famous, boarded a rum runner 48 miles off East Lake Worth Inlet. The black had a cargo of liquor; her crew were placed under arrest, and taken on board the patrol boat. The alert prize crew discovered that the rummies had poured gasoline and oil into the bilges so that, had an attempt been made to start the motor, an explosion would have certainly followed with serious results.

Cutter *Yamacraw,* very active on southern patrols, was cruising off the Florida coast near Fernandina to check up on the auxiliary schooner *Charles H. Hyde.* *Yamacraw's* captain had information that *Hyde's* registry at Nassau as a British vessel was legally doubtful. The schooner was sighted and overhauled, and found to be loaded with 1,000 bags of fine liquor. Though just outside the international limit, the schooner was seized because of the questionable registry rather than the liquor, and towed to Savannah. This was done with full knowledge that she might have to be towed out again and released—as was the case.

A large portion of the liquor which got to Key West was transported by small craft from Havana. But there were other ways. A car ferry running between Key West and Havana carried cars and freight. It was involved in one little racket which Coast Guard cutters found difficult to counter. Men in Havana would pick up a supply of bottled liquor and put it in bags which were tied to a long line buoyed at both ends. Confederates on the ferry would then take over, and when the ferry reached Key West Reef the bag-carrying line would be paid out over the stern to lie on the bottom in relatively shallow water. Men from Key West would then go out under cover of darkness, retrieve the cache, and take it to a ready market in the town.

One of the most persistent rum runners in the Gulf of Mexico was the two-masted British schooner *Island Home.* She made it a habit never to deliver liquor at the point called for in the manifest. She was seized with a full load of liquor, taken into Galveston, and all hands were given sentences ranging from 4 to 18 months, and fines of $250 to $5,000. This discouraged her not at all; she was still running rum 3 years later when *Yamacraw* examined her in outside waters. Her name had become *Madam,* but there was no change in her operations.

By the beginning of 1925, the rum row off Chandeleur Island, Louisiana, had become quite formidable; there were seven vessels doing business with contact boats. Virtually all of this liquor was destined for the New Orleans market. The area was patrolled by cutters *Comanche* and *Tallapoosa.*

After the six-bitters came on the scene in 1925 and 1926, they were very active in patrolling these waters, intercepting blacks from Bimini, Nassau, and Havana, and in making seizures. One of the most outstanding of these patrol boats was *CG–249.* After she had been on the job for many months, she was patrolling one night about 10 miles off Gun Key. Soon after dusk, this vessel stopped and drifted. She was rewarded by the faint sound of motors in the direction of nearby Cat Key. Boatswain Harry Ball, commanding, went ahead full speed in that direction and stopped again. The sound of motors was more distinct and to the south. Again *CG–249* proceeded. In the light of a rising moon the 30-foot motorboat *V–13574* was observed making for Miami.

The patrol boat's searchlight brought her into full view, and three men stripped to the waist were seen in the beam beginning to throw sack after sack overboard in a desperate effort to lighten their burden and put on greater speed. Boatswain Ball ordered a Springfield rifle tracer bullet sent across her bow. Mr. Edward Mayl of the *Miami Daily News* was a guest on board *CG–249,* and in the *Daily News* he gave this description of what followed:

"A flash: a loud report and a blazing tracer bullet struck the water astern and leeward of the racing 'rummy'. Six more gunny sacks of liquor went overboard. Another flash, another shot, and a second blazing ball struck the water at the bow of the fugitive craft. More gunny sacks went overboard. The distance lessened by one-half, giving the Coast Guard 1-pounder easy range at 200 yards.

" 'Man the gun' cried the Coast Guard skipper. The crew jumped forward. More gunny sacks went to keep company in Davey Jones' locker.

"The ship's gun boomed; the bullet dropped before the bow of the little white launch. She was an easy mark on the phosphorescent sea, caught between the beams of a full moon and the powerful searchlight of our rum chaser.

"Again, the 1-pounder barked, and spashed its bullet beside the liquor carrier. A bare back disappeared into her hold. Twice more the Springfield rifles sent tracer bullets around the desperate vessel.

"Only 100 yards separated the vessels at the finish. Three army Colt automatics spat in the waters within a yard of the quarry and still the boat kept on and the gunny sacks went overboard.

"Boom! A third 1-pounder belched death at the tiny liquor transport. 'Hello aboard!' came Boatswain Ball's even voice through our ship's megaphone. 'All hands stand by or we'll send you and your ship to the bottom.'

"Four hands shot toward the moon which had discovered them but another pair of ambitious arms sent still another gunny sack to the bottom. A single automatic barked, and the third pair of arms lifted weakly overhead as the body wilted and dropped in a heap at the stern.

"The motors of the smaller vessel had died. The Coast Guard searchlight played upon the beaten crew of three as our cutter drew alongside.

" 'We're beat, Cap. We're through. Don't shoot!' cried a husky voice in heavy gutterals."

The three were taken on board the patrol boat and arrested—a 12-year-old boy, a man about 55, and a younger man of around 30. Still unjettisoned were about 90 sacks of whiskey. *V–13574* was seized and tied astern, and all were taken into the Miami Coast Guard Base.

There was nothing particularly unusual about this chase and seizure unless it be the presence of a 12-year-old boy. It was typical of hundreds of cases which might be considered routine.

There were often minor events in this grim business which caused amusement. A rum runner was calmly unloading cargo on a Florida beach where cars were waiting to transport it, when the operation was pounced upon by the Coast Guard's shore patrol. Amid some wild confusion, the liquor, cars, boat, and some of the men were captured; a few men escaped. Articles found there were also seized. Among them was an ear trumpet. This was known to have belonged to a rum runner called "Deafy." Now Deafy needed this ear trumpet, and several times he appealed to the local Coast Guard to let him have it back. He was politely told on each occasion that the Coast Guard would be glad to return it if he would say when and where he lost it, and if it tied in with the Coast Guard's knowledge about it. This, Deafy was unwilling to do, of course, as he could then be involved in the incident.

As we know, prohibition was unpopular with the American people and the press, and while neither, with very few exceptions, had any dislike for the Coast Guard as such, they were ready to discredit the Service in order to destroy the prohibition movement and cause the constitutional amendment to be rescinded. This was especially true at Key West.

The Coast Guard Base there was very active since the town was a big "port of entry" for liquor. Even so, an amazing amount of contraband got through. The population of Key West was almost 100 percent against prohibition and those whose duty it was to enforce it. This produced a very uncomfortable situation for the Coast Guard. Here, as in many other widely scattered places, feeling ran high at times, and there were demonstrations against the coast guardsmen.

For example, in 1932 one of the six-bitters was patrolling off Key West when her skipper, Chief Boatswain's Mate Bowery, sighted a rum runner and signaled him to stop. The signal went unheeded, so a burst of machine gun fire brought the speeding rummy to a halt. Upon seizing the boat, Bowery was told that his bullets had killed the skipper who, when hit, had fallen overboard. The man's name revealed that he was one of a family of notorious rum runners. Bowery took the boat in to Key West. Word quickly got around, animosity ran rampant, and there was much talk of lynching Bowery. This was not new; he had been threatened many times before, but this looked very serious.

Bowery was charged with first-degree murder by the father of the rum boat's skipper. A hearing was held by a justice of the peace. Fearing trouble, Lt. Comdr. Harley E. Grogan, who had been sent to sit on the case, discovered that since the local police wore no side arms and were friendly with the rum runners, they would not be helpful. He tried unsuccessfully to obtain National Guard troops to keep order. Then he sent from the base a truck load of coast guardsmen with a machine gun and had it park nearby. The hearing was open, and everyone who entered the room was searched; quite a collection of knives, guns, and blackjacks resulted. Since the body of the "victim" had not been found, the charge was changed to manslaughter, and Bowery was released on bond.

Investigation which followed disclosed that the skipper had disappeared before in a similar manner and had reappeared in Cuba. After things quieted down, it was learned that in this instance he had jumped overboard, made shore, and proceeded to his girl friend's home at Tampa.

The case went before the grand jury some months after the hearing, and as no witnesses for the prosecution attended, the case was dismissed. Bowery continued to capture rum runners off Florida, turned in a creditable record, and escaped lynching.

Special events sometimes induced special campaigns. In the spring of 1928 the Shriners were scheduled to hold a convention at Miami. Such a market was enticing, and the rum runners greatly increased their efforts to assure that the supply of liquor would not become exhausted. Coast Guard activities were also increased as a countermeasure. Small, fast boats made the crossing from Florida to Bimini in the daylight hours, returning with their loads at night. Coast Guard craft began intercepting these runners on the east-bound trips, and if the men were found with substantial sums in their pockets, usually around $1,200, they were held for investigation. This interference with their plans brought about a change, and east-bound trips were then made after dark. This, however, delayed their west-bound crossings; the slower boats lost a day unless they wished to chance a daylight return with their liquor loads, with disastrous results, which a few did.

Two of the 75-footers operating in the Gulf of Mexico became involved in a unique rum running episode. *CG–302*, commanded by Boatswain B. Paulson, and *CG–246* were patrolling the waters between the Mississippi Delta and Timbalier Island when *CG–302* sighted the French three-masted schooner *Arsene J.* and stood toward her. Three motorboats were observed in the deepening dusk leaving the schooner's side in a hurry. One of these was seized, and information was obtained about the purchase of liquor from *Arsene J.*

On the basis of this, *CG–302* proceeded to the schooner, and Boatswain Paulson and his chief engineer, A. Handley, went on board. Her papers were examined, the liquor checked, and the master was transferred to *CG–302*. Paulson returned to his patrol boat, and J. D. Mathews replaced him in the schooner. Handley and Mathews remained in the three-master to supervise things there.

Meanwhile, *CG–246* had come up alongside the schooner. *CG–302* and *CG–246* began towing *Arsene J.* toward Timbalier Lighthouse, with New Orleans as their destination. Just before midnight *CG–302* suffered some damage, and it was necessary to part the cable and steer for shore. *Arsene J.* remained under tow by *CG–246* for a while, but the latter soon received a signal for assistance from *CG–302*. The schooner was left where she was and, preoccupied with their own difficulties, the patrol boats departed.

For 3 nights and 2 days, *Arsene J.* with Handley and Mathews on board, drifted or sailed in circles in the general area where she had been left. At first, the coast guardsmen were confident that *CG–302* or another boat would return, but as time went on their hopes first dimmed and then vanished. The schooner's mate decided to make port. Handley and Mathews wanted to be taken to Havana, but this was refused. The vessel went instead to Coatzacoalcos,. Mexico. There, the schooner was held pending negotiations between the United States and Mexico. In the meantime, it was considered that the coast guardsmen had been shanghaied.

Shortly afterward, cutter *Tallapoosa* steamed to Coatzacoalcos to retrieve the two coast guardsmen. As she entered the port, she boiled along astern of the Mexican steamer *El Superior* which was also entering. Lt. (j.g.) George B. Gelly of *Tallapoosa* was ashore that night and fell into conversation with representatives of the Standard Oil Co. of California who lived across the street from the Federal barracks. They had seen the cutter enter the harbor, thought she was chasing *El Superior,* and suspected that the United States was going to war with Mexico because of an incident 2 weeks earlier. It seemed that the U.S. Marines were fighting the insurrectionist General Augustino Sandino in Nicaragua. A company of Federal troops had entered the barracks before daybreak one morning, had marched out in peasant clothes with rifles and cartridge belts, and had boarded *El Superior* to join Sandino. The oil company representatives had sensed retaliation!

Handley and Mathews were returned to the U.S.A. in *Tallapoosa*.

The Honduran oil screw *Aurora* was a notorious rum runner which had long operated in the Gulf of Mexico. The 100-foot cutter *Forward*, Boatswain W. C. Hart, was cruising in March 1933 off Pass a Loutre of the Mississippi Delta, well inside the 12-mile limit. Hart sighted *Aurora* which was then headed toward the Delta and within 10 miles of the coast. *Aurora*, also sighting *Forward* at about the same time, turned and fled southeastward. *Forward* chased her in continuous and hot pursuit. The vessel was overhauled and stopped outside of the 12-mile limit. The Boatswain reported the circumstances to his Division Commander who directed him to seize the liquor-laden vessel, which had sailed from Belize, British Honduras, ostensibly for Nassau, but without proper manifest.

Aurora was an old and unseaworthy vessel. At the time of seizure her master was maneuvering her in a circle, operating the engine to free his ship of water. Hart placed a prize crew of three in the vessel and took her in tow. During the night she leaked persistently, and the prize crew manned the pumps. To complicate things, the sea began making up. In the morning, it was necessary to transfer one of the prize crew to *Forward*, and while maneuvering to bring *Aurora* close enough, the towing hawser became fouled in the cutter's propeller. *Aurora* ranged up out of control and collided lightly with the Coast Guard vessel. The rummy's stem head was caught by *Forward's* guard as the cutter rolled. The condition of the stem and wood ends of the planking, revealed by the damage, was very poor.

The leaking increased, and so the 502 sacks of liquor were transferred to *Forward*, as well as the ship's gear and the eight members of her crew. *Aurora* sank about 25 miles south of Mobile Bay. *Forward* then proceeded to Mobile and turned the crewmen, gear, and liquor over to customs authorities.

Later, the court found as to facts that evidence failed to show that *Aurora*, when sighted, was within 12 miles of the coast; and as to conclusions of law that seizure was not in accordance with the process of laws of the United States nor by virtue of any treaty and was therefore illegal and unauthorized, and that there was no authority to seize the liquor. It is of interest that one of the proctors for the claimants was the son of the judge before whom the trial was held. The salvaged cargo was released to the claimants, and the prisoners were released and returned to Honduras. An appeal by the Government was dismissed.

The vast majority of seizures were made without violence, but it was inevitable that some fights would occur. Rum runners were about the same everywhere, and southern waters had their share of hijacking, doublecrossing, gangland reprisals, and flying bullets. Whenever the Coast Guard made a seizure there was always the possibility that those captured would resort to violence.

Perhaps the most notorious incident of this sort involved the 75-foot patrol boat *CG–249*, operating out of the Coast Guard Section Base at Fort Lauderdale, and commanded by Boatswain Sidney C. Sanderlin.

As we know, Bimini had maintained a flourishing liquor business with rum runners supplying the Florida trade. In 1927, it developed that rummies had been purchasing liquor there with counterfeit American money, and the U.S. Government decided to track this down if possible. To that end, Secret Service Operator Robert K. Webster had been assigned the job of going to Bimini to locate, if possible, the plates and presses involved and catch the counterfeiters through the British authorities. Webster had been sent to Fort Lauderdale, and Boatswain Sanderlin had received orders to take him to Bimini for this purpose.

CG–249 started out from Fort Lauderdale at about noon on 7 August 1927 with its seven-man crew, and Mr. Webster as a passenger, and headed for Bimini. After having proceeded for a few miles, *CG–249* sighted a motorboat which looked suspiciously like a rum runner, heading for the Florida coast. Sanderlin decided to investigate. He altered course toward her and ordered her to stop. This went unheeded, and several shots were fired across her bows before she hove to.

Boatswain Sanderlin boarded *V–13997* to search it for contraband, and found 160 cases of liquor. The boat's crew consisted of two men, Horace Alderman and Robert W. Weech, both of Miami. The boatswain seized the craft and placed the crew under arrest; he then searched both prisoners for arms and found none. Alderman and Weech were then ordered to go on board *CG–249*. However, before boarding the patrol boat Alderman managed to pick up a gun which he had hidden in his engine room. The coast guardsmen began transferring the liquor from the rum runner to their own vessel.

Sanderlin recognized the complication in his situation, since his orders were to go to Bimini, and he did not have men enough to spare for a prize crew. He therefore went into the pilot house to radio his base for instructions. Alderman and Weech, presumably unarmed, followed him.

As the boatswain began working his key, Alderman shot him in the back, killing him instantly. Victor A. Lamby, motor machinist's mate first class, witnessing this murder, started aft toward the armory to arm himself; now that the die had been cast, Alderman immediately shot him in the spine, wounding him mortally. The murderer then picked up a pistol from the pilot house and armed his partner Weech.

The two murderous rummies now had control of the situation. Lamby was taken to the engine room, threatened with death, and otherwise treated brutally. Brandishing his gun, Alderman ordered the coast guardsmen to return the cases of liquor from *CG–249* to *V–13997*, and this they did. He then ordered the remainder of the crew of the patrol boat as well as Mr. Webster to go on board his boat; there he lined them up, saying that he intended to shoot them all or, perhaps, make them walk the plank farther at sea, and burn *CG–249*. Thus, all evidence of the crime would be destroyed. This was no idle threat; Weech was agreeable to the plan. Alderman told Weech to go to the engine room of *CG–249* and break the gas lines preparatory to setting the patrol boat on fire. Weech did as he was told, and completely tore off the port and starboard main gas lines, flooding gasoline into the bilges. With Lamby lying in the engine room, Weech then threw a lighted match in there and he and Alderman jumped into their own boat. Fortunately, the engine room failed to ignite.

All but Sanderlin and Lamby were now in the rum boat. Alderman instructed Weech to start the engine in order to get away from the expected explosion when the fire in *CG–249* got underway. However, something went wrong with the motor, and it would not start. This distracted Alderman's attention from the coast guardsmen, who availed themselves of the opportunity thus presented, and they rushed the killer. In the rush Alderman began firing; his spewing revolver shot Mr. Webster through the right breast and killed him instantly, and then shot Acting Ship's Cook Jodie L. Hollingsworth, hitting him in the shoulder and eye. But Frank L. Tuten, boatswain's mate first class, and Frank Lohman, motor machinist's mate second class succeeded in overcoming Alderman who was stabbed and beaten unconscious. Weech came up the companionway and was knocked over the head, rolled overboard, and again taken prisoner as he came up.

Tuten, Lohman, and the other two uninjured coast guardsmen, John A. Robinson and Hal M. Caudle, were now in control. *CG–249* was still floating, she was not burning, and her radio was operative. The base was notified, and assistance was rushed to the scene.

A Coast Guard Board of Investigation convened at the section base at Fort Lauderdale at which it was found that it was the intent of Alderman and Weech to kill all hands and burn *CG–249*, destroying all evidence of their crimes; that Weech, while he committed no actual shooting, was equally as guilty as Alderman; and that Alderman and Weech were guilty of murder and piracy on the high seas.

More than 2 years were required to convict Alderman and Weech. Trial was at Miami; Weech became somewhat cooperative, and was given a prison sentence. Alderman was convicted of murder and was sentenced to be hanged. Alderman paid for his crimes by hanging— at the Coast Guard Section Base, Fort Lauderdale.

Another very famous case was that of the rum runner *I'm Alone*. This involved international complications of a serious nature. *I'm Alone* was a two-masted knockabout schooner of the fisherman type, built at Lunenberg, Nova Scotia, in 1924. She was sound and seaworthy, and beautiful to behold. Twin 100 horsepower auxiliary motors moved her along at about 12 knots; her holds could accommodate about 2,800 cases of liquor. She had been built for the liquor trade, which she pursued vigorously.

I'm Alone brought her first load to the New England coast and disposed of it easily; she used St. Pierre et Miquelon as her chief source of supply, and made many trips to Rum Row and other points, successfully carrying out her missions for 4 years. This schooner assiduously kept to the high seas where she was immune from seizure, but she was often picketed and trailed by Coast Guard cutters to keep shore-based rummies from making contact. This annoyed her, but she did a big business in spite of it. It is said that she earned more than $3 million for her owners. Until 1928 her principal area of operations was between Gloucester and the Virginia Capes. The Coast Guard watched for an opportunity to take her in, but not once during her Atlantic coast operations was she found in waters where seizure would be legal. Hijackers knew her, too; on several occasions she beat off pirates who tried to board her.

In the fall of 1928 *I'm Alone* was sold and new owners took over, but her mission remained the same. Capt. John T. Randall was given command, and her scene of activity shifted to the Gulf of Mexico. Forty-nine years old, Randall was a good seaman; he had served as an officer in the Royal Navy in World War I, had received wartime decorations, and held a master's license. He was a hard-boiled skipper, with a stubbornness that contributed greatly to ending his days at sea.

For her first trip south, *I'm Alone* loaded 1,500 cases of assorted liquors at St. Pierre. Her rendezvous was at a spot more than halfway from the Mississippi Delta to the Texas border—well south of Trinity Shoal. On arrival, Captain Randall awaited contact boats which could match his torn dollar bills. Instead, cutter *Wolcott* appeared and picketed and trailed the schooner for 2 days. Randall became annoyed and, in disgust, set out for Belize without having disposed of a case.

I'm Alone cruised about from Belize to Nassau, and then returned to the same spot off Trinity Shoal. This visit was more successful. A contact boat appeared and came alongside, matched some dollar bills, and departed with a load. The schooner went out to sea and returned 5 days later, disposing of more liquor to the same boat. Then at daybreak on 20 March 1929 *Wolcott* came up from the west. *I'm Alone* got under way but *Wolcott* was close by. Boatswain Frank Paul, commanding the cutter, checked his position and placed the point of contact at 10.8 miles from shore—within the 12-mile limit. Randall placed it about 15 miles away. Such positions, as we know, were extremely difficult to prove to the satisfaction of courts. The two vessels were now on a southerly course, and Boatswain Paul signaled Randall to heave to.

Randall refused, and *I'm Alone* continued on her way. Meaning business, Paul then fired several blank shots across her bows, and finally the vessel stopped. Randall called over that Paul, if unarmed, could come on board, and the boatswain boarded the schooner. The two captains had a long talk over a table in the master's cabin during which Randall was reproached for his stubbornness. Paul looked over the craft and its cargo, and then returned to *Wolcott*. *I'm Alone* headed southward with *Wolcott* trailing. The latter's commanding officer thought things over further.

Several hours later *Wolcott* drew close, and again signaled the schooner to heave to. Randall refused once more, and was given 15 minutes to change his mind. He didn't. After a warning, *Wolcott* opened fire in earnest; shells from her 4-pounders screamed through the rum runner's sails, rifle fire sang overhead, and a bullet grazed Randall's right thigh. Shoal water caused the cutter to fall astern, but the chase continued that night and the next day, with *I'm Alone* using her motors and turning up 12 knots. By the second morning, the two vessels were 220 miles south of the Mississippi Delta. The weather became nasty; the wind increased to a moderate gale, and the sea made up. Over the horizon from the southwest appeared cutter *Dexter*, a sister ship of *Wolcott*, and she closed in. *Dexter* signaled *I'm Alone* to heave to but Randall continued on. From fairly close range *Dexter* let go with her guns scoring several hits. Firing grew hotter and hits were more numerous; splinters flew, sails became tattered, the hull was holed. The rummy was now leaking copiously, and she slowly settled.

When the forward deck was awash, Randall ordered abandon ship, ducked below for his books and papers, and went over the side. As he and his men reached *Dexter* with the aid of a floating cabin door, *I'm Alone* disappeared beneath the waves. One man, French-born Leon Mainjoy, was done in when he was hauled on board the cutter; efforts to revive him were fruitless.

Dexter and *Wolcott* headed northward, and reached New Orleans with seven surviving crew members of the late rum runner. All were marched ashore, and turned over to customs authorities.

The incident had immediate and serious repercussions in British, Canadian, and Washington diplomatic circles. Because of Mainjoy, France joined in the protests against the alleged high-handedness. The British Parliament was the scene of speeches. A member of the Canadian House of Commons claimed an act of war if the "attack" had been carried out under official Government instructions—an act of piracy if on Boatswain Paul's initiative. The Coast Guard maintained that *I'm Alone* was first contacted in territorial waters and that hot and continuous pursuit followed, that the schooner was armed, and that she refused to heave to when so ordered. The international legal aftermath blew hot and cold, mostly hot, for several years.

Not until 1935 was the incident closed. A judicial commission consisting of a U.S. Supreme Court Justice and the Canadian Chief Justice convened; as a result Canada received a settlement of $50,666 (as against $386,000 asked), and an official apology from the United States. There was no award to the owners of *I'm Alone* either for the vessel or its 2,000 cases of liquor, but Captain Randall and his crew were awarded $25,666 and exonerated. Captain Randall never went to sea again.

Though far removed from the main theatre of rum running operations, the waters of Florida and the Gulf of Mexico were alive with illicit trade from almost the beginning to the end of prohibition. They gave the Coast Guard no rest from vigilance, no freedom from gang-controlled arrogance and violence, no respite from the worry of international incidents and rationalized court decisions.

Nevertheless, the Coast Guard's campaign slowed the flow, discouraged many, and caused numerous runners to give up the traffic. It inspired admiration even from a sometimes hostile public which determined to have its liquor regardless of the gangsterism, graft, murders, and corruption which it fostered, and the coincidental flouting of this controversial, unenforceable, and unpopular law of the United States.

Rum runner *Mary Langdon* flanked by *Redwing*, left, and *CG-237*, right; guarding her after seizure.

Hohenlinden at anchor following seizure. She made a most daring attempt to land her own liquor.

Artemis finally located in boat yard. Showing damage sustained from gunfire and collision.

Paulding at Boston. Only three stacks standing after attempt to rescue *CG–238*.

CG–403, one of the new 78-foot patrol boats. Speedier than the 75-footers, these were the best of the anti-smuggling boats.

Whispering Winds at New London after capture. After conversion, she became CG–986.

Bullet holes and Highland Still. A close-up of *Whispering Winds'* pilot house.

The four-master *Arco Felice II.* She smuggled both liquor and aliens.

Lieutenant Commanders John S. Baylis and Robert C. Jewell relax in icy surroundings after the ordeal.

Rum ship *Audrey B.* She was captured by the intrepid *CG–290*.

Mary, **a typical contact boat.** This 43-footer was powered with a 100-horsepower engine.

A die-hard rum runner, *Miserinko,* of the *Popocatapetl* group.

Captain Frank M. Meals. As a lieutenant, he was greatly responsible for the success of radio communications in the fight against the smuggler.

Seventy-five foot patrol boats from Gloucester base.

Cruising cutter *Yamacraw*, one of the cutters active in southern waters.

***Yamacraw* and three prizes.**   A nest of contact boats testifies to a good day's work.

***Arsene J* took Coast Guardsmen for a ride.**   Here she waits for another load.

Island Home, **rum runner of the Gulf.** She was seized by *Yamacraw* off Edmont Key, Florida, in 1926.

Annetta I was seized by *Ericsson*—one time she did not pass.

Rum runner *Linwood* burning. The crew of this rum-laden vessel set her afire to destroy evidence before seizure.

Mistinguette picketed by *Terry.* Lying to outside the 12-mile limit.

A deck load of liquor. Rum runner *Kirk and Sweeney* with cases and barrels of rum ready for quick transfer.

Firelight **in her happier days.** This troublesome black finally sank herself by ramming.

Notorious rum runner *Vinces.* This vessel, photographed from *Gresham,* was captured by *Mascoutin* off Charleston.

Cutter *Redwing.* *Redwing* towed *Homestead* after her capture.

Diatome, a high-speed rum runner. Captured off Los Angeles, she was converted by the Coast Guard and became *CG–827.*

Nola, heavily protected by steel armor plate. She was lost in a running battle with three Coast Guard patrol boats near Vineyard Sound Lightship in December 1931.

Rum running steam yacht *Surf* at anchor after her seizure.

The official United States Coast Guard ensign.

British schooner *Pesaquid* of Nassau waiting for business off Cape Henry, Virginia.

CHAPTER X

Ships That
Did Not Pass

THE NUMBER OF VESSELS that eluded the Coast Guard patrols during the entire period of prohibition will never be known, of course. Yet, despite the vigilance and aggressiveness of the Service, it is certain that the number of those which successfully landed their cargoes was very considerable. Some were caught on their first venture; many made numerous successful landings only to be apprehended eventually; an inexcusable total represents rum runners, both vessels and men, who were caught and released several times. A large number escaped seizure altogether. Throughout the era it was a battle of wits, and it is to the Coast Guard's credit that its seizures went into the thousands.

At one time, cases involving liquor violations of all types comprised 40 percent of all those before courts in the United States. This partly explains why sometimes it took 2 or 3 years before cases could be finally disposed of. It may also account to some extent for rapid and superficial trials. It does not account for the fact that while some trials were conducted on a fair and conscientious basis, others were treated as if they were nuisances, and still others were carried out where the court obviously seized upon the slightest technical detail to find in favor of the lawbreakers. This could have disheartened a service less dedicated to its duties than the Coast Guard.

One of the most troublesome and important types of evidence needed in the trials was the exact location of a seizure. Perhaps Coast Guard evidence of this sort was the easiest for the defense to refute. In foreign vessel cases where there was the remotest possibility of question, and there were many, the defense would offer evidence apparently equally good that seizure had been made on the high seas and, therefore, outside of Coast Guard jurisdiction. Even the most carefully prepared evidence of position sometimes proved fruitless, but it was always to the best interests of the Coast Guard to use the greatest care in determining position when any seizures were made.

131

As an example, destroyer *Ericsson,* Lt. Comdr. Lloyd T. Chalker, was cruising about 100 miles off Cape May, when the steamer *Andora* of Oslo, Norway, was sighted. On closer approach, it was seen that a smaller vessel was alongside; *Ericsson* headed toward her and increased speed. The smaller vessel left immediately, but after a three-quarter hour chase, *Ericsson* overhauled the boat and stopped her. She was *Annetta I* of New York, formerly a U.S. Navy subchaser, with seven men on board.

It was found that she had a cargo of champagne in cases apparently just received from *Andora* and hastily stowed. She had no papers of any sort. Since an American vessel with liquor could be taken on the high seas, *Annetta I* was seized.

Lieutenant Commander Chalker determined his position at the point of seizure by three independent means: first a sight of the sun was taken; next the dead reckoning position was established; then four radio compass bearings were recorded. In this case, high seas or territorial waters were not a factor, but meticulous establishment of position was.

Not only was the exact location of seizure important, but it was essential to make a thorough search of the vessel under examination. Destroyer *Porter* was cruising off the entrance to Long Island Sound when she sighted the two-masted auxiliary schooner yacht *Consuelo II* of New York, presumably on her way from Miami to City Island. This vessel appeared heavily laden, and *Porter* trailed her until she reached sheltered waters. When about 2 miles north of Little Gull Island, the destroyer overhauled the schooner which hove to on orders. The boarding officer discovered liquor on board, as well as a crudely forged paper. No documents had ever been issued to a vessel named *Consuelo II,* but the original registry number was discovered; she was really the yacht *Louise,* a former Boston pilot boat. The vessel was thereupon seized together with its cargo, the crew were transferred to *Porter,* and a prize crew were placed on board. *Consuelo II* was towed to New York, where the men and their vessel were turned over to customs authorities.

Then came some surprises. At the time of seizure the Coast Guard found a moderate amount of liquor and looked no further. Customs inspectors found 923 bags of 6 bottles each and were about to call it a day when a concrete floor aroused suspicions; investigating, they found under it another 1,200 bottles. On close inspection another concrete floor was discovered together with 1,350 more bottles. The additional cargo had been almost undetected!

This vessel was in excellent condition and the Coast Guard felt it would be useful in its fleet. It was taken over and became *CG–806.*

Cutter *Legare* left Block Island one winter evening on patrol and noticed a faint glow on the horizon. Heading toward it, she soon came up to the schooner *Flor Del Mar* of Halifax ablaze, abandoned by her crew, and with lifeboats missing. She was a well-known rum runner.

Legare searched unsuccessfully for the crew, then stood by the burning vessel, not daring to go alongside for fear of a fuel tank explosion. However, she held her bow against *Flor Del Mar* and fought the flames with her fire hose. After fighting this fire for 4 hours, during which there were several minor explosions, the flames were brought under control, and attempts were made to salvage the vessel and her cargo.

In an effort to lighten the ship, the coast guardsmen transferred the liquor to the cutter. But *Flor Del Mar* was waterlogged and in danger of sinking. Removal of cargo alone proved insufficient to keep her afloat, so handpumps were worked and fire buckets were used for bailing. At daybreak *Legare* took the schooner under tow; flames broke out frequently but both vessels arrived safely at New London.

Coast Guard officers and men, when boarding vessels, received good cooperation in some cases, hostile resentment in others, and everything between these extremes. Generally, most seamen were resentful of the law enforcement measures necessarily taken by the Coast Guard. This was particularly true of yachts. Whenever there was the slightest ground for suspicion, the Coast Guard had every right, under U.S. and international laws, to require a vessel to heave to for boarding and inspection. Perhaps stopping for the purpose was an annoyance, but if no laws were being broken the vessel boarded had nothing to fear, and cooperation was certainly the best policy.

Cutter *Seneca* met with resentment at boarding in the following instance. While cruising off the New Jersey coast in the vicinity of the rum ships in April 1929, she sighted the American collier *T. A. D. Jones,* bound from Norfolk to New Haven, Conn. Colliers had, for good reason, been suspected of unlawfully transporting whiskey. *Seneca* signaled *T. A. D. Jones* to heave to for inspection, using whistle and visual signals to no avail. Only after three blank warning shots from the cutter's 6-pounder had screamed across her bows did the collier obey.

Lt. Frank M. Meals and Ens. Kenneth P. Maley were sent to board the vessel. The master of *T. A. D. Jones* placed every possible obstacle in the way of these boarding officers. Usually a vessel being boarded at sea makes a lee for the boarding boat; the collier was not only headed directly into the sea but the Jacob's ladder was put over well toward the bow where the choppy sea made boarding uncomfortable, difficult, and hazardous. When finally on the collier's deck, the officers were greeted by the master with a continuous stream of profanity and insults directed at the Coast Guard in general and boarding officers in particular.

It was impracticable at the time to make a detailed search of the vessel at sea, and since the papers were found to be in order, the master was told he could proceed when the boarding officers had returned to *Seneca.* But the moment the officers were in their small boat, *T. A. D. Jones* got under way. The master's actions, language, and lack of cooperation prompted Lieutenant Meals to recommend that the vessel be reported by radio and searched upon arrival in port.

When *T. A. D. Jones* arrived at New Haven, where "Tad" Jones coached football at Yale and owned a coal business, the master heatedly reported being fired upon three times after the three warning shots. This erroneous report caused adverse publicity and a great furor on a wide front. The vessel was searched as Meals had recommended, but given a clean bill of health insofar as liquor was concerned. How much better it would have been had the master taken a few minutes for courteous cooperation with Coast Guard officers who were merely performing their duty!

The French auxiliary two-masted schooner *Mistinguette* of St. Pierre was a veteran rum runner of the fisherman type. Once she had been hijacked, and Coast Guard destroyers had trailed her often. On a stormy night in March 1926 she was standing along the southern shore of Long Island. Destroyer *Porter,* Lt. Comdr. Leroy Reinburg, was proceeding eastward in the same waters and sighted *Mistinguette* running without lights. When *Porter* put her searchlight on her she turned southward, and Reinburg gave chase, finally stopping the vessel. A boarding party discovered 3,000 cases of liquor, seized the craft, and arrested the crew of 10. These smugglers, who offered no resistance, had planned to deliver the cargo at a point 20 miles off Montauk. The weather was nasty with rain, snow, and a heavy swell. With Lt. Norman R. Stiles in charge, *Mistinguette* proceeded to New York under *Porter's* escort. Stiles, who navigated the schooner for 36 uninterrupted hours exposed on deck in the storm, displayed great devotion to duty.

The Great Lakes were the scene of a heavy illicit rum trade, mostly with small craft; the Detroit River, with Canada on one side and the United States on the other, was alive with the business. The Coast Guard was active in these areas, and made innumerable seizures, mostly routine, but sometimes with gun play. Some larger vessels were involved, however. One seizure of a sizeable ship was made by the 110-foot patrol boat *Cook,* Chief Boatswain's Mate Herbert Oddy. Procedure in this instance varied from the usual.

The Coast Guard had information that the Canadian steamer *Geromino* was enroute from Windsor, Ontario, presumably for Chicago with a cargo of liquor, and wished this vessel to be apprehended, boarded, and seized. Boatswain W. A. Skeen was at Sault Ste. Marie, and so was *Cook.* Skeen received orders which directed him to proceed in *Cook* to a point 3 miles south of Detour Passage entrance, where the waterway opens into Lake Huron; there, as directed, he opened sealed orders which had been given him.

In obedience to these orders, Skeen had *Cook* proceed to Mackinaw City, Mich., on the south side of the 5-mile-wide Straits of Mackinac, and tie up at the State Pier. Skeen contacted Mr. F. Yount and Mr. F.

134

Thropp, special customs agents, who arrived by train the next morning. After a conference, Boatswain Skeen learned the further details of his assignment, which was to capture *Geromino*. The two agents joined Skeen on board *Cook,* which then went to a vantage point affording a good view toward Lake Huron, and anchored. A sharp lookout was kept. The suspect vessel had not appeared by late afternoon, and *Cook* shifted to a position at the southwest end of the Straits and again anchored. From that position, there was an unobstructed view of the Straits of Mackinac.

Later, in the gathering dusk, the lookout reported the lights of an approaching vessel which answered the description given by the agents. This vessel was closely watched and permitted to make her way well into the Straits. *Cook* then quickly got under way, and after a half-hour run she signaled the steamer to stop; the whistle signal went unheeded. After a second signal, the steamer laid out a dense smoke screen. Fearful of losing the quarry, Skeen ordered one shot across her bows with the 1-pounder. The ship continued on, and a second shot was fired just ahead of the pilot house. The vessel then reversed engines and stopped.

Cook laid alongside *Geromino,* and Skeen with three armed men together with Yount and Thropp, boarded the vessel without opposition. She carried no licensed officers, and no official papers of any kind, but her holds and even her decks were loaded with beer, champagne, and assorted liquors. No name appeared on her bows or stern; her name boards on either side were reversible, with *Geromino* of Kewanee on one side, and *Arbutus* of Kewanee on the other!

Geromino's entire crew were mustered on deck, searched, and questioned. Letters, papers, and anything else which might throw light on the case were confiscated. Seizure was made at a point 4⅝ miles northwest of Mackinac Point Light, the position being determined by Chief Oddy by bearings, soundings, and distance run. Skeen then placed an armed party of three on board *Geromino*, and the customs agents remained on board to assist. With the ship's crew working the ship and *Cook* escorting, both vessels proceeded to the State Pier at Mackinaw City where they tied up. They remained for the night with the prisoners confined below decks under heavy guard.

The next day *Geromino* was returned to Detroit, and the Coast Guard marked down one more mission accomplished.

The British auxiliary schooner *Pesaquid* was a persistent and troublesome rum runner. For years she hovered off the coast, usually outside the 12-mile limit, discharging her cargoes to contact boats. She had been captured once by *Acushnet* off Block Island and again off the North Carolina coast by *Mascoutin*. Many destroyers and cutters had picketed her. She was in for more trouble.

Many cutters, destroyers, and six-bitters went for long periods without an opportunity to make seizures; this made for monotony and discouragement. Boatswain Teevens, skipper of *CG–236* had seen other patrol boats bringing in prizes, but he had captured none. Though he had boarded many vessels, no liquor had been found. Teevens, with greater determination than ever, approached Comdr. Fred H. Young, commanding officer of the New London Base, and said: "I am going out tonight and stay out until I get something." Commander Young acquiesced, and replied: "You are on your own until you bring one in. Good luck to you."

Teevens went out and had two more discouraging days; but on the third, while off Block Island, he sighted *Pesaquid,* overhauled her and, since the seas were too rough for boarding, he picketed her for 2 more days. The weather finally moderated, and Teevens mustered the courage to go on board. Perhaps he should have waited longer, for while *CG–236* was alongside, her guard rail was smashed by impact against *Pesaquid,* and she suffered other damage. But Teevens found 3,500 cases of whiskey, promptly seized the vessel, and placed her crew under arrest.

The boatswain reported the capture to his base, and also the fact that he was practically out of gasoline. He managed to get more, however, and began towing *Pesaquid.* Other patrol boats offered help, but the boatswain was proud of his catch and waved them away. *CG–236* had towed the schooner a considerable distance toward New London when the sea began making up and Teevens had to turn the job over to a destroyer. The six-bitter went to drydock for repairs. The boatswain's grim determination, however, had paid off in an important capture.

Firelight of Halifax, one of the smaller vessels, was another troublesome rummy. The 125-foot cutter *Harriet Lane* was patrolling off Gloucester one cold January night when she sighted an apparent rum runner proceeding without lights fairly close off the starboard bow. She put her searchlight on the black, found to be *Firelight,* which immediately put on speed; *Harriet Lane* gave chase illuminating her own ensign and giving whistle signals for the runner to heave to. The vessel finally stopped, displayed her stern light, and immediately forged ahead again. The cutter rang up full speed and resumed the chase; once more *Firelight* hove to. A boarding party was sent over; contraband was evident, and the vessel was seized within the 12-mile limit.

The master and crew were taken on board *Harriet Lane.* Coast guardsmen then searched the ship, found no manifest, carefully checked bearings and determined the point of seizure as 7.8 miles from the Londoner beacon. The court later upheld the seizure, but *Firelight* went to work again.

Destroyer *Conyngham* was picketing and trailing *Firelight* a year later about 40 miles south of Nantucket. Patrol boat *Eagle,* a 100-footer, was ordered from New London to relieve her, and arrived at the scene about midnight. She drifted in the vicinity of the black. After 20 minutes, *Firelight* suddenly came about as if to strike *Eagle* on the starboard bow. The patrol boat immediately went astern to avoid contact if possible, but *Firelight* struck her a glancing blow on the starboard side. *Eagle* stopped while an inspection was made for possible damage; fortunately there was none.

This little operation boomeranged on the rummy. In the collision she had broken her planking from below the waterline to the deck. A half-hour later *Firelight* was settling rapidly. The crew of eight abandoned her, drew away, and watched her sink stern first. *Conyngham* was standing by as she had not yet received orders to go to New London. *Firelight's* crew, therefore, were taken on board the destroyer, which later transported them to New London.

The gruelling duty of the destroyers eventually told on them, and during the fiscal year 1931 twelve had become unfit for further antismuggling operations. Accordingly, *Ammen, Beale, Burrows, Downes, Fanning, Jouett, McCall, Monaghan, Patterson, Paulding, Roe,* and *Terry* were decommissioned and returned to the Navy. Five other destroyers, all flush deckers, were overhauled and reconditioned at the Philadelphia Navy Yard, and taken over by the Coast Guard; these were *Badger, Herndon, Hunt, Welborn C. Wood,* and *Abel P. Upshur.* We shall become familiar with some of these new names.

A number of rum ships committed suicide somewhat in the manner of *Firelight.* The destroyer *Davis,* attached to New London, was both witness and victim in an incident of this type. Destroyers and six-bitters operating out of the New London Base worked on a grid system; various patrol areas were designated Area Baker One, Baker Two, Baker Three, Affirm One, Two, and so forth. On 8 June 1931, *Davis* was assigned to patrol Area Baker Two, *Tucker,* Baker One, *Badger,* Baker Three, *Ericsson,* Baker Four and Five, and 125-foot *Marion,* Baker Two. These vessels went to their areas, relieving others which had been on duty there.

In Baker Two, *Davis* encountered 2 days of foggy weather, and northeast gales on the third day, but then the weather cleared. Shortly before noon on the fourth day the destroyer found the British oil screw *Shubenacadia* of St. John's drifting about 60 miles south of Martha's Vineyard. *Davis* continued to scout, but *Marion* was directed to proceed to *Shubenacadia's* position and keep her under surveillance.

In the early evening, *Davis* came up to the rummy, which *Marion* was picketing. *Shubenacadia* then went ahead at 9 knots, and both Coast Guard vessels trailed her. As dusk closed down, the black decided to try an escape. She doused her running lights, emitted large clouds of smoke from her exhausts, and began circling in an effort to get out of range of the Coast Guard searchlights. Being unsuccessful, she stopped and switched on her running lights; suddenly, dousing lights, she ran away full speed in a cloud of smoke. *Davis* and *Marion* increased speed and kept the black in the range of their searchlights. *Shubenacadia* changed course often and drew away from *Davis* because of that vessel's large tactical diameter, but gained little on *Marion* whose greater maneuverability was an asset. *Davis* finally straightened out and put on speed, gaining on both.

Shortly the three vessels were in the same relative position as when the black began her escape try. *Shubenacadia* then repeated her original maneuver by heading toward *Davis* and cutting astern, but the two Coast Guard vessels hung on. The same frantic attempts were made six or eight times before midnight. Next the black changed course toward another rum runner which destroyer *Welborn C. Wood* was trailing. *Shubenacadia* dodged between *Wood* and the other black in its escape effort, but *Wood* kept a searchlight on the rummy and contact was maintained.

About an hour later, *Davis* was steaming at 10 knots on a steady course, with *Shubenacadia* 200 yards off her starboard bow swinging around toward *Davis*. When 50 yards off, the black blew a passing signal of one blast, indicating a port-to-port passing and consequent crossing ahead of the destroyer. Sensing that the rummy could not possibly cross the destroyer's bow, the latter's officer of the deck signaled stop, then full speed astern. *Shubenacadia* also realized that she could not cross, and put her engines in reverse while making 10 knots; nevertheless, she struck bow on against the starboard side of *Davis* abreast the No. 1 waist gun.

The bow of *Shubenacadia* was badly shattered, and the vessel began to settle on an even keel. Since the rummy was in a sinking condition, her crew abandoned ship and went on board *Marion*.

The officer of the deck in *Davis* sounded the siren and general alarm promptly upon being hit, and preparations were made for placing the collision mat which, however, was not needed. In examining damage, it was found that the force of the blow had opened bulkhead seams of the forward fuel oil tank, and that the guard rail and the ship's side were deeply dented. Fuel oil from the rupture ran into the after compartment of the forward berth deck and accumulated to a depth of about 8 inches. To ease this situation, oil was transferred from the starboard to the port fuel tank.

Two hours after the collision, *Shubenacadia* sank, with *Marion* and *Davis* standing by. As she went down, many large liquor-filled kegs floated away. About 40 of these were broken open by *Marion's* crew causing them to sink and constitute no menace to navigation.

By mid-morning, the destroyer's crew had finished bailing out the fuel oil from the compartment and virtually all traces had been cleaned up. *Davis* received permission to proceed to New England and, in company with *Marion,* reached the base in mid-afternoon.

While resentment at boarding was rather general, there were occasions when a rum runner's master would be cooperative and talkative if he felt secure. One example was Watson Wagner, master of *Mareuilendole,* an ex-Navy 110-footer which had been converted for the liquor trade.

One summer evening, destroyer *Henley,* Lt. Comdr. R. E. Hunter, was cruising westward in low visibility and approaching Cape Cod. Through the murk a suspicious looking vessel was sighted, and the destroyer changed course toward her to investigate. The vessel also sighted *Henley* at about the same time and abruptly headed for the open sea. Hunter swung around her stern and identified her as the Nova Scotia oil screw *Mareuilendole.* The destroyer stopped and secured radio bearings and soundings placing *Henley* 8.7 miles from the Pamet River Coast Guard Station. Meantime, *Mareuilendole* was proceeding rapidly eastward.

Henley then gave chase at full speed, and after a run of 4 miles ordered the black to heave to, which she did. The boarding officer, finding a cargo of liquor and a fraudulent manifest, immediately seized the vessel. Hunter placed an officer and four armed men on board, reported to his base commander at New London, and was instructed to remain in his position until arrival of the patrol force commander in *Cassin.*

That destroyer arrived 2 hours later after a run from Provincetown, and the force commander and Hunter went on board *Mareuilendole* to talk with the master. Wagner talked very freely. He said his soundings showed he was more than 12 miles offshore, that he knew he was subject to seizure if closer than that, and that he had not been nearer to the coast at any time. Though his manifest called for "general cargo," he said that meant liquor. The master said he had no radio transmitter on board, and that he knew the penalty for rum runners having one was a fine of $7,000 and a sentence of 5 years for the operator. He discussed freely the method of delivering his cargo; he did not sell for cash within 50 miles of shore, and delivered his cargo only upon orders. Wagner mentioned having been in various rum vessels. He claimed that *I'm Alone* had been built for him personally, but that he had sold her after several years.

Getting really chummy, Wagner said that if the officers would let him go, he would return immediately to St. Pierre. In reply to this, Hunter removed five of the rum runner's men and placed them in *Henley.* On arrival at Boston both vessels were met at the anchorage by the deputy customs collector and several inspectors, who searched the black again. It was thought originally that the only grounds for seizure that would "stick" related to the improper manifest. But customs authorities discovered other evidence, and *Henley*'s chief radioman found a radio transmitter which apparently had been tampered with since seizure. The case was upheld.

. Among the more persistent rum runners was the British three-masted auxiliary schooner *Vinces*. She had long been on the suspected list; the Coast Guard received word in March 1927 that the British schooner *Dorothy M. Smart* had been transferring a large cargo to *Vinces*, and that the latter might be expected to enter waters of the Norfolk Division to dispose of it. The division commander was alerted to enable him to distribute his forces in order to effect capture.

Mascoutin, Lt. O. Egeland, was among the cutters alerted; the division commander ordered her to maintain radio silence, inasmuch as *Vinces* was known to be equipped not only with a spark transmitter and receiver, but a radiotelephone as well. *Mascoutin* scouted to the southward of Charleston, S.C.

While running northeastward toward Charleston Lightship, the lookout discovered what appeared to be a small fishing vessel coming out of a bank of mist. With the aid of binoculars, Lieutenant Egeland made the vessel out to be a three-masted power schooner crossing astern under power alone. He headed northwestward.

At that moment, *Mascoutin* placed the schooner at 10.5 miles from the nearest shore line, and immediately turned about, steaming on course 208° true to the eastward of the schooner to cut her off. Ten minutes after having been sighted, the suspected ship apparently discovered the cutter, turned about when 9.2 miles from land, and headed for sea.

Mascoutin changed her course to 193° true, to 164° true, and again to 140° true, swinging in a slight arc and finally coming up astern of the vessel which proved to be *Vinces*.

The cutter blew stop whistles which were ignored, and then fired a blank shot across her bows without effect. To show that he meant business, Egeland sent four service shots over the mastheads of the schooner. The cutter then drew abreast of the vessel and slowed down to her speed.

"You have been within the 12-mile limit," called the cutter's skipper, "Stop your vessel. I am coming on board." The defiant master replied that he would not stop. Two more shots, with lower elevation each time, were sent over the schooner, and Egeland again asked the master if he intended to heave to. The latter said he would not unless his ship were damaged. This invitation was accepted by *Mascoutin*. Since the rummy's crew were all aft, a shot was carefully aimed forward; the shell crashed through the bulwarks, hit the rail, a dory and a hatch, but did only minor damage. The rum runner then hove to at a point 15.1 miles from the South Carolina shore line.

A boarding party found *Vinces* liquor-laden; she had no log book and no bill of health, and her papers appeared to be irregular. The master, mate, engineer, cook, and three deck hands were arrested, the vessel was seized, and various papers and articles were taken into custody. Thereupon, *Vinces* was taken in tow to Charleston, and later to Savannah. This seizure resulted in a prolonged court case, with volumes of legal proceedings, in which the Government finally won.

The steamship *Homestead,* 1,321 tons, was a marked rum runner. Her skipper, M. L. Gilbert, was wanted to answer an indictment on a rum running charge dating back to 1923. The vessel was wanted in her own right as a dedicated and pestiferous runner of illicit liquor. Coast Guard vessels had been alerted to be on the lookout for her and to bring her in. Brought in she was, after one of the most troublesome captures on record.

Headquarters had sent secret instructions to the Destroyer Force commander at New London who, in turn, had instructed his commanding officers in the Destroyer Force to bring *Homestead* to New York if found on the high seas. Early in the afternoon of 4 February 1925 destroyer *Jouett,* Lt. Comdr. Raymond L. Jack, found *Homestead* at anchor some distance from Montauk Point. The destroyer began circling slowly. Her commanding officer sent word to the force commander that he was picketing the vessel which was anchored "in the lee of Montauk Point" without giving the exact position; he requested that cutter *Redwing* be sent to his assistance to tow the vessel to New York. The force commander replied that *Redwing* would be sent to join him.

Redwing had just brought another vessel in to New London and turned her over for customs investigation, when she received orders to go out again to join *Jouett.* The problem for the cutter seemed simple, for it should not be difficult to locate *Homestead* in the lee of Montauk Point. *Redwing,* under command of Ens. Raymond V. Marron, accordingly put to sea. The weather was nasty, and by early evening the cutter neared Montauk where *Jouett* and *Homestead* were supposed to be. At that point Ensign Marron received a radiogram from *Jouett* directing him not to come out since the sea was entirely too rough in which to work, and to seek shelter for the night. Comdr. W. H. Munter, force commander, did not receive this message.

Marron turned *Redwing* about and returned to anchor near New London. *Jouett* continued to picket. Soon after midnight, however, the destroyer was forced to leave *Homestead,* whose actual position was 25 miles 188° true from Montauk Point Light (not strictly "in the lee of Montauk Point") and proceeded to Melville, R.I. to make repairs to leaky condensers and change the water in her boilers.

The situation was made partially clear to the force commander by two messages at 8 a.m.; one from *Jouett* reported her on the way to Melville, and the second from *Redwing* indicated that cutter was anchored near New London. In the meantime *Homestead,* free of *Jouett,* remained riding at anchor in a heavy sea with strong southeast winds.

Commander Munter was naturally upset; he immediately ordered *Redwing* to port, boarded a patrol boat, and met the cutter in the river below New London. He then boarded *Redwing,* ordered Ensign Marron to steam at full speed for *Homestead's* position, and asked why he had not proceeded as ordered. Only then did he learn of *Jouett's* radiogram. *Redwing,* with Commander Munter on board, reached *Homestead* in the early afternoon and found her at anchor. The heavy easterly swell was still running, but Ensign Marron lowered a boat and sent an armed party to take charge of the vessel.

Homestead was hailed and her master told she was to be boarded, whereupon she immediately got under way with anchor dragging. This frustrated the attempt to board, and the boat returned to *Redwing;* the latter set out in pursuit, and quickly overtook the steamer. Her master was informed that the Coast Guard had orders to board her whenever and wherever found except in foreign territorial waters, and he was ordered to stop his vessel. His refusal was given in a flood of seagoing profanity.

Captain Gilbert was then warned of Marron's intention to use guns if necessary. The master again refused to stop, saying that he would resist all attempts to board or interfere with the movement of his ship. During these exchanges, *Homestead* was making 5 or 6 knots and still dragging her anchor, though attempts were being made unsuccessfully to take in the chain.

Words having proved futile, *Redwing* manned her guns and fired three warning shots from her 1-pounder. *Homestead* disregarded these and steamed on. Three shots across her bows from a 3-inch gun followed, without effect. *Redwing* was brought abreast of *Homestead* and close to her port to have the best control of gunfire, and avoid injury to any crew member. Since the cutter had only shrapnel, great care had to be used. A shot carefully aimed near the waterline at the bow fell short. *Homestead* kept on, but raised Costa Rican colors on her after staff.

Redwing dropped astern and came up on the starboard quarter in a position to disable the steering gear. A second shot struck the quarter within an inch of the wheel chains at the quadrant. *Homestead* proceeded as before, but a lifeboat was lowered to the rail and it appeared that the crew members were putting into the boat a mattress with a man on it. Colors aft were lowered to half mast.

Commander Munter thought it possible but improbable that someone might have been injured by shrapnel, reported his situation to Headquarters, and requested instructions indicating how far he could go. He was instructed to bring the vessel to New York regardless of the master's protests and resistance. Headquarters then ordered *Seminole* at New York to proceed to *Redwing's* assistance.

Homestead's master was then warned that his ship would be fired upon to compel him to stop. Commander Munter ordered a shot to disable the steering gear aft. From about 300 yards, *Redwing* fired 11 shots separated by intervals sufficient to determine if the vessel were stopping. The tenth shot was aimed at the pilot house; it struck the upper side of

the chart house and, exploding, completely wrecked the interior including steering compass and wheel. The eleventh shot, aimed at the stack,
hit a stay and exploded. The vessel was now disabled, and the master
was finally forced to heave to. Miraculously, no one in the pilot house
had been hit or injured by the shrapnel.

The steamer's men placed their dunnage in two lifeboats, which were
lowered with men in them. The boats were told to come alongside
Redwing; the starboard boat never left *Homestead's* side, but the port
boat lay about 50 yards away. The steamer signaled by flashlight that
she was slowly sinking and that one man had been killed and several
wounded. Both reports proved entirely false. *Redwing* stood by with
her searchlight on the rum runner, noting no change in draft; in about
2 hours *Homestead's* port boat returned to the ship, and both boats were
hoisted and secured. Gilbert was asked if he was ready to take a tow
line; he replied that he was not. And so the night was spent.

Meanwhile *Seminole,* Capt. Philip H. Scott, had left New York and
had notified *Redwing* of her expected arrival the next morning. Soon
after daybreak, *Seminole* reached the area but, because of heavy haze
and lack of a radiocompass, did not make contact until 11 a.m. Meanwhile, *Redwing* lowered a boat with an armed boarding party to board
the rum runner and handle a tow line. The sides of *Homestead* were too
high to climb, and the master refused to put over a line or sea ladder.
The swell was considerable, and it was still deemed unwise for *Redwing*
to attempt to go alongside. Furthermore, the cutter was short-handed
by 12 men, leaving an insufficient number to handle both ships and the
large number of prisoners.

Seminole finally found *Redwing,* and after the sea moderated it was
decided to board. A boarding party was made up from both cutters,
and *Redwing* went alongside; *Seminole* lay astern with guns trained on
the vessel. Boarding was accomplished without resistance. It was found
that no one had been killed or wounded. The master and crew of 24
were taken prisoner and transferred to *Redwing,* the vessel was seized,
and a prize crew of men from both cutters were placed in *Homestead.*
Redwing towed and *Seminole* escorted, and all reached the anchorage
off the Statue of Liberty. *Homestead's* master was placed in leg irons
and handcuffed, and the vessel, crew, and cargo of 12,000 cases of liquor
were turned over to customs. Commander Munter received commendation from the Commandant, Admiral Billard.

The cold winter night of 24 January 1931 was a busy one off the
entrance to New York Harbor. A single incident involved three related
rum runners and six Coast Guard vessels. Boatswain Karl Schmidt,
commanding six-bitter *CG–145,* took charge and coordinated the activity. When it ended, three rum runners had been turned over to
customs officials at New York.

Early in the evening *CG–145* was patrolling outside Ambrose Light-ship when Schmidt sighted a vessel to the eastward apparently going nowhere. Chief Boatswain's Mate Wilbur Tally was on watch; as Schmidt went below to read, he told Tally to check the vessel and see what they were doing there.

A half hour later Tally sounded the general alarm bell and informed Schmidt that the vessel was the barge *Brooklyn* of Newark, and that there was a speedboat alongside her. As *CG–145* came around the stern of the barge, Schmidt sighted through the darkness another object on the starboard side. The searchlight beam revealed a schooner from which sacks and packages were being loaded onto the barge. The six-bitter attempted to go alongside the schooner, but the latter's lines were cut with a hatchet and the vessel went away at full speed. Observing a number of men standing on the barge, where sacks and packages were piled high on the deck, Schmidt turned *CG–145* about and chased the schooner.

Drawing abreast, *CG–145* sounded her klaxon horn with no visible effect; Schmidt then fired three blank shots from his 1-pounder and these were ignored. Three service shots were then put over the vessel's bow without result. Aiming amidships in an attempt to disable the craft, two more shots rang out, found their mark, and stopped the vessel. Coming alongside, the searchlight revealed the name *Josephine K* of Digby, Nova Scotia. She was recognized as a famous rum runner which Coast Guard vessels had often trailed.

As *CG–145* approached, a man in the schooner called: "You lousy . . . ., you shot a man." The patrol boat made fast, and Schmidt went on board. Several men were standing about, and one was lying on the deck near the pilot house. This man was William P. Cluett, the master, and he had been wounded by a shot.

Boatswain Schmidt had to do some fast thinking. He put Chief Tally and Chief Motor Machinist's Mate Stephen Heck, both well-armed, in the schooner, and as soon as possible transferred Cluett to *CG–145*. He told Tally to anchor or drift in the area until his return. The patrol boat then proceeded at full speed toward Ambrose Channel with the injured man. Schmidt informed his base and requested that a doctor be sent to meet *CG–145* in the channel. He also radioed *CG–180* and *CG–161*, known to be in the vicinity, and asked that they go to his assistance.

Schmidt met these two patrol boats near Ambrose Lightship, and requested *CG–180* to come alongside, planning to transfer Cluett to that craft for a trip to the base. The man's condition combined with the swell, however, made this inadvisable. So the boatswain sized up his complicated problem, and came to a quick decision. He and Chief Boatswain's Mate James Axel, in charge of *CG–180*, exchanged com-mands temporarily, and Schmidt took one seaman from *CG–145*. With

144

Axel in charge, *CG–145* proceeded with Cluett to the base, watching in the meantime for the doctor.

Schmidt then went alongside *CG–161* and asked her skipper to find *Josephine K* and stay with her. Schmidt, now with *CG–180,* set out to search for the barge *Brooklyn.* This barge was sighted shortly afterward in tow of the tug *Dauntless No. 6* about a mile from Ambrose Lightship. *CG–161* found the schooner drifting, got a line on board, and anchored to keep the schooner from drifting further offshore. Thus, at this time, Cluett was on his way to medical assistance at New York, and *Josephine K* was secure.

Schmidt in *CG–180* went alongside *Brooklyn* and boarded her with four men. There was no resistance. The boarding party was met by the master who had an interesting story to tell, most of which was borne out by the evidence. The master showed the boatswain the pile of sacks on the deck, took him below and displayed a hold full of contraband, and talked freely. Asked where he got the cargo, the master said that earlier in the evening a speedboat had come alongside with 20 to 25 men; they boarded the barge, and two with revolvers forced him into the pump room and told him to shut up. Another vessel, *Josephine K,* tied up and men started throwing sacks onto the barge—so many that the master feared his barge would turn over, and he protested to the man guarding him. The men stowed the sacks below. Then *CG–145* had come along, and *Josephine K* had departed post haste.

The boatswain arrested the master and his two crewmen, and seized the barge. Leaving the others of the boarding party in charge, and giving them a machine gun, Schmidt instructed them to allow no one but coast guardsmen on board; he took with him three sacks as evidence.

CG–180 then proceeded full speed to *Josephine K,* which was under surveillance of *CG–161,* and where Tally and Heck guarded eight prisoners in the forecastle. Schmidt boarded the schooner and ordered *CG–180* to go back to the barge *Brooklyn,* and to instruct *CG–145,* if she met her, to go to the schooner. *CG–180* was to stay with the barge and try to have her anchored at Red Hook Flats.

A search of the schooner revealed that she had no ship's documents or manifest, that she had come from St. Pierre, and that the forward hold was still partly filled with contraband. *CG–145* arrived after midnight and made fast to the schooner. The 125-foot patrol boat *Reliance,* which had been sent out to assist, arrived at *Josephine K's* position soon after *CG–145.* Three hours later, the new 250-foot cutter *Sebago* reached the scene. All four Coast Guard vessels stood by until noon.

In the morning, several officers and men boarded *Josephine K* to assist in closing and sealing the hold and to make repairs, but the engines defied their efforts; the schooner's crew had deliberately disabled her motors. It was found that a shell from *CG–145* had crippled the black's steering gear.

Reliance towed *Josephine K* to New York, and *Dauntless No. 6* and *Brooklyn* were anchored at Red Hook Flats for attention by customs officials. The other Coast Guard vessels resumed their patrols and settled down to less arduous duties.

A great deal of liquor was taken in to New York by harmless appearing tows. The alertness and resourcefulness of Boatswain Schmidt frustrated this attempt with marked success, though the injury to the schooner's skipper was regrettable. In most cases, barges were loaded much farther offshore than in this instance.

CHAPTER XI

"Black Duck" and
Other Tales

IN ITS CONSTANT EFFORT toward better vessels for the anti-smuggling business, the Coast Guard built, and placed in commission during the fiscal year 1932, nine new *"Thetis* Class" 165-foot patrol boats. These had the necessary speed, seaworthiness, and maneuverability to cope with the best of the liquor supply vessels. They were *Argo, Aurora, Calypso, Daphne, Galatea, Hermes, Icarus, Perseus,* and *Thetis.*

The Coast Guard, however, needed additional fast vessels to cope with the ever speedier rum ships. It was unable to procure these in the normal manner. The rum runners had developed their own high powered, speedy craft for the express purpose of running liquor. A good number of these were seized. The Coast Guard found it expedient to acquire many of these captured rum runners for its own anti-smuggling operations. A gratifying number were used to good advantage as "CG" boats throughout the remainder of the prohibition era.

Over 500 of the boats seized between 1925 and 1935 were thought useful, and after due process of law they were assigned to the Coast Guard. In numerous cases overhauling and remodeling was necessary. Rum runners already mentioned which were taken over by the Coast Guard were:

RUM RUNNER	BECAME	RUM RUNNER	BECAME
Alice	(*)	Mareuilendole	(*)
Anna	(*)	Marianne	(*)
Black Duck	CG–808	Mary	CG–988
Cigarette	CG–911	Matilda Barry	CG–9268
Com-An-Go	CG–908	Over The Top	CG–8009
Consuelo II	CG–806	Ruth	CG–9073
Gemma	(*)	Victor	CG–943
Helen	CG–8000	Vinces	CG–821
Idle Hour	CG–918	Warbug	CG–928
Lilly of the Valley	CG–823	Whispering Winds	CG–986

*Disposed of before receiving CG numbers.

After acquisition, many of the seized vessels were found unsuitable for one reason or another. In some cases the boats were sold; in a few they were turned over to other Government agencies; a great many of them were condemned and burned. In cases where the boat was condemned, the action was taken after a survey of commissioned officers, and after approval by Coast Guard Headquarters, it having been determined that the boat was not only unfit for service duty, but also unsafe for use by other Government departments or private individuals.

The boats acquired ran all the way from dories to yachts and large vessels. Of these 500-odd boats, 196 were surveyed and condemned almost immediately after having been taken over; most of them were burned, although a few were towed to sea and sunk. Forty were promptly sold. Some seemed more suitable for use by other governmental departments, and 22 were transferred directly to them. The rest of these vessels, totaling 232, were useful to the Coast Guard in varying degrees. Of this number, 101 were in commission throughout the rest of the prohibition period, and many beyond that. Seventy-four were "C.G." boats for varying periods and then, having outlived their usefulness, were burned. A total of 43 were useful for a while and sold when proved unsuitable. Fourteen ex-rum runners were commissioned for a time and then transferred to other governmental agencies for which they were more appropriate. For greater detail, see appendix A.

One of the condemned vessels was used as a float to a target screen. Our friend *Mareuilendole* was condemned, towed to sea, and sunk. Two of the vessels were lost by sinking, two were wrecked in a hurricane, and three were wrecked otherwise. Eight were accidentally destroyed by fire.

One of the fast rum runners taken over by the Coast Guard and found highly useful became *CG–808*. It will be remembered that she was involved with *Artemis*. *CG–808* had been *Black Duck*, a notorious rum runner captured by Boatswain Alexander C. Cornell. This skipper of *CG–290* made many seizures including that of *Idle Hour*, which became *CG–918*. The *Black Duck* capture was one of the most publicized during the Rum War.

Boatswain Cornell was an experienced officer; he held a chief mate's license in the U.S. Merchant Service, had resigned his commission as lieutenant, junior grade, in the Navy to join the Coast Guard as a boatswain, and his combined Navy and Coast Guard service totaled over 16 years. *CG–290* departed the New London Base in mid-afternoon of 28 December 1929 to maintain patrol in the Eastern Passage of Narragansett Bay, jointly with *CG–241*, specifically to prevent any smuggling vessel from entering the area. Cornell's crew consisted of seven other men. His patrol boat reached the vicinity of Dumpling Rock in the evening, and because of the depth of the water was unable to anchor;

therefore, she tied up to Dumpling Rock Bell Buoy, heading toward sea, and in accordance with orders, doused her lights. *CG–241* was on the other side of the channel near Fort Adams.

Meanwhile, *Black Duck* (*C–5677*) was offshore taking on a cargo of liquor from the British oil screw *Symor*. She was of the speedboat type, lightly but strongly built, and painted grey. Powered with two 300 horsepower engines heavily muffled and with a smoke screen device, she was a very fast rum runner, and had eluded Cornell for over a year. When loaded, she cast off from *Symor* and headed into Narragansett Bay with 383 sacks of assorted liquors.

Boatswain Cornell, standing watch in his pilot house, noticed nothing out of the ordinary until 2 : 15 a. m. The night was calm, visibility was poor with patchy fog, and audibility was excellent. The increasing sound of powerful motors, coming from sea, reached his ears. He peered intently into the murky black of the night. Suddenly the speedboat became visible, moving rapidly without lights. Cornell put his searchlight on the vessel and immediately recognized her as *Black Duck;* sacks of liquor could be plainly seen piled on the after deck. He swung his searchlight alternately on his Coast Guard ensign and the rum runner, at the same time sounding his Klaxon horn as a signal to stop. The rummy's response to this was a burst of speed. *Black Duck* passed within 75 feet of *CG–290's* bow, and as she passed, Cornell hailed her and ordered her to stop. No one was visible on her decks.

The black kept up her increased speed. As she was drawing away, Cornell ordered the seaman who was alert at the machine gun to "let her have it." He opened fire, aiming astern of the craft in accordance with his previous orders, and his burst consisted of 21 shots in about 3 seconds. At the same time, *Black Duck* swerved sharply to the left, with the result that, instead of going astern, the shots raked the port side of the craft and penetrated the pilot house. There was no intent to fire into the vessel, but that is what happened. Then the gun jammed. *Black Duck* disappeared toward the shore.

A short time afterward, the black reappeared out of the fog heading toward *CG–290*. She turned on her lights, and drew alongside the patrol boat with some difficulty, bumping the latter on the starboard quarter, and was finally secured with help from the six-bitter. The vessel was immediately boarded by the coast guardsmen, who found a man crumpled up on deck near the wheel, and two more on the deck of the pilot house. Struck by machine gun fire, two had died instantly, and the third nearly so. A fourth man had been shot in the hand, and he was given first aid on board *CG–290*. The other three were beyond help. Under these circumstances, *Black Duck's* men were not searched and nothing was taken off the vessel except one bag of liquor which was held for safekeeping.

149

Cornell proceeded immediately in *CG–290* to Fort Adams. After a request for medical assistance the doctor arrived, pronounced the three men dead, and bandaged the wounded man's arm. The boatswain then reported the incident by radio to his base and proceeded to patrol in accordance with his orders.

A Coast Guard Board of Investigation found neither Cornell nor the gunner culpable, and cleared them completely. Later, a special grand jury at Providence found no true bill against the crew of *CG–290*. *Black Duck* was turned over to the Coast Guard for conversion into a patrol boat.

The *Black Duck* episode had some unpleasant repercussions; shortly afterward, Coast Guard recruiting posters in Boston were torn down by a mob after a protest meeting. Recruiting in Boston was suspended for a time. In New London, a gang brutally beat two coast guardsmen, and this resulted in fines for three of the attackers. In official circles, however, the Coast Guard was strongly upheld.

Boatswain Cornell was one of the most outstanding skippers in the Rum War, and a terror to the rummies. He had *Black Duck, Idle Hour, Del Ray II, Helen, High Strung, Audrey B,* and many others to his credit. And between the final capture of *Vinces* and his *Black Duck* exploit, he added *Beatrice K* to his long list of seizures.

Cornell in *CG–290* went out on special orders from his base commander one night, finished patrolling Gardiner's Bay and anchored against a dark shore background near the entrance to Shelter Island Sound. Vessels trying to enter would have to pass close by him.

One hour later, a vessel running without lights was sighted, headed toward nearby Cedar Island Light. *CG–290* slipped her anchor and lay to with engines stopped, awaiting passage of the vessel. Soon the craft crossed her bows only a short distance away. The patrol boat went full speed ahead after signaling, and *CG–290* pulled alongside splitting a rail on the rum runner. The skipper identified the craft as *Beatrice K* of Gloucester. The rummy was ordered to anchor, which she did, and two men boarded her to interview her captain and search her holds.

The captain, O. Nelson, produced papers including a license for mackerel and cod fishing. Boatswain Cornell stood at his rail and talked with him. The master felt friendship was the best strategy. He told of having been boarded by destroyer *Fanning*, thoroughly searched, and given a clean slate. This was true. Nelson claimed he had 60,000 pounds of fish on board for New York and that they would spoil if he were detained, that his generator was inoperative and his batteries dead— the reason he was running without lights—and that *Beatrice K* was leaking badly. He said he was a stranger in the locality, and had picked Sag Harbor as a most likely place to get things repaired. On questioning, he said he had fished off George's Bank for 15 years. The men who searched the hold then reported the vessel loaded with fish and ice.

Cornell carefully considered these things which did not quite ring true. No liquor had been found, but why should a vessel needing repairs and going from George's Bank to New York run 20 miles off course to a small hamlet such as Sag Harbor when she had passed up such facilities as those at New Bedford, Newport, and New London which were nearer? The batteries were found to be perfectly dry, indicating the water probably had been dumped out. A bucket was over the exhaust and manifold to keep sparks from betraying her position; when asked about his, the captain became angry and threw it overboard but did not mind the split rail. Cornell could not conceive of a man being unfamiliar with Long Island Sound if he had been fishing for 15 years on George's Bank.

These discrepancies aroused Cornell's suspicions, and the boatswain decided the vessel should be searched more carefully under better conditions. He placed a man on board and ordered *Beatrice K* to proceed to New London.

At Base Four her holds were opened, and three bin boards were removed, as well as fish and ice to a depth of 18 inches; at that point tar paper was discovered, under which were about 1,600 sacks of Meadville Pure Rye Whiskey! When the liquor was found, Cornell addressed Nelson as "captain." Nelson replied: "Don't call me captain, I am not the captain; he left in a dory before you came on board." The crew were arrested and the vessel was seized for probable cause. Cornell received commendation from the base commander and a Commandant's Letter of Commendation for this exploit.

What case could have been clearer and more watertight? It went to court, of course. The judge held that the Coast Guard had no right to arrest *Beatrice K* for running without lights (the reason was "probable cause") and no right to search the vessel without a search warrant, agreeing with attorneys for the defense that the vessel, being the "home of the crew members," was inviolable for the purpose of extensive search. *Beatrice K* was released on bond and her crew found not guilty. It was a preposterous ruling! But it stood.

This aroused indignation of Coast Guard officers, far and wide. It made probable the release on bond of other vessels similarly seized.

Keen observation resulted in another important capture on 14 June 1931. Destroyer *Cummings,* Lt. Comdr. Elmer F. Stone of *NC–4* fame, was cruising about 40 miles offshore from Montauk Point. Not long after daybreak Lt. Kenneth P. Maley was on watch and sighted a beautiful white steam yacht heading toward Shinnecock Light on the south shore of Long Island. She was about 165 feet long. He admired her sleek lines, but as *Cummings* drew nearer, he noticed that she seemed to labor in the swells as if she were heavily laden. He decided to trail her for a while and keep her under observation.

151

The "owner" and a few "guests" in yachtsmen's attire were soon served breakfast on the afterdeck. *Cummings* drew close. Maley watched this with interest, and noticed that afterward they smoked long cigars; but through his glasses he could see that the cigars were held in toil-blackened hands! It was noticed that the portholes were covered and that the sides of the vessel bore large scrape marks, indicating the vessel had been tied up alongside another. The steam yacht, identified as *Surf* of New York, was flying the flag of the New York Yacht Club.

His suspicions now thoroughly aroused, Stone decided to board, but to bide his time. *Surf* continued on her course at modest speed, with *Cummings* closely trailing, until the two vessels were 1.7 miles off Montauk Point. *Cummings* then drew alongside and Lieutenant Maley asked her master for permission to board. It was readily granted.

Maley boarded *Surf* and found most of the ship's papers in order, but the master could produce no manifest. The vessel was licensed for pleasure purposes only. He then requested permission to go below. The master said he had no objections, but would prefer his going later because there were some ladies on board who had not dressed. The lieutenant expressed regret, but insisted upon going below.

The master then drew Maley aside and said that all his money was tied up in the 4,000-case cargo of liquor which they had on board. He offered to pay Maley $10,000 if he would let *Surf* proceed. Maley refused this bribe and made a quick examination of the cargo. He then placed the master and his crew of 14 under arrest, and seized the vessel. It was found that the master was wanted on another charge of attempted bribery. *Surf* was taken into New York and delivered to customs. Even this apparently watertight case got nowhere when it came to trial.

A great many yachts figured in rum running. Another was the American yacht *Allegro* of Philadelphia, a typical private yacht with white hull, varnished deckhouses, and a spar-colored stack. Her capture required several Coast Guard craft and local police.

At daybreak one placid August morning the six-bitter *CG–103*, Chief Boatswain's Mate Alfred P. Becker, headed eastward from Absecon Inlet to examine an area frequented by smuggling vessels. Three hours later the helmsman sighted a vessel apparently stopped about 3 miles ahead, and held his course. Soon it was observed that there were two vessels alongside each other, and that they were separating. One was a black hulled schooner; the other was *Allegro*. The latter stood southeastward zigzagging at 15 knots and showing no flag; *CG–103* gave chase and gradually gained on her, but fire was withheld.

When the patrol boat was close enough to hail her, the vessel stopped as ordered. *Allegro* hoisted the American yachting ensign and a yacht club pennant. Her hull showed scrape marks. Becker sent two men to the yacht to examine her papers.

Shortly afterward one seaman returned, requesting Chief Becker to go on board. He did so and noticed an odor of liquor, and the seaman showed him a hatch which recently had been nailed fast. The presumed owner and skipper of the yacht went forward also. Becker told him he wanted the hatch opened, but this the man refused. He then called Becker aside and said confidentially that he had taken 10 cases from the schooner, and offered to pay the chief an unspecified amount for releasing the yacht. Becker's reply was that the yacht was under seizure and would be taken to Cape May. The section at Cape May was informed by radio, and *CG–103* was directed to bring *Allegro* in. A seaman was left on board in charge, and both vessels proceeded. Later examination revealed a large cargo of liquor, stored in the forepeak, bilges, and staterooms.

In the afternoon the 125-foot patrol boat *Pulaski* hove in sight and was requested to accompany the vessels, since *Allegro* appeared to be having engine trouble. She did so, and some time later *Allegro* was taken in tow by *CG–103*. A choppy sea developed, and after an hour of towing the line parted. *Pulaski* took over the tow, with *CG–103* following astern, and the three vessels proceeded thus throughout the night.

In the morning *Allegro* got her engine fixed and cast off the tow. She proceeded under her own power toward the Cape May Harbor jetties. Then came a surprise. A boat was suddenly lowered from *Allegro,* and seven persons jumped in and rowed toward the beach. *Allegro's* engine had been stopped, and the yacht drifted. *Pulaski* lowered her boat to pursue the escaping prisoners, and radioed the base to inform it of the situation. With *Pulaski's* boat in pursuit of the escapees, *CG–103* stood toward *Allegro,* made fast to her, and finally towed her to the base. The two Coast Guard stations at nearby Wildwood were notified by telephone and a fast boat was dispatched to the scene. Wildwood police assisted. Between these forces all of the escaping prisoners were apprehended and jailed.

Destroyers and six-bitters often spent weeks on end patrolling their assigned areas without effecting a capture—just picketing and trailing under circumstances which permitted no other action. Such patrols were monotonous and uninteresting and made the personnel concerned feel that they were accomplishing next to nothing. There was recognition, however, that always there might be an "incident" just ahead which would justify the monotony of the past weeks.

It was after such a period that *Abel P. Upshur* made an important seizure. This flush decker, under command of Comdr. Frederick A. Zeusler, was one of the later acquisitions of the Coast Guard, and was attached to the New London Base..

In September 1932 *Abel P. Upshur* was patrolling about 30 miles south of Shinnecock Light when the officer of the deck sighted two vessels some distance off his port bow lying very close together. The larger one was a two-masted black vessel having the appearance of a foreign rum runner, and the other was a white single-masted yacht. Commander Zeusler was notified of the suspicious appearance of the craft and immediately ordered the destroyer to head toward them.

On sighting *Upshur* the two vessels parted, the black vessel heading southeastward and the yacht northeastward. Destroyer *Shaw* was about 7 miles to the northwest of *Upshur*; she was requested to pursue the black vessel while *Upshur* chased the yacht. The former proved to be the Canadian oil screw *Walter Jr.*, and she was overtaken. *Upshur* overhauled the white vessel and identified her as the 55-foot yacht *Sea Urchin* of New York; she had been running rum for some time. The yacht hove to promptly. She was low in the water and had a big black smear on her port side.

Commander Zeusler sent Ensign Maloney by dory to board the yacht. The master presented him with the ship's papers consisting only of enrollment and license, which seemed in order, but he had no manifest. The master said he was bound from New York to Montauk. He accompanied Maloney who went below and found 354 cases of liquor which, the master revealed, had just been taken from *Walter Jr.* The vessel was seized, and the skipper and his three crew members were arrested. The boarding officers returned to *Upshur,* and were replaced by Lt. A. L. Ford and Machinist J. H. Decker.

In addition to the arrested men, there were two women passengers about 27 years of age, who gave a New York hotel as their address. Ford engaged the women in conversation. As a result, he learned that upon departure of the yacht from port its activities were unknown to them, and he firmly believed them when they said they were glad to see the Coast Guard intervene. Perhaps the rum runners took them along to camouflage their illegal trade, and to make it look more like a yachting party!

The next task was to get *Sea Urchin* to New York. Decker satisfied himself that the yacht had sufficient fuel and oil for the trip, and Lieutenant Ford ordered him to get under way. This was done with considerable difficulty; the engineer of *Sea Urchin* was badly under the influence of liquor and finally was removed from the engine room. With Ford and Decker in the yacht, *Upshur* departed on patrol. The yacht's engine proved to be in very poor operating condition and the vessel could proceed at only 7 knots.

During the trip to New York, Ford and Decker stood watches alternating at the wheel and guarding the prisoners. The two women were greatly in fear of bodily injury from the crew of *Sea Urchin,* especially the engineer; they were kept constantly in the company of the Coast Guard officers. The yacht arrived at the barge office in New York the following morning after a slow trip.

154

Much has been said in these pages about the need for convincing proof of the position of seizures and the presence of liquor, and the tendencies of various courts to grasp upon minor technicalities to find against the plaintiffs. One of these minor technicalities seemed far fetched in the extreme, and yet it had constructive results for the Coast Guard.

In the middle 1920s a seizure case was in court. One of the Coast Guard vessels had taken in a foreign rum runner. A smart attorney for the defense challenged the legality of the seizure on the grounds that the Coast Guard vessel had not at the time of seizure displayed the proper Coast Guard ensign as required by law. Under international law a vessel stopping another for investigation must display its own national ensign, and Coast Guard Regulations further require that the Coast Guard ensign and commission pennant be displayed. The seizing vessel had shown both.

The attorney pointed out that on the Coast Guard ensign flown by the seizing vessel the eagle held in its right claw an olive branch with an indeterminate number of olive leaves, and that in the left claw it held only three arrows. According to law there should have been 13 olive leaves and 13 arrows. He asked just where in law could be found a description of the "distinctive Coast Guard emblem" authorized by President Taft to be embodied in the ensigns flown from Coast Guard vessels? It is said that he produced in court a number of Coast Guard ensigns, no two alike. In some the eagle looked to the left, others to the right. The numbers of olive leaves and arrows varied from flag to flag. Just what *was* the official Coast Guard ensign, and how was an honest rum runner to know it when he saw it? The prosecution was hard put for an answer!

The original flag of the service, known as the "Revenue Ensign," was authorized by Congress on 2 March 1799, and was originally flown as authorized by revenue cutters in lieu of the national ensign. It was the same flag which is now flown over customhouses and recognized as the "Customs Flag." Early collectors of the customs had jurisdiction over the revenue cutters and this flag was a symbol of their authority. But over the years indiscriminate use ashore caused its significance as an emblem of a sea-going service to become lost. Accordingly, during the Taft Administration, the Revenue Cutter Service, formerly known as the Revenue Marine, was authorized to display on the old Revenue Marine flag a "distinctive Revenue Cutter emblem" to distinguish it from the customs flag. A distinctive device was, therefore, placed on the flag over the vertical red and white stripes, and this was the flag questioned by the rum runner's attorney.

Obviously, something definite had to come out of this. It will be recalled from chapter VIII that Lt. Frank M. Meals had been assigned to the Communications Office at Headquarters in the middle 1920s. Since flags come under communications, the job of straightening out the flag discrepancies fell upon this officer. He soon discovered that the variations from the original design had come about through manufacturing difficulties and multiplication of errors by using old flags as patterns for new ones, instead of always going back to the original design. Here and there an arrow or an olive leaf would be eliminated or the eagle would look the other way and many variations resulted.

After months of research, Lieutenant Meals unearthed the original design of the Revenue Marine flag made by Alexander Hamilton and described in his own handwriting. The existing ensign of 1925 followed Hamilton's design very closely, except for the distinctive emblem authorized during the Taft Administration. Nowhere could a sketch or written description of that emblem be found. This, of course, laid the Coast Guard open to innumerable challenges in future seizure cases! An official and accepted design was a must.

Mr. Oscar Kee, then a draughtsman in the Communications Section at Headquarters, was assigned to improve the design then in use with particular reference to any manufacturing difficulties brought to attention by manufacturers. When Kee had completed the design, Lieutenant Meals had to describe it in words sufficiently clear so that a person could reproduce Kee's design from Meals' description.

Both the design and description were approved by Secretary of the Treasury Andrew W. Mellon, and authorized by President Coolidge for use by the Coast Guard. Since then, the emblem as specified has also been used on official letterheads, seals, and other items where the Coast Guard emblem was appropriate. Never again was there a question about the authenticity of the Coast Guard ensign. New flags were distributed to the fleet all in accordance with the approved design.

CHAPTER XII

The End of
Prohibition

THE COAST GUARD waged its Rum War in this manner, beginning with 4 years of incidental operations and then 10 years of intensive and aggressive action, as long as the 18th amendment remained in force. There was no let-up until 1933 when appropriations were drastically reduced and Coast Guard operations against the rum fleet were curtailed; many units were placed out of commission.

It should not be assumed, however, that during this 14-year period all went serenely with the 18th amendment and the Volstead Act. Quite the contrary. These remained the law of the land, and it was the duty of all enforcement agencies, including the Coast Guard insofar as anti-smuggling operations were concerned, to enforce the law without qualification.

As time went on, what prohibition was doing to the United States became increasingly apparent. The underworld controlled the liquor business with an ever-tightening grip; control of the liquor traffic had its corollary grip on many other forms of crime and corruption; gangsterism spread across the country and reached undreamed of proportions. Corruption grew at virtually all political levels. The enforcement agencies were overwhelmed.

Effects of prohibition have been felt down to the present time and will probably continue to be felt for decades yet uncounted. Prohibition made the "Roaring Twenties" roar. It engendered the spirit that to beat the law was smart. Almost everyone was doing it, and it became an accepted part of life. Even citizens who otherwise would not think of deliberately breaking the law became willing lawbreakers when it came to having their liquor. So a widespread disrespect for law was born, and it flourished; it has filtered down through the years.

These trends were obvious, of course, almost from the beginning. No one could prophesy at any given time how far they would carry, but they persisted and intensified year by year.

The wets were never happy with prohibition, and it was not to be expected that once the law became effective they would stand placidly aside and accept it. However, they found themselves unorganized and without adequate spokesmen. At first there were no funds, and there was no real leadership except what the liquor interests themselves provided.

There were some relatively unsuccessful early attempts to organize. The Association Against the Prohibition Amendment was founded in 1918 and was incorporated in the District of Columbia in December 1920. It continued for many years. The Crusaders, mostly young men, were established in 1922, and the following year the Moderation League, and the Constitutional Liberty League of Massachusetts, were founded. These associations grew, but they accomplished next to nothing until 1926. At that time their importance increased when they combined with the American Federation of Labor to give evidence to a congressional committee holding hearings on enforcement problems. In these first 6 years of prohibition, the efforts were chiefly toward modification of the Volstead Act, for nobody had the slightest idea that repeal could be achieved. It had been discussed, however, as early as 1924.

The labor unions had for some time demanded beer, but between 1927 and 1930 this was abandoned in favor of all-out repeal of the 18th amendment. The American Legion, too, came out for repeal. In 1927 a group known as the Voluntary Committee of Lawyers proclaimed opposition to the amendment, and the next year the Bar Association of New York favored repeal and return of the liquor question to the States. Little by little other organizations joined the movement and pressure for repeal began to mount and to be felt.

The Women's Committee for Modification of the Volstead Act changed its name in 1927 to "The Women's Committee for Repeal of the Eighteenth Amendment," and campaigned accordingly. Another association, the Women's Organization for National Prohibition Reform, was established in 1929 with 17 members; by 1932 membership had grown to more than 1,325,000.

Liquor cases filled the court dockets, as we know, and demanded a large percentage of the time the courts were in session. The pros and cons of prohibition and modification or repeal became part of every political campaign. While this was going on, Congress and the executive branch of the Government did little to resolve the question one way on the other. President Harding did nothing, of course, in the early days of prohibition. President Coolidge did little to relieve the situation, but did expand the Coast Guard to improve anti-smuggling procedures at sea.

The first constructive steps to remedy matters were taken after President Herbert Hoover assumed office in 1929. By this time, it was crystal clear to many millions of Americans that the "cure" was worse than the "disease," and that a nationwide change in public sentiment was occurring. Official referendums and unofficial polls left no doubt.

Despite all this, however, the drys were able to maintain large majorities in both Houses of Congress until 1932; the wets never held more than 30 percent of the seats, and usually less. National voting did not reflect the true temper of the American public to the extent that was revealed in local elections. The latter left no doubt that the people generally were becoming fed up with their dry paradise.

The wet leadership, at first lodged mostly in the brewers and distillers, had changed with the years; by the very late 1920s it had shifted to large numbers of highly influential business and professional men. Dry leadership was showing deterioration. Finances of the wets improved while those of the drys became sadly strained. With prohibition in force, the drys had nothing to be aggressive about, whereas the growing number of Americans who were disgusted and alarmed with the turn of events had a full belt of ammunition.

Before Herbert Hoover was nominated by the Republicans in 1928, he mentioned prohibition as "a great social and economic experiment, noble in motive and far-searching in purpose." In his later acceptance speech, he spoke against repeal of the 18th amendment. When he was elected with 444 electoral college votes to Al Smith's 87, the Senate was dry with 80 seats against 16, and the House was dry 328 to 106. But sentiment was on the march.

On assuming office, President Hoover promptly appointed the National Commission on Law Observance and Enforcement. It comprised many leaders in the legal profession and became known as the Wickersham Commission. This body studied the problems of prohibition enforcement for nearly 2 years and reported in January 1931. The voluminous report made no radical recommendations, but did suggest a few changes in judicial procedures and methods. The report pleased no one, and in a few months it was virtually forgotten; the rum runners continued to run rum, and the public grew more restive.

On 3 September 1929 the stock market reached its then all-time high, tapered off and, in October, crashed. For nearly 3 years stock prices declined irregularly, losing almost 90 percent of their 1929 values. During this process business suffered severely, unemployment reached disastrous proportions, and the Great Depression was on. Of all the influences to bring about repeal, this was probably the greatest. The growing army of wets found new arguments which not only held water, but alcohol as well, and they exploited the national disaster to the best of their ability.

The repeal movement accelerated rapidly. When the Democratic Convention met in 1932 it adopted a plank for repeal. There was more than a moral issue in this. Like every other financial segment of our country in those deep depression years, the U.S. Treasury encountered rough going. A flow of legal liquor to be taxed would swell the Treasury's receipts, and this was a bright spot in the heavy overcast. The Republican Party in its Convention did not commit itself or its candidate to repeal—merely taking a negative stand.

When Franklin D. Roosevelt made his nomination acceptance speech in 1932 he announced that from then on the 18th amendment was doomed. In the period between his election and his inauguration, the Senate passed on 17 February 1933 a resolution submitting an amendment for repeal to State conventions, followed 3 days later by passage in the House. Fights for delegates to these conventions commenced immediately.

On becoming President, Roosevelt reduced the appropriation of the Prohibition Bureau by 57 percent and that of the Bureau of Industrial Alcohol by 37 percent. He requested that Congress modify the Volstead Act to allow manufacture and sale of "3.2 percent beer." A month after Roosevelt's inauguration Congress did so. No more did the speakeasies operate in pseudo-secrecy; their doors were flung open for the sale of legal beer. Trucks could transport beer without fear of apprehension and without gangster escorts.

Michigan was the first State to hold its convention; on 10 April 1933 the repeal amendment was unanimously ratified by that State. Ratification was needed by 36 states and Utah, the 36th to ratify, did so on 7 November 1933. On 5 December the 21st constitutional amendment, which repealed the 18th amendment, became effective and prohibition came to an end.

With this came also an end to rum running as it had been known for 14 years. During prohibition the rum runners had been concerned with getting the liquor ashore to the market at a handsome profit and with calculated risk. Now that the transportation and sale of liquor had become legal, other means of transportation wholly within the law largely replaced the rum runners. For the most part, the rummies gave up. The syndicates found that, under the circumstances, greater profits lay in other fields of crime. The now powerful and wealthy underworld, through its gang combines and interlocking directorates, followed these other fields from coast to coast.

But running liquor had become a deep-seated habit with some. These men could still make a good profit by buying liquor as before and landing it surreptitiously, thus avoiding payment of the Federal tax. This merely reverted to the older type of smuggling and was, for the most part, a minor operation. Yet, the Coast Guard had to prevent smuggling in all its forms to the extent possible. It found that it was still at war with the rum smuggler, though this might be termed a mopping up operation.

Coast Guard appropriations were severely reduced for the fiscal year 1934, and this meant a drastic cut-back in the Service. In 1933, seven destroyers had been returned to the Navy. Now, the remaining eight were decommissioned and returned, and a large number of smaller craft were disposed of. With a reduced fleet and personnel, the Coast Guard was required to maintain the Block Island-Montauk-Cape May patrol against the die-hards. Smuggling of liquor continued moderately off the Atlantic coast north of the Chesapeake Capes; the volume of liquor running was considerable in the Carolinas and Georgia, and quite heavy in Florida and along the Gulf coast. Occasional rum runners were found and seized and often savage resistance to arrest was still encountered.

Some smuggling of liquor, aliens, and a variety of goods has kept on through the years; the Coast Guard and customs officials keep alert against it as part of their regular duties. But the big business of running liquor came to an end.

EVALUATION

Evaluation of the Coast Guard's activities and effectiveness during the years of the "Noble Experiment" involves obvious difficulties and challenges. In the first place, he who undertakes evaluation must do so from the standpoint of conditions which existed at that time entirely without the benefit of hindsight. Secondly, he must also be able to look back with the perspective of the historian upon the whole operation and its relationship to subsequent events. Thirdly, he must reconcile the two viewpoints without emotion, partiality, or bias.

At the outset of prohibition, no one had any idea that the smuggling of liquor from the sea would ever reach the proportions later attained. Small law enforcement forces with modest appropriations to back them seemed in those days sufficient, and Coast Guard personnel and floating equipment were deemed adequate to cope with what little smuggling might be done. Smuggling liquor was akin to the smuggling of any other commodity or article—something to be alert against and to prevent in the regular course of duty.

Not until Capt. Bill McCoy set the pattern was there much more than a trickle from the sea, and at that time, the pattern was not recognized. From then on, the pattern gradually unfolded; as the Coast Guard saw it develop, it exercised greater vigilance and the cutters became more active in going after and seizing the violators. By late 1922–23, the need for an aggressive war against the rum runners became apparent; the forces at hand were completely inadequate to control the rising tide of seaborne liquor which few had foreseen. Ways and means were discussed and weighed but little was done. By 1924 the rum traffic had overwhelmed its opposition and the Coast Guard could not intercept more than perhaps 5 percent of the flow of liquor. Something had to be done and done quickly.

The great expansion of the Coast Guard followed. In 1924 and 1925 the Service was forced to adopt the Rum War as a major activity without any sacrifice whatever of its other important functions. From then on the prevention of liquor smuggling on the sea was the chief concern of the cutters, and of the destroyers and patrol boats which were acquired for the purpose.

The Coast Guard undertook these operations with some distinct and important limitations. While appropriations were greatly increased to permit the expanded fleet and personnel, there was no limitless outpouring of funds. The new vessels could not be procured or built overnight; a year was needed, at best. With funds so limited, and with the need of faster craft, the Service was astute to avail itself of some of the captured rum runners.

The early 3-mile limit and the later 12-mile limit, beyond which foreign vessels could not be seized, provided an important and constantly exploited immunity for the liquor supply ships. Legally, the Coast Guard was powerless to molest them, and could only picket and trail to try to prevent contact with shore-based runners. This proved generally successful. Some seizures of foreign vessels were unwisely made beyond these limits, and often international complications followed. But to discover and keep under surveillance every offshore rum runner in the vast coastal waters of the United States would have required a fleet far greater than the Coast Guard could muster. Thus, many succeeded in supplying the contact boats and a large number of the latter were continually slipping through the "second line of defense" to land their cargoes. However, from 1925 onward, the flow was slowed measurably.

This was no easy time for coast guardsmen. From start to finish, the prohibition law was unpopular. Citizens of the United States could have been divided into two groups—wets and drys. So far as their tastes and sympathies were concerned, personnel of the Coast Guard also could have been divided the same way, as could every other large group of people. Temptations placed in the way of the coast guardsmen through seized liquor and rum runners' attempted bribes were great. It would be straying from the truth to say that all coast guardsmen were able to resist these temptations. Some bribes were taken, and some liquor was destroyed through internal consumption. In a few isolated cases, coast guardsmen ashore even cooperated with rummies. The truly amazing fact is that those who succumbed to the temptations comprised such an extremely small proportion of the whole. When infractions of the rules were discovered, the offenders were dealt with promptly and severely. The overwhelming majority of officers and enlisted men were dedicated to their task no matter what they personally thought of the 18th amendment.

The disheartening number of releases and acquittals by certain courts, when there should have been forfeitures and convictions, had a distinct effect upon the morale of the Coast Guard officers and men, and greatly complicated their task. It is to their everlasting credit that, despite this ever-present threat of having their efforts go for naught, the officers and men carried on conscientiously and diligently.

The public generally wanted its liquor, and took a very dim view of all enforcement agencies. The press was mixed; while the Coast Guard received a "good press" in many quarters, it was by no means good in others. The Service did not enjoy popularity with either wets or drys; the wets criticized it, of course, because it was carrying on a campaign against the rum runners; the drys criticized it since it did not completely stop the flow of liquor from the sea. It was a cross which the coast guardsman had to bear, and he bore it well.

But many good things for the Coast Guard came out of these 14 years of rum warfare. The Service was greatly expanded, and while it became reduced at the end of the period, it remained larger and more important than it had been previously. Instead of a service known for the most part locally along the coast, it became internationally known. Much of the experience gained by its personnel was immensely valuable. Its *esprit de corps* was immeasurably enhanced and that enhancement has persisted down through the years. Intelligence became highly developed and has remained so. Standardization of communications procedures in line with those of the Navy was a strong plus factor in World War II.

Some Coast Guard officers of the rum running days, now retired, will say that the Service was not even indifferently successful in catching the rummies. Perhaps these officers are perfectionists and were disappointed that all the rum runners were not caught. Like many, they may have served in vessels which effected very few captures. Others are of the opinion that the Coast Guard succeeded in reducing the flow of liquor to a mere trickle, and that success was great. Other opinions range all the way between the extremes. In these reflections, much depends upon what each individual considers par for the course, influenced somewhat by the successes, or frustrations personally encountered.

However, we can get down to some very convincing data and a sound conclusion. The Atlantic, Pacific, and Gulf coasts of the United States, not including the shores of bays, rivers, and so forth, exceeded 5,000 miles in length. When the Coast Guard's floating equipment was at its numerical peak, there were approximately 330 vessels 75 feet or more in length. These comprised destroyers, first-class cruising cutters, second-class cruising cutters, harbor cutters, and launches, and 75-foot, 100-foot, and 125-foot patrol boats.

The Coast Guard had other duties to perform besides chasing rum runners, and some of these vessels were always so engaged. All had periods in port for liberty and rest, as well as occasional times of availability for overhaul and repairs. It is perhaps likely that 200 vessels were at sea attending to the rummies at any given time.

If these 200 vessels could have spread a cordon along our coasts, that would have meant about one vessel in the line every 25 miles. But coastal waters had width as well as length; and it would have meant one vessel to every 300 square miles of ocean within the 12-mile limit alone! That certainly would not have been a tight blockade; in fact, a real blockade with 200 vessels covering 60,000 square miles would have been completely impossible.

Even such a disposition of vessels was not possible, however, because there were concentrations of rum ships and contact boats, requiring concentration of Coast Guard vessels at certain points, particularly off New York and New Jersey. Furthermore, picketing was vital, and theoretically 25 large rum ships hovering outside the 12-mile limit supplying the New York market tied up 25 Coast Guard vessels. It is readily apparent that while the Coast Guard succeeded in intercepting and seizing a tremendous total of rum runners, it did not have the physical means with which to bring about a complete stoppage in the flow of liquor from the sea.

Considering the numerical strength of the adversaries, the immunity of the foreign rum runner beyond the legal limit, and the great expanse of ocean in which operations were carried out, one can only conclude that the Coast Guard did a highly creditable piece of work in making its thousands of seizures. The amount of liquor successfully landed was greatly reduced; the life of the rum runner was made uncomfortable and hazardous; and in the later years the business became almost unprofitable.

Coast Guard personnel almost to a man rose above the frustrations and discouragements offered by unsympathetic courts, unpopularity with the public, and the temptations of the period. Their dedication to a duty which was often distasteful, their conscientiousness in carrying out their assignments, and their courage in meeting the challenge of violence, was a credit to them and in accordance with the high standards of the U.S. Coast Guard.

Rum Runners Taken Over

By Coast Guard

1925 to 15 April 1935

A LIST OF BOATS seized for violations of laws of the United States and, after due process of law, assigned to the Coast Guard for its use. In cases where boats were disposed of by burning, such action was taken after a survey by commissioned officers, and approval thereof by Coast Guard Headquarters. It had been determined that the boat was not only unfit for use or further use by the Coast Guard, but also was unsafe for use by other Government departments or private individuals.

Name or number of rum runner	Became—	Used	Used, then sold	Used, then burned	Used, then destroyed	Used, then transferred	Transferred to another Government agency	Sold	Burned	Destroyed
Aceal.............	CG–8002...		X							
Ady...........									X	
Agnes W.........									X	
Alena..........	CG–978...				X					
Alice..									X	
Alma..........	CG–950...		X							
Althenia Jane.....	CG–992...								X	
Angelica.									X	
Ann...									X	
Anna.........							X			
Annabelle........	CG–955...		X							
Annie.				X						
Annie F.				X						
Antigostima	CG–937...	X								
Ark.	CG–9160..			X						
Arrow.	CG–804...			Xª						
Astra..								X		
Auf Weidersehen..	CG–9251...	X								

ª Burned accidentally.

Name or number of rum runner	Became—	Used	Used, then sold	Used, then burned	Used, then destroyed	Used, then transferred	Transferred to another Government agency	Sold	Burned	Destroyed
Baboon	CG–973					X				
Baby Bottleman				X						
Barcarole	CG–9064					X				
Barney Google									X	
Bella Marie								X		
Belle				X						
Bill	CG–831	X								
Black Duck	CG–808	X								
Blaimore I								X		
Blanche Marie	CG–983						X			
Blanche R	CG–951	X								
Bonnie				X						
Bozo	CG–9009			X						
Butterfly									X	
Cacoethes	CG–837	X								
Caloba	CG–807			X						
Carolyn								X		
Catherine M	CG–9275	X								
Cecil S									X	
Charlotte S	CG–8024					X				
Chickie	CG–822			X						
Chief	CG–9194		X							
Chippewa	CG–9013		X							
Cigarette	CG–911				X					
Cinderella	CG–963		X							
Com-An-Go	CG–908							X		
Congress								X		
Constance	CG–919			X						
Consuelo II	CG–806	X								
Crow	CG–9108			X						
Daisy T	CG–957								X	
Dante								X		
Dart	CG–904	X								
Dart	CG–8007	X								
Dawn	CG–9262						X			
Dewdrop										X
Diana II			X							
Diatome	CG–827	X								
Dodge	CG–9116						X			
Don	CG–946									X
Dorothy and Audrey	CG–920							X		
Dot	CG–8035					X				
Dot	CG–8012			X						
Edith	CG–938	X								

Name or number of rum runner	Became—	Used	Used, then sold	Used, then burned	Used, then destroyed	Used, then transferred	Transferred to another Government agency	Sold	Burned	Destroyed
Edna	CG–936				X					
Elenora	CG–800		X							
Elizabeth	CG–917								X	
Elk	CG–924								X	
Ellen	CG–9252		X							
Elma	CG–9079			X						
El Toro	CG–977	X								
Emmy								X		
Ermis									X	
Ethel May	CG–9010				X					
Fatima									X	
Fay	CG–9117			X^a						
Fidelia	CG–996						X			
Fior de Italia			X							
Florence	CG–9001		X							
Fly	CG–8030	X								
Gaviota	CG–802	X								
Gemma			X							
Gene Tunney	CG–984			X						
George E. II	CG–828	X								
George and Earl	CG–9277	X								
Gipsy Sue	CG–8013			X						
Gloria S									X	
Good Luck	CG–835					X				
Halcon	CG–979		X							
Hammitt L. Robbins	CG–954								X	
Happy Parrot	CG–961			X						
Harbor Trader	CG–934		X							
J. M. Hathaway	CG–948	X								
Hawk									X	
Helen	CG–8000		X							
Helena	CG–829			X						
Hiawatha	CG–834	X								
Hilda	CG–9250	X								
Homebrew									X	
Ida C. Robinson			X							
Idle Hour	CG–918							X		
I. H. Tawes	CG–953									X
Ike	CG–923			X						
Imp	CG–952			X						
Inia II					X					
Inverness	CG–990	X								
Irish Luck	CG–8006		X							

ᵃ Burned accidentally.

167

Name or number of rum runner	Became—	Used	Used, then sold	Used, then burned	Used, then destroyed	Used, then transferred	Transferred to another Government agency	Sold	Burned	Destroyed
Isabel			X							X
Italian Beauty	CG–9152									X
Jackie	CG–902		X							
Jedson	CG–8032		X							
Je T'Aime	CG–833	X								
Jim LuLu	CG–2380			X[a]						
John D	CG–9127	X								
Julia	CG–940				X					
Karankawa	CG–9012			X						
Kathryn	CG–9255	X								
Killarney	CG–970				X					
Kiyokawa	CG–9274	X								
Lady Lou	CG–906							X		
Laura	CG–9264	X								
Laura L	CG–956	X[b]								
Leo V	CG–8005			X						
Liberty	CG–824	X								
Lilly of the Valley	CG–9265		X							
Lincoln		X[a]								
Little Gussie	CG–9011							X		
Little Josephine									X	....
Lucky Star								X		
Lucky Strike								X		
Main	CG–960						X			
Malvina E	CG–958						X			
Mardelle	CG–832	X								
Mareuilendole										X
Margaret D									X	
Marianne				X					X	....
Marija	CG–942								X	....
Marjorie	CG–809	X								
Marta	CG–966								X	
Mary	CG–988		X							
Mary Joy	CG–995	X								
Mary Lou										X
Matilda Barry	CG–9268	X								
May B	CG–998			X						
Metmuzel	CG–815						X			
Mianus	CG–967		X							
Micky								X		
Mike									X	....
Mimi	CG–8026	X								
Miss C. B	CG–985		X							

[a] Burned accidentally.

[b] Sank.

Name or number of rum runner	Became—	Used	Used, then sold	Used, then burned	Used, then destroyed	Used, then transferred	Transferred to another Government agency	Sold	Burned	Destroyed
Miss Palm Beach..	CG–9115...								X	
Mizpah...........	CG–838....	X								
Moto Morovich...	AB–25.....							X		
Mystery Girl.....	CG–944....				X					
Neptune.........	CG–912..		X							
Njord...........									X	
Nordeda........									X	
Norman D.......	CG–9145...								X	
Onagara........									X	
Onaway.........	CG–9256...			X						
Osprey.........									X	
Osprey.........	CG–905....					X				
Over the Top.....	CG–8009...								X	
Pat.............	CG–9138...	X								
Patara...			X							
Patsy...........				X						
Phantom........	CG–962....							X		
Phantom II......	CG–939....						X			
Pip.............	CG–9156...			X						
Porpoise........	CG–914....	X								
Princess.........	CG–964....			X						
Pueblos.........	CG–9271...						X			
Quetzaicoatl......	CG–972....								X	
Rainbow II......	CG–9005...			X						
Redwood.......	CG–9272...							X		
Rene-B.........	CG–916....		X							
Resolution.......										X
Rethaluleu.......								X		
Righto..........	CG–9006..								X	
Robert B........	CG–935....						X			
Roven Gambler...	CG–997....		X							
Russel...........	CG–8008..				X					
Ruth...........	CG–9073.						X			
Ruth J..........			X							
Safe and Sane....									X	
Sal Lal II........	CG–8001.		X							
Sambo G........							X			
Sayona II........	CG–930....			X						
Scout...........	CG–9001.			X						
Sea Gull........	CG–933....			X						
Sea Hawk.......	CG–968....		X							
Seger...........	CG–9173..						X			
Seno Isla........	CG–8003..					X				
Shark...........			X							
Sharpie..	CG–9209...	X								

Name or number of rum runner	Became—	Used	Used, then sold	Used, then burned	Used, then destroyed	Used, then transferred	Transferred to another Government agency	Sold	Burned	Destroyed
Skip	CG–8011		X							
Star	CG–903		X							
Stephanotis, O. N.	CG–975					X				
Sumatra	CG–836	X								
Talvez	CG–959						X			
Teddy P.	CG–826	X								
Thomaston			X							
Tornado	CG–981		X							
Tramp	CG–813			X						
Tuna	CG–980								X	
Venar	CG–9133								X	
Vera	CG–9112			X						
Victor	CG–943		X							
Vinces	CG–821	X								
Violet	CG–9269							X		
Virginia I	CG–801		X							
Warbug	CG–928				X					
Whatzis	CG–9266	X								
Whippoorwill	CG–987	X								
Whispering Winds	CG–986	X								
Winnie	CG–9267					X				
Wyona	CG–9057		X							
Wild Rose	CG–9278	X								
Yvette June	CG–994	X								
Yulu			X							
Zebadiah	CG–9263					X				
Zev	CG–816	X								
No identification	CG–2248				X					
Do	CG–9041			X						
Do	CG–9090								X	
Do	CG–9102								X	
Do	CG–9120			X						
Do	CG–9122	X								
Do	CG–9123	X								
Do	CG–9134			X						
Do	CG–9139	X								
Do	CG–9140	X								
Do	CG–9141	X•								
Do	CG–9142								X	
Do	CG–9146								X	
Do	CG–9147	X								
Do	CG–9151			X						
Do	CG–9154			X						
Do	CG–9155			X						

c Used, wrecked.

Name or number of rum runner	Became—	Used	Used, then sold	Used, then burned	Used, then destroyed	Used, then transferred	Transferred to another Government agency	Sold	Burned	Destroyed
No identification..	CG–9168...		X							
Do	CG–9180...					X				
Do	CG–9181...					X				
Do	CG–9186...			X						
Do	CG–9195...	X								
Do	CG–9196...	X								
Do	CG–9197...	X								
Do	CG–9198...			X						
Do	CG–9199...								X	
Do	CG–9206...								X	
Do	CG–9207...	X								
Do	CG–9208...	X								
Do	CG–9210...			X						
Do	CG–9211...	X								
Do	CG–9212...			X						
Do	CG–9213...	X								
Do	CG–9214...	X								
Do	CG–9215...			X						
Do	CG–9216...			X						
Do	CG–9217...	X								
Do	CG–9218...	X								
Do	CG–9219...								X	
Do	CG–9223...	X								
Do	CG–9224...			X						
Do	CG–9227...								X	
Do	CG–9229...		X							
Do	CG–9230...					X				
Do	CG–9233...	X								
Do	CG–9234...			X						
Do	CG–9240...	X								
Do	CG–9241...			X						
Do	CG–9242...	X								
Do	CG–9254...			X						
Do	CG–9259...	X								
Do	CG–9260...	X								
Do	CG–9273...	X								
Do	CG–9276...	X								
579	CG–9003...			X						
4133	CG–830...		X							
4149	CG–9175...								X	
4291	CG–9176...								X	
4320	CG–9182...								X	
231490	CG–9261...							X		
294–A	CG–9257...							X		
336–A	CG–2254...		X							

Name or number of rum runner	Became—	Used	Used, then sold	Used, then burned	Used, then destroyed	Used, then transferred	Transferred to another Government agency	Sold	Burned	Destroyed
510–A					X					
723–A	CG–9008			X						
1280–A	CG–9157		X							
1810–A	CG–9159		X							
1464–A	CG–8031	X								
2085–A	CG–9055			X						
3802–A	CG–8010	X°								
4710–A	CG–9231			X						
4784–A	CG–9158			X						
4835–A	CG–9193			X						
A–658	CG–8022								X	
A–1181	CG–8034						X			
A–1365	CG–9162			X						
A–1674	CG–999		X							
A–3636	CG–8023		X							
A–8718	CG–929		X							
A–9960	CG–969			X						
936–C	CG–9045			X						
C–5698	CG–989		X							
C–5883	CG–993			X						
C–6200	CG–910			X						
C–8348	CG–991	X								
417–D	CG–2251		X							
Dory 1	CG–9220	X								
Dory 2	CG–9221	X								
Dory 3	CG–9222			X						
K–1231	CG–947		X							
K–5021	CG–9190			X						
K–5403	CG–9030			X						
K–5691	CG–982	Xᵃ								
K–8343	CG–9095								X	
K–13367	CG–9130	X								
K–14775	CG–2379		X							
K–14987	CG–932			X						
K–17435	CG–9243			X						
K–18967	CG–8025						X			
K–19825	CG–921	X								
K–22632	CG–9244	X								
K–22845	CG–8028		X							
L–4806	CG–9188			X						
L–9938	CG–922			X						
L–11503	CG–8029	X								
729–M	CG–2377								X	

ᵃ Burned accidentally.

ᶜ Used, wrecked.

172

Name or number of rum runner	Became—	Used	Used, then sold	Used, then burned	Used, then destroyed	Used, then transferred	Transferred to another Government agency	Sold	Burned	Destroyed
1619–N..........	CG–9192...		X							
N–322...........	CG–971....		X							
N–2382..........	CG–9074...								X	
N–2526..........	CG–9270...	X								
N–2618..........	CG–9056...			X						
N–2702..........	CG–9258...	X								
P–108...........	CG–2249...	X°								
P–309...........	CG–9235...			X						
6694–T..........	CG–9153...	X								
U–1111..........	CG–9249...	X								
USC–489........	CG–9015...								X	
USC–4255.......	CG–814....					X				
USC–4331.......	CG–9237...								X	
USC–4351.......	CG–9253...	X								
V–293...........	CG–9228...	X								
V–943...........	CG–9113...								X	
V–1158..........	CG–9089...								X	
V–1468..........	CG–9029...			X						
V–2206..........	CG–9078...			X						
V–2316..........	CG–9050...			X						
V–2774..........	CG–9100...								X	
V–2793..........	CG–8020...		X							
V–2980..........	CG–9232...			X						
V–3042..........	CG–9245...								X	
V–3044..........	CG–9098...								X	
V–3483..........	CG–9144...								X	
V–4434..........	CG–9072...								X	
V–5920..........	CG–9106...								X	
V–6622..........	CG–9028...			X						
V–6845..........	CG–909....								X	
V–7008..........	CG–9027...			X						
V–7691..........								X		
V–7741..........	CG–9105...								X	
V–8155..........	CG–9047...			X						
V–8457..........	CG–9128...								X	
V–9074..........	CG–9097...								X	
V–9424..........	CG–9026...			X						
V–10962.........	CG–9163...								X	
V–10980.........	CG–9136...								X	
V–11173.........	CG–9189...								X	
V–11498.........	CG–9171...								X	
V–11941.........	CG–812....	X								
V–12216.........	CG–8004...			X						
V–12541.........	CG–9066...			X						

° Used, wrecked.

Name or number of rum runner	Became—	Used	Used, then sold	Used, then burned	Used, then destroyed	Used, then transferred	Transferred to another Government agency	Sold	Burned	Destroyed
V–12734	CG–9109			X						
V–13619	CG–9202		X							
V–13774	CG–9051			X						
V–13797	CG–9025			X						
V–14120	CG–9118								X	
V–14177	CG–9049								X	
V–14228	CG–9024			X						
V–14233	CG–9022			X						
V–14316	CG–9023			X						
V–14408	CG–9062								X	
V–14509	CG–2261							X		
V–14568	CG–9021	X								
V–14615	CG–9174		X							
V–14682	CG–8015				X					
V–14690	CG–9019			X						
V–14708	CG–8014			X						
V–14720	CG–9081			X						
V–14838	CG–9088								X	
V–15021	CG–8021		X							
V–15042	CG–9017			X						
V–15086	CG–9178						X			
V–15113	CG–9110			X						
V–15140	CG–9042			X						
V–15280	CG–9046	X °								
V–15301	CG–8018	X ᵃ								
V–15428	CG–9121								X	
V–15474	CG–9092								X	
V–15495	CG–2260	X °								
V–15670	CG–9065								X	
V–15739	CG–9004			X						
V–15764	CG–9103								X	
V–15773	CG–9107								X	
V–15828	CG–9172			X						
V–15847	CG–9135						X			
V–15867	CG–2256								X	
V–15891	CG–9070								X	
V–15944	CG–9031			X						
V–16069	CG–9067			X						
V–16109	CG–2257			X						
V–16174	CG–9164								X	
V–16212	CG–9119								X	
V–16360	CG–9084						X			
V–16365	CG–9032			X						

ᵃ Burned accidentally.

° Used, wrecked.

Name or number of rum runner	Became—	Used	Used, then sold	Used, then burned	Used, then destroyed	Used, then transferred	Transferred to another Government agency	Sold	Burned	Destroyed
V–16484	CG–9143								X	
V–16626	CG–8016				X					
V–16654	CG–9052			X						
V–16700	CG–9033			X						
V–16727	CG–9034			X						
V–16847	CG–9044			X						
V–16865	CG–8017			X						
V–16952	CG–9035			X						
V–16967	CG–9201								X	
V–17108	CG–9071			X						
V–17205	CG–9238								X	
V–17261	CG–9161								X	
V–17341	CG–9191	X								
V–17400	CG–9036			X						
V–17428	CG–9091	X								
V–17430	CG–9063			X						
V–17454	CG–9037			X						
V–17489	CG–9061								X	
V–17515	CG–9053			X						
V–17533	CG–9184								X	
V–17576	CG–9038			X						
V–17586	CG–9060								X	
V–17648	CG–9142			X						
V–17769	CG–9111			X						
V–17884	CG–9039			X						
V–18031	CG–9040			X						
V–18082	CG–9132								X	
V–18177	CG–9068								X	
V–18325	CG–9126			X						
V–18371	CG–9043			X						
V–18378	CG–9131			X						
V–18387	CG–9085								X	
V–18398	CG–9125			X						
V–18471	CG–9086								X	
V–18480	CG–9054		X							
V–18520	CG–9058								X	
V–18522	CG–9059			X						
V–18560	CG–9080			X						
V–18615	CG–9169								X	
V–18697	CG–9048			X						
V–18714	CG–9137								X	
V–18754	CG–9148								X	
V–18790	CG–9075					X				
V–18871	CG–8019	X •								

• Burned accidentally.

Name or number of rum runner	Became—	Used	Used, then sold	Used, then burned	Used, then destroyed	Used, then transferred	Transferred to another Government agency	Sold	Burned	Destroyed
V–18906	CG–9104			X						
V–18963	CG–9096								X	
V–18987	CG–9114								X	
V–19141	CG–9093								X	
V–19142	CG–9101			X						
V–19223	CG–9150			X						
V–19265	CG–9087								X	
V–19337	CG–9204								X	
V–19377	CG–825	X								
V–19445									X	
V–19573	CG–9124			X						
V–19593	CG–9170								X	
V–19779	CG–9187			X						
V–19793	CG–9226								X	
V–19995	CG–9203								X	
V–20104	CG–9149								X	
V–20137	CG–9177								X	
V–20162	CG–9165								X	
V–20163	CG–9200			X						
V–20185	CG–9183			X						
V–20227	CG–9166						X			
V–20280	CG–9167								X	
V–20467	CG–9236			X						
V–20577	CG–9179			X						
V–20531	CG–9185					X				
V–20678	CG–8033	X								
V–20947	CG–9247			X						
V–21142	CG–9219								X	
V–21183	CG–9239								X	
V–21252	CG–9248			X						
V–21389	CG–9246								X	
1220–Y	CG–9076			X						
1693–Y	CG–9014			X						
Z–62	CG–9007			X						

Index

Vessels listed in Appendix A are not included in this Index unless they are otherwise mentioned.

Union Temperance Society, 4
Upshur, 137, 153, 154

V

Vaughan, 80, 81
Vereign, 53, 57
Victor, 35, 147
Vigilant, 89
Vinces, 93, 94, 140, 147, 150
Virginia, 57
Volstead Act, 9, 11, 54, 157, 158, 160
V–13574, 121, 122
V–13997, 126, 127

W

Wagner, Watson, 139
Wainwright, 49
Walter Jr., 154
Walton, CDR John Q., 47
Warbug, 57, 147
Webster, LT E. M., 106, 110
Webster, Robert K., 126, 127
Weech, Robert W., 126
Welborn C. Wood, 137, 138
Wheeler, CAPT William J., 28
Whispering Winds, 95, 147
Whitbeck, LCDR J. E., 64
Wickersham Commission, 12, 159
Wilkes, 49
Wilkes-Barre, 57

Wilkin II, 27, 28
Wilkinson, William D., x
Willard, Frances W., 6
William Malloney, 57
Wilson, Captain John, 53
Wilson, President Woodrow, 9
Winnisimmet, 89
Wissahickon, 89
Wolcott, 89, 128
Women's Christian Temperance Union, 6
Women's Committee for Modification of the Volstead Act, 158
Women's Committee for Repeal of Eighteenth Amendment, 158
Women's Organization for National Prohibition Reform, 158
Woodbury, 89
Woods, BSN W. A., 99, 100
Woolard, BSN Thomas G., 91

Y

Yamacraw, 23, 89, 120, 121
Yankton, 37, 38, 39
Yeaton, 89
Young, CDR Fred H., 136
Yount, F., 134, 135

Z

Zeussler, CDR Frederick A., 153, 154

☆ U. S. GOVERNMENT PRINTING OFFICE : 1971 O - 413-463

NEW ORLEANS

GALVESTON

Gulf of Mexico